Digital Asset Management

Content Architectures, Project Management,
and Creating Order Out of Media Chaos

Elizabeth Ferguson Keathley

Digital Asset Management: Content Architectures, Project Management, and Creating Order Out of Media Chaos

ISBN-13 (pbk): 978-1-4302-6376-0

ISBN-13 (electronic): 978-1-4302-6377-7

President and Publisher: Paul Manning
Lead Editor: Steve Weiss
Intel Project Manager: Sarah Yost
Technical Reviewer: Henrik de Gyor
Editorial Board: Steve Anglin, Ewan Buckingham, Gary Cornell, Louise Corrigan, Jim DeWolf, Jonathan Gennick, Jonathan Hassell, Robert Hutchinson, Michelle Lowman, James Markham, Matthew Moodie, Jeff Olson, Jeffrey Pepper, Douglas Pundick, Ben Renow-Clarke, Dominic Shakeshaft, Gwenan Spearing, Steve Weiss
Coordinating Editor: Jill Balzano
Copy Editor: Christine Dahlin
Compositor: SPi Global
Indexer: SPi Global
Artist: SPi Global
Cover Designer: Anna Ishchenko

Distributed to the book trade worldwide by Springer Science+Business Media New York, 233 Spring Street, 6th Floor, New York, NY 10013. Phone 1-800-SPRINGER, fax (201) 348-4505, e-mail orders-ny@springer-sbm.com, or visit www.springeronline.com. Apress Media, LLC is a California LLC and the sole member (owner) is Springer Science + Business Media Finance Inc (SSBM Finance Inc). SSBM Finance Inc is a Delaware corporation.

For information on translations, please e-mail rights@apress.com, or visit www.apress.com.

Apress and friends of ED books may be purchased in bulk for academic, corporate, or promotional use. eBook versions and licenses are also available for most titles. For more information, reference our Special Bulk Sales–eBook Licensing web page at www.apress.com/bulk-sales.

Any source code or other supplementary material referenced by the author in this text is available to readers at www.apress.com. For detailed information about how to locate your book's source code, go to www.apress.com/source-code/.

This book is dedicated to all my friends and relatives who believe in me,
but most especially Winn Keathley, who reads to
our kids every night (often with voices).

Contents at a Glance

Contents

About the Author

Elizabeth Ferguson Keathley is a board member of the DAM Foundation and has chaired both the Human Resources and Education committees. Currently Elizabeth is working with the DAM Foundation to establish the first official certificate program for digital asset managers. She has written, taught, and been actively a part of conferences related to the arrangement, description, preservation, and access of information for more than 10 years. Her ongoing exploration of digital asset management and its relationship to user needs can be followed at her homepage for Atlanta Metadata Authority: http://atlantametadata.com. Those interested in following her digital asset management feed on Google Plus can find her at +EKeathley.

About the Technical Reviewer

Henrik de Gyor is a consultant working in the field of digital asset management (DAM) for a wide variety of organizations. Henrik is the director of DAM Services at Marlabs Inc., where he leads a practice of professionals who assist, advise, and advocate for DAM clients. Previously, Henrik managed the daily operations of a DAM solution for a number of years.

Henrik is very active in the global DAM community and co-organizes the world's largest DAM Meetup group in New York City every month. He writes a vendor-agnostic blog about DAM from the user and administrator perspective. He hosts a podcast series about DAM that has audio interviews with other DAM professionals. When he is not traveling, Henrik resides in Northern Virginia with his wife and stepdaughter.

Acknowledgments

This book would not exist without the work of the dozens of DAM gurus and mentors who publish, present, and blog on this new profession. In particular, the works of Mark Davey, Jeff Lawrence, Peter Krogh, David Diamond, Henrik de Gyor, and Teresa Regli were foundational to the content of this work. I would also like to acknowledge the work of every DAM programmer and consultant I have ever had the pleasure of working with for informing my view of DAMs and the industry, with particular thanks to Chad Sears, Tom Buekers, and Mark LaFrenz. To every presenter at a DAM conference that has stood up and shared their work fearlessly, thank you; I learn more from those few days of peer-to-peer sharing each year than during months on my own, and this book would not exist without you. To those who put together DAM conferences, and in particular those at Henry Stewart, thanks for putting together an environment that fosters learning, debate, and growth in the field.

Foreword

I was invited to attend the NYC Digital Asset Managers Meetup cocktail party. I showed up at the trendy little bar, and the room was packed with DAM professionals from around the world. In the middle of the crowd was Elizabeth, actively working the room, advocating for DAM education and encouraging all the DAM attendees to participate in a DAM salary survey she was conducting for the DAM Foundation. Picture one of the nicest people you know, someone who is intellectual, driven, passionate, well connected and with a charming personality, and you've met Elizabeth. She spent the evening mentoring DAM professionals and also evangelizing the importance of DAM education and the often-overlooked value of having well-trained DAM professionals on staff. It was by chance that we met at this meetup, many years ago. I quickly discovered that we had very similar beliefs about the DAM profession and the need for better DAM education.

I have had the privilege to work with Elizabeth on several occasions including her latest project, a collaboration with the DAM Foundation to establish the first official certificate program for digital asset managers.

The volume, velocity, variety, and complexity of digital information require highly skilled DAM professionals to develop digital strategies to maintain a strong competitive edge in the emerging digital marketplace.

Digital asset management is a rapidly emerging technology that provides opportunities for companies to unlock the hidden value of their archived digital assets and to leverage information from big data sources to drive business successes. Many companies lack well-trained DAM professionals who can provide digital strategy in this highly complex and rapidly challenging field.

Elizabeth is a true DAM advocate. She is an active board member for the DAM Foundation and has chaired both the Human Resources and Education committees. If you attend a DAM conference, there is a good chance you will find Elizabeth on the speaker list. Elizabeth brings years of experience when speaking on topics such as controlled vocabularies, metadata modeling, and digital preservation. Elizabeth advocates for DAM systems that provide easy access of information and creative materials. She teaches educational seminars and has authored numerous articles on DAM topics. It is my pleasure to introduce Elizabeth's first book.

Elizabeth brilliantly introduces the reader to the complex notions and exciting world of digital asset management in this book. She translates the complex concepts of DAM solutions into an accessible and guided educational experience that builds understanding.

Elizabeth uses analogies to illustrate DAM concepts. She uses the analogy of a mechanical clock to provide an overview of the complexities of a modern DAM system. When the clock was first invented, they were sophisticated pieces of technology and weren't welcomed universally. Elizabeth winds a story around this analogy to explain how DAMs are often misunderstood and not initially widely accepted or appreciated by everyone in the organization. Her approach to educating the reader about DAM technologies and the business value of the DAM make this book a must to anyone interested in learning about DAM, while providing information for anyone considering a DAM project.

Elizabeth's extensive knowledge and experience shine in this book. She provides real-world sample job models, case studies, business cases, ROI models, and quotes from leading DAM experts. This book delivers a well-rounded understanding of DAM systems, including DAM technologies, staffing, DAM usability, content architecture, search and indexing, and business, legal, DAM workflows and many other core topics. She also explores, in detail, DAM roles, job descriptions, and salary scale and advice on hiring and staffing DAM professionals.

The information included in these pages is fundamental for any DAM user.

If you are considering a career in digital asset management or are planning a DAM project, this DAM book is a must!

—By Jeff Lawrence
Engagement Director at Celerity—Business Acceleration Consultancy
http://celerity.com/blog/authors/JeffLawrence/

CHAPTER 1

■ ■ ■

Introduction to DAM

Chapter Goal: *An introductory chapter defining digital asset management (DAM) systems and the purpose of the book, with an overview of topics to be covered.*

Twenty-Five Years Ago, Email Was New

When I am asked to explain what a DAM system is and why an organization might need one, I frequently refer to our recent history with email. DAM systems are highly analogous to email systems, both in the complexity of their initial deployment and in the way they will change and shape our work environments in the next few decades. Both email programs and DAMs require a substantial investment in hardware, software licenses, and the hiring of specialized staff. Both can cause skepticism among communications staff because they involve a change in regular work routines. Because the technology is new and rapidly evolving, both require substantial training and commitment on the part of management. Finally, both technologies are the inevitable result of our need to pass information more quickly and efficiently throughout the Internet.

Imagine that it is 1989. At a conference, or in a meeting, someone brings up the idea of a new interoffice electronic mail system. Your IT people and a few key staff have been sending each other messages through the local area network (LAN) for a few years, but computers on every desk are still a relatively recent phenomenon, and the idea that something as critical to business as daily memos and project communications could be trusted to the rather unreliable new technology seems an expensive and risky proposition. Besides, how would you know when to check your electronic mail? Better to keep those internal documents circulating from the copy center, on good old reliable paper from the Xerox machine. No one remembers that when the Xerox machine first arrived in the office 25 years earlier, the same concerns about expense, reliability, and the need for the technology were also suspect. The idea of electronic messaging is waved off; if something is really important and needed quickly, people can just pick up the phone. If the tech guys keep bringing up the new Microsoft Mail system, send them the message loud and clear that your organization has spent enough on computers lately. You'd have to be crazy to spend millions of dollars *again* on a system that doesn't seem to work several times per year. Many of those whom you work with are convinced that computers at every desk is just a temporary fad anyway.

Because it is 1989, the news has been full of information about the Iran-Contra Affair, and key to the public's understanding of the evidence is an explanation that the White House staff uses a system called IBM Notes for sending each other quick messages and brief memos via computers. Colonel Oliver North assumed that when he hit the "delete" command for his electronic messages, they were gone forever, but records of his transactions still existed on backup files stored on magnetic tape. The newscasters boil the Iran-Contra Affair down to clips of the testimony of the attractive Fawn Hall, and they mention that Colonel North is being prosecuted for the destruction of documentation. A few articles and broadcasts mention that this information was known to have existed and to have been destroyed at North's direction, because of electronic mail backups. True news junkies and IT nerds take note, and this is the birth of what will become known as email in the general public consciousness. In October 1989, Apple Link is relaunched as a new company: America Online. For the first time, email and the Internet are commercially available in homes that love new technology. I went online for the first time that holiday season, in the house of an uncle who worked for Unisys, and my cousins and I spent our time merrily flaming each other on the BBSwhile searching for video-game cheat codes.

```
REMOTE ACCESSIBLE DRIVEN BBS V4.5CG
    CONFIGURATION/SETUP EDITOR
  (1)  SETUP YOUR SYSTEMS DISK
  (2)  CONFIGURE SYSTEM & HARDWARE
  (S)  CREATE V4.2-4.5 NMR SUBBOARDS
  (E)  MODIFY SUBBOARD DATA
  (R)  SEQUENTIAL FILE READER
  (O)  HOW TO REGISTER FOR RAD
  (S)  VIEW DIRECTORY (8)
  (G)  DOS COMMANDS    (8)
  (W)  SEQUENTIAL FILE WRITER
  (L)  TEXT FILES LIST NEEDED
  (H)  SETUP HACKING QUESTIONS
  (C)  CONVERT V3.8-4.0 TO 4.5 SUBS

REMOTE ACCESSIBLE DRIVEN BBS V4.5CG
```

Figure 1-1. *Bulletin Board Systems (BBS) were common information and file sharing sources for internet users in the 1980's. This screenshot of the RAD BBS is of version 4.5, released in July of 1989* Source: http://rachelbythebay.com/w/2013/02/12/rad/ *Retrieved 12/31/2013*

The current equivalent to the Iran-Contra Affair is that of WikiLeaks. Those who understand what, exactly, happened with Private Manning and how it happened know that it all boils down to a lack of clear user access control within DAM systems. Still, just like Iran-Contra, the details are difficult to understand, there are interpersonal relationships involved, and the whole mess will be clearer 25 years from now. We may not even refer to DAMs in the same language we do today; email was called electronic mail until about 1993. Still, the clear progression and proliferation of email and DAMs make it clear that these are two workplace tools that have parallels in their histories of development and adoption. Somewhere this holiday season some young people will log on to DAMs and merrily use them in ways for which they were clearly not designed, and in 25 years I look forward to reading their books about whatever technology comes next.

> *As I've looked at [DAM], beyond the initial benefits of creating libraries, centralization of knowledge, and sharing, **I've found incredible opportunity throughout automation.** Tying it with other content so some of the manual production work of getting assets into layouts or to websites, managing workflows, managing approvals, the act of centralizing assets and metadata has been an incredible benefit to further automation. Getting the centralized library offers money savings on the business case is giving tens of millions of dollars to the organization through asset reuse, speed to market, and delivery of marketing materials. (Source: William Bitunjac, Group Manager, Target Technology Services and Target Mobile, "Another DAM Podcast Transcribed," p. 162)*

This Book Is an Introduction Itself

The book you're now reading, in physical or digital form, was written as a guide to those wishing to learn about, deploy, or work with a DAM. In the following chapters, information about these complex systems will be discussed at a high level, without getting into specific systems now on the market or how they are coded. I made this choice simply because the technology related to DAMs is moving so quickly as to make any in-depth treatment of the subject obsolete by the time of this publication. Systems are only called out by name rarely, and instead the text will focus on the needs and actions of a digital asset manager in his or her day-to-day work in any DAM.

In a survey conducted by the DAM Foundation in 2012, digital asset managers reported doing roughly the same tasks related to their DAMs no matter what system they used or what industry employed them ("Results of the DAM Foundation Salary Survey: Who We Are, What We Do, Where We Work and How We Are Paid," *Journal of Digital Media Management*, vol. 2, issue 1, 2013). This high uniformity of reported tasks suggests that these tasks are both needed and necessary for companies with DAM systems.

Based on this information, gathered from digital asset managers, this book will walk you through common questions related to DAMs and this new career field. The appraisal, selection, and housing of DAMs and the assets to be put in them will be discussed first, followed by an examination of the technical requirements related to the searchability of the system. Chapters on DAM metrics, workflows, rights management, system migration, and digital preservation will round out the big topics reviewed as part of DAM work.

What a DAM Is and Isn't

A DAM system is a software system that, in combination with other systems, stores and distributes digital assets in a controlled and uniform way. DAMs arrange, describe, store, and provide access to digital assets that are linked to metadata models, which allow a digital asset manager to work with the assets in desirable ways. The DAM itself should function with a search engine to provide results for assets, and it should include workflow capabilities that document and regulate the creation, review, and approval of new digital assets. Common systems connected to a DAM might be an email server for the distribution of assets and workflow alerts; an index engine like Solr for generating search results; a transcode engine that generates several versions of the master file for easier playback and distribution of video; and custom **application programming interfaces** (APIs) that allow uploading or downloading to the DAM from web sites. Mature DAMs often have a dozen or more other systems connected to them in order to serve their asset ingestion and retrieval needs. DAMs allow for the creation and maintenance of access control lists (ACLs) that reserve some content for specific groups of users, while releasing other content in search results for all users. All true DAMs are capable of generating detailed metrics on all system actions, in order for digital asset managers to know which assets are in the system, who is working with those assets, and how assets are being used within the DAM.

Types of DAMs

Because the field of digital asset management is so new, there is variability in the terms used to describe both DAM systems and systems that are DAM-like. Below are some thumbnail definitions of systems that are similar to DAMs or are offered in the DAM marketplace. Due to the endlessly imaginative minds of those marketing these systems, the terms are often open to interpretation. However, all the systems below are subsets of DAMs, as a DAM can be programmed to do all of these things, while some of these systems cannot accomplish larger tasks that a more flexible DAM system might.

- **Media asset management (MAM) systems**: These types of DAMs exclusively deal with images and video. They may have workflow tools or may be focused on providing a centralized library of assets. Often systems that use the term "MAM" are sold in the video or television creation space, and they are made to link with video-editing bays.

- **Brand asset management (BAM) system**: These DAMs focus on aspects of brand management, including brand workflows and the maintenance of brandmarked, copyrighted, or intellectual property. These systems may include HTML interfaces that are meant to guide external users through the brand request process for licensing purposes.

- **Document management (DM) systems**: These systems are really just DAMs by another definition of the acronym, but they are marketed with a focus on managing assets for legal or human resources purposes. They may be limited in their capabilities by their focus on documents only, but most are able to attach images to files, whether or not the images are viewable.

- **Enterprise content management (ECM) systems**: These DAMs are sold as a way of linking many different systems. For instance, a company might refer to the overarching DAM that governs both its MAM, which is used by the video team, and its DM system, which is used by its legal team, as the ECM. Because very large organizations—especially media companies—often have more than one type of DAM in play, the term "ECM" is meant to convey the larger system that allows for all the others to work together. Some DAM vendors label their product as an ECM to convey how it is designed to link systems that might otherwise be considered separate.

Systems That Are Not DAMs

Systems that are called **content management systems** (CMSs), as the term is commonly used at the time of the writing of this book, are generally those that allow for shortcuts in the publication of web pages through entry forms. Because a sophisticated CMS might contain a small image library, and because these systems are commonly used in web publication, there is often confusion about the differences between a CMS and a DAM. A DAM stores assets, and it may offer up a URL containing an image or content for a web page to hotlink to, but it is not a web-page creation machine by itself. A CMS is a web-publication tool for those who wish to create web pages in a quick and relatively easy way. A CMS is not designed for use in the long-term storage of digital assets, nor is it typically able to handle workflows or complex searching and sharing functions.

Web content management systems (WCMs) usually only store images and content for publication on web sites. While these systems often lack more robust metadata creation and search capabilities, they excel at keeping images organized for web publication. However, they are not designed for the long-term storage of digital assets, and they do not provide a user-friendly environment for the complex searching and sharing needs of designers. Some handle workflows, and some do not, but none are true DAMs.

DAMs Are Part of a DAM Strategy

DAMs should be part of a holistic digital asset management strategy: one that looks both to the future need for data migration and updating of systems as well as to continually bringing digital content from the past forward to continue accessibility. Identifying your organization's needs and wants in its overall treatment of digital assets should be considered when planning a DAM.

Digital content is just as fragile as physical artifacts and it requires the same kinds of unique considerations. Just as the long-term storage and accessibility of physical photographs in an archive require specialized training, an investment in proper climate controls, and premium housing materials, the long-term storage and accessibility of digital images in a DAM require specialized training, investment in a secure server environment, and proper digital preservation planning. Those in charge of a company's business continuity planning (BCP) should be aware of digital asset management efforts and should be involved in discussions of return on investment (ROI) and hardware investment planning (see Chapter 10 for ROI formulas).

Digital assets are constantly created and constantly destroyed. In many ways, DAMs are necessary in the information age to ensure the integrity of digital assets and to reduce risk. To this end, digital preservation strategies are discussed at length in Chapter 12. Be aware that just as the acts of digital creation and destruction never end, digital asset management is also a never-ending process. There is no finish date for a DAM, just a series of accomplished projects and tasks within the system.

> *If you're not familiar with a DAM at all and once you install it, it's a big piece of software. It's going to be something intimidating to some people, some of your users. Other users are going to dive right in and love it. Also a piece of advice to buyers, once you purchase the DAM, it's not going to be set and you can walk away from it. Your DAM will always be morphing, changing as new groups are added. As the needs of your users expand, there's going to be meta fields constantly be added. . . . The DAM's never, "Build it and there it is and walk away." **It's going to be changing with your business needs.** (Source: David Fuda, Digital Asset Manager at Ethan Allen, "Another DAM Podcast Transcribed," p. 170)*

DAMs Have Stages of Maturity

When you evaluate an existing DAM or plan for one of your own, it is helpful to know that these large systems exist in various forms of deployment. In 2012, the DAM Foundation released the first version of the DAM Maturity Model, and with feedback from the global community new iterations of the evaluation tool continue to be released. Housed permanently at `http://dammaturitymodel.org/`, the model evaluates many different facets of DAM systems and operations into five levels of maturity.

The five levels of DAM maturity are as follows:

1. Ad hoc: Unstructured meeting of organizational needs; no value applied to user scenarios

2. Incipient: Project-level requirements gathered, but with no end-to-end context

3. Formative: Program-level requirements gathered; beginning to apply end-to-end context

4. Operational: Use cases are well structured, organized, and prioritized; all users identified with known input and output expectations; dependencies, prerequisites, and interrelationships identified

5. Optimal: Framework in place to define, measure, and manage existing and new use cases; systems validated against use cases

These five levels of maturity are broken out for 15 different areas that are organized under four main headings, as seen in the following graphic.

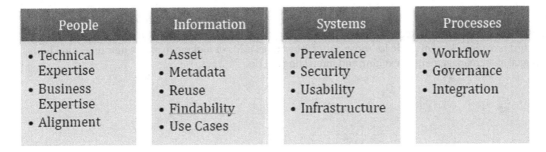

Figure 1-2. *The four DAM Maturity Model focuses and dimensions. Graphic by Mark Davey, CC-BY-SA 2.5.* `http://dammaturitymodel.org/` *(retrieved 11/15/2013)*

Whenever someone asks about DAMs, I first point them to the Maturity Model to use as a gauge both for existing systems and for writing the goals for their own. The DAM Maturity Model not only defines many of the challenges of DAM implementation, but also puts into succinct words the ultimate goals of many digital asset managers.

Conclusion

There will be some creative destruction during the birth of your DAM; older systems and web sites will be retired as their content is folded into a central repository. So too will older habits of working change, just as they did with the adoption of email. The process of arranging and describing digital assets for access and preservation is a rewarding one though, and any "war stories" you may build up in the process of deployment will one day be told with humor and honor, just as those who deployed and implemented email systems 25 years ago may speak of their experiences networking the workplace for the first time.

As someone who has watched the emergence of DAM systems into the mainstream over the past decade, I can honestly say that I have never been more optimistic or excited about a tool for the workplace. While the explosion of documents born in digital form over the past 30 years has been fun to watch, the disorganization presented by this arm of the information age has been a bit crazy-making for those of us for whom the organization of information is a passion, not just a job. DAMs offer us the chance to once again bring order out of the chaos of offices and their work products in a logical fashion, an order long since missing as paper-filing systems and professional secretaries have become ever more rare.

Further, the transparency and accountability offered by the workflow tools present in DAMs promise us a flexible work environment enabled by the Internet. Through DAM workflows, tasks may be accomplished anywhere at any time where the proper tools and people exist. As long as items and tasks are checked in and out of the centralized system in the way the job requests, it doesn't matter if the job is done while the baby naps, while you visit a sick relative, or while you're on a plane to somewhere exciting. Work in a DAM can be done without reliance on the workplace, and as a former dweller in a cubicle, I'm very grateful.

> *Explain issues and their solutions to the people who need to know about it, in their perspective. Keep in mind who your audience is. Use visuals to explain as needed. Document how to resolve issues often, then share this documentation openly and often. Repeat. Simplify. Do not over complicate unless you like confusion, fixing errors, and having delays. Be an agent of change.*
>
> ***Change not because it's shiny, new, cool, but needed for increased effectiveness and efficiency across the organization****. (Source: Henrik de Gyor, Author and Podcaster, "Another DAM Podcast Transcribed," p. 383)*

Those who work as advocates for DAMs must be many things: educators, information professionals, change agents, archivists, reference librarians, records managers, proofreaders, conflict resolution experts, and more. It is hoped that this text provides a kind of guide for those either inheriting DAMs or looking to start a new one, and I hope that you find digital asset management as exciting and interesting as I do.

CHAPTER 2

When It's Time for a DAM: Identifying a Need

Chapter Goal: *Explanation for identifying the need for a DAM system within the organization.*

Figure 2-1. *An old-fashioned, mechanical analog clock*

In the previous chapter, it was helpful to use the analogy of email in 1994 to discuss where digital asset management systems (DAMs) are in their development in 2014. In the identification and implementation of a DAM, I'd like to use the analogy of an old-fashioned, mechanical analog clock. All most people see of an analog clock is its face, which tells us the time. Quite a bit of user education went into people reading analog clocks. In order to understand the device, one had to learn that there were 60 seconds in a minute; that though our day is divided into 24 hours we count them by 12s, twice; that though most of the system is base 12, the increments between each hour are counted off by 5s; and of course, on your fancier clocks, you might see roman numerals, which requires a whole other set of knowledge in order to interpret the time of day. DAM systems are much like these clocks, in that all most people ever see are their faces (user interfaces), and some training is required to interpret those effectively. Just as opening the back of an analog clock will reveal a complex system of gears, so too will investigating a DAM reveal that it has many moving parts working together to present the user experience. Most people with clocks in their homes had no idea that the *escapement* was the bit of clockwork that connected the wheelwork with the pendulum; most people who use a DAM don't realize that there's a separate email service provider sending them alerts when they get a message from the system.

Anchor, or Recoil, Escapement :
a, escape-wheel ; *b, c*, pallets.

Figure 2-2. *Illustration from Chambers's Twentieth Century Dictionary of the English Language (1908). Escapement , n. act of escaping: means of escape: part of a timepiece connecting the wheelwork with the pendulum or balance, and allowing a tooth to escape at each vibration.* `http://commons.wikimedia.org/wiki/File:Chambers_1908_` `Escapement.png` *(retrieved 8/13/2013)*

There were centuries when a clock was a sophisticated piece of technology that wasn't welcomed universally, and you should keep this in mind when pitching a DAM adoption to your organization. Before railway schedules, the time of day was determined by local authorities (`http://www.webexhibits.org/daylightsaving/d.html`). It took decades of work by dedicated individuals to make the keeping of time uniform and to institute international time zones; people complained about centralized control of timekeeping technology dictating the way that they worked. Just as not everyone was ready to use synchronized clocks on an everyday basis, not every company is ready for a DAM. Those companies that are ready to make this jump forward will realize benefits that will give them a competitive edge in the marketplace. What follows in this chapter will be an examination of the why and what of DAM. After unpacking why your business needs a DAM and what exactly it has to offer, we'll examine why DAMs succeed or fail.

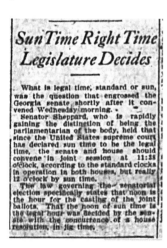

Figure 2-3. *Implementing a DAM is no small effort. When you put in place a technology that centralizes assets, it can be helpful to remember that people once resisted agreeing on a centralized way to tell time. This clipping from the front page of the July 12, 1911, issue of "The Atlanta Georgian and News" shows an argument typical of that era in American state governments. While railways and telegraphs used standard time from 1883 on, the U.S. government officially used sun time until the Standard Time Act of 1918*

Why Do We Need a DAM?

The real costs of unmanaged digital assets to a company are many, but I'll outline only the most common here. All of these topics are worthy of their own chapters and are discussed elsewhere in this text, but for the sake of generating quick talking points when petitioning for buy-in to a DAM project, here are the reasons your company may need a DAM.

Brand Management and Rights Management

While at first it may seem odd to link brand management and rights management, the two are in fact strongly interdependent as they rely on the same technical solutions and can strongly influence each other. Brand management is the applied strategy of controlling the way your organization or a particular product/service is presented to the public. Rights management, as used when discussing DAMs, refers to the linking and cross-referencing of licenses, releases, and contractual information needed when using digital content.

A good brand manager will tell you that his or her job is heavily dependent on the legal ability to track copyrights on things like brandmarks, branded imagery, and licensed properties such as music and visual content generated for advertising. All of those tasks can be managed within a DAM, and they are issues of rights management. If your current document or visual content system isn't linking the releases, contracts, and other legal documents to each asset, then that system isn't a DAM. The popularity of DAM systems has led several large corporations to claim that their asset-storage solutions are DAMs when they really aren't. If the system can't track rights and assist brand managers with their needed tasks, then it isn't a DAM.

Information Silos

As an organization grows, different teams and departments will invent their own ways of storing and searching for visual content (photos, graphics, videos, etc.) and documents. Because these storage and search strategies are unique to the groups of people who invent them, new employees or people from other departments will not be able to find what they need on each custom-organized shared drive or SharePoint-type solution. The person searching in a custom storage solution may not even be able to access the shared drive or system due to lack of permissions! If you've ever been unable to find an asset because someone was on vacation or out sick, you've run into an information silo.

Information silos generate a host of problems as side effects, including but not limited to the following:

Versioning Issues: Part of the life cycle of a digital asset includes multiple versions, whether because of corrections made in Photoshop or because versions were changed in response to user needs. When information silos exist in an organization, a file with multiple versions can quickly muddy basic search strategies and lead to confusion between departments. If you have information silos, odds are you've distributed or used the wrong version of an asset at a critical time, and a DAM can help prevent this from happening.

Redundant Systems: It's likely as you embark on your effort to implement a DAM that others in your organization have seen the problems before you and have attempted to deploy systems that organize files or access to them with limited success. When information silos have grown so large as to present problems for the people working with them everyday, it's common for companies to look for a quick fix first–and when it comes to a DAM, a quick fix will never last. Without a robust system with full-time attention and good planning, companies will end up building multiple information silos instead of a DAM. If your organization has the same assets stored in several different systems with no governance, leading to information silos and lots of versioning issues, then you have redundant systems that need to be consolidated with DAM. The cost of maintaining redundant systems is potentially very high when compared to the cost of an overall digital asset management solution.

The above problems that can be solved with a DAM are also closely tied to the issues surrounding **search costs** and **digital preservation**. Putting a value on the time your organization spends on inefficient searches is discussed in depth in Chapter 10, where proposed formulas for calculating a return on investment (ROI) are presented. Without going into the monetary valuations, if you're considering a DAM deployment it's likely that there have been instances in your organization where important assets simply could not be found when needed, costing your company money. Likewise, digital preservation is examined in depth in Chapter 11. If your organization lives and dies by its visual assets, then without a DAM strategy you'll lose content as time goes on unless you make plans for the curation of older files and formats. When discussing digital preservation as an issue in a high-level discussion, ask your management if there are any videos, graphics, or images that have already been lost due to the lack of a digital preservation plan–more than likely the answer is yes.

What Do You Want to Do with a DAM?

Now that we've gone over the most common reasons for implementing a DAM, let's examine strategies for developing high-level use cases and start the process of building justification for a DAM formally. How you do this will be determined by the size of your organization. If you work for a university or a smaller advertising agency, a simple list of needs and use cases may be all the outline you need to make your case for the purchase of a DAM. If you're part of a large organization, you may be requested to write a request for proposal (RFP). In an RFP, the long-term and short-term objectives of your DAM will be outlined, along with any strategies the DAM will support. By outlining your needs, the RFP will give you a better idea of what to ask each DAM vendor who wishes to sell your organization a system, and when you can hand each vendor the same list of needs for your DAM, you give them something uniform to respond to.

Because DAM systems are actually complex ecosystems of software and application programming interface (APIs) working together, it's very common to hire consultants familiar with DAMs to write RFPs. A quick look around at any DAM conference or on LinkedIn will turn up a dozen of these consultants quickly, and frankly they are often a solid investment for those looking to implement a DAM. Product offerings in the digital asset management space are diverse and ever-changing. It is the job of DAM consultants to be familiar with all the best offerings and to be agnostic as to which are best: every system is best for *some* company, but that means every offering is possibly a mistake for *your* company.

Do We Need a Consultant?

Unfortunately, the digital asset management space is also one with a history of vendors who oversell or misrepresent their products to buyers. This has led to a corporate landscape littered with failed DAM initiatives over the past decade. Some failed due to a lack of understanding by buyers of what exactly they were purchasing (see Chapter 10 for more on this), but some actually failed due to promises that vendors made that their DAMs couldn't possibly keep. While product research can be done on your own, investigate hiring a vendor-agnostic consultant to walk you through the RFP process. When interviewing consultants, ask them about the last few systems they've implemented, and call those customers to see how the DAMs are doing. Also, ask them what solution they ended up purchasing; hopefully the answers will be at least slightly different, showing that the consultant doesn't come to your table with a preconceived notion of what DAM system would best fit your organization's needs.

Needs Assessment for Your DAM

Often the best strategy for identifying what you want your DAM to do will come from outlining the real and potential problems arising from the current method of digital content management. To do this, it is helpful not only to talk and write about the scenarios already mentioned in this chapter but also to formally outline the processes that led to breakdowns in the management of digital assets. Set up interviews with different teams in your organization to gather information for your outlines and charts. When interviewing internal resources regarding the generation, storage, and distribution of assets before the implementation of your DAM, ask your colleagues the following questions:

- Which assets does your group use and produce?

- What are the sources of the assets used and produced?

- What are the destinations of assets used and produced?

- Where are the assets stored?

- What are the common problems encountered in the use, production, delivery, and storage of your digital assets?

Below is an example of three departments that might generate, store, and use assets in an organization plagued by the siloing of information:

Department X Assets

Asset Sources	Storage	Destination
Getty/iStock Self-Created assets Shared Drives of other departments	Hard Drives CDs/DVDs on shelves Legacy System	Departments Y & Z Website 1 Website 2 Outside Agencies

Department Y Assets

Asset Sources	Storage	Destination
Department X Self-Created Assets Untracked Employee Photos Outside Agencies	Hard Drives Outside Agencies	Website 2 Older CMS Newer CMS Outside Agencies Department Z

Department Z Assets

Asset Sources	Storage	Destination
Self-Created Assets Outside Agencies Untracked Internet Sources	Newer CMS Hard Drives Outside Agencies	Departments X & Y Website 3 Customers Outside Agencies Newer CMS

Figure 2-4. *A needs assessment chart can be laid out in spreadsheet form or in custom tables, as above; all needs assessments should track asset sources, where they are stored, and their final destination*

By surveying each department or source of assets, how assets are stored, and the final destinations for assets, you can begin to identify what legacy systems could be folded by putting their assets into the DAM, what process pain points can be solved, and where the low-hanging fruit for DAM content might reside. You can also ask others to help you build a priority list for assets they'd like to have more easily searched and shareable. While this is preliminary, a full audit will very likely reveal other sources and assets not previously mentioned by each department. Consider your survey a starting point, and don't be surprised when more assets and sources are discovered once your DAM project actually gets under way.

Archiving Versus Asset Management

If your background before working with DAMs has been working with archives or records management, you probably recognize the process above as the first step in the appraisal and acquisition process. There are key differences, however, in appraising digital assets for the archives and traditional records management roles versus evaluating the same sorts of items for ingesting within a DAM.

Traditionally, an archivist or records manager is only concerned with the assets at the **end of the life cycle**; the role of a digital asset manager is to assist with the arrangement, description, preservation, and access of assets that never have a clear end-of-life status. This includes assisting in the (legal) reuse and sometimes repurposing of assets as they are involved before, during, and after asset **creation/acquisition**. Because DAMs can be focused on the preservation of digital assets, this distinction between digital asset managers, records managers, and archivists may begin to seem like splitting hairs. As this book is released, universities are still teaching archivists and records managers how to deal with past assets, while information technology and graphic design programs are teaching students to deal with newly created and in-process assets.

This division of thinking about the life cycle of documents is rooted in the past, when paper-based files made the generation of new content continually necessary. In practice, the versioning and reuse of digital assets have always involved the repurposing of past materials and multiple versioning. It could be said that DAMs were created to solve the issues created by thinking of and treating digital assets as paper ones. Digital assets are not just flat pieces of paper with their surface content only; they are complex files layered with meaning regarding their creation, creators, and the way language shapes our understanding of the concepts the asset strives to convey. Only once a digital asset manager has understood that a digital document is all of these things can he or she truly understand the ways in which the information/asset should be treated in searches, workflows, and storage for the future.

When outlining the everyday workflow of assets from the point of creation forward, keep in mind that a creative asset never truly reaches the end of its life for dead storage, as was the practice in the last century. Digital files can and should live forever with the ability to be searched and reused as needed. For many types of creative files, there is no end of the life cycle, and so we must bring the practices of archivists and records management out of basements and into the everyday working environment.

Let's review some of the problems that can arise from nonstructured or poorly structured content management strategies. In the examples of the flow charts above, we see linear processes reflective of the linear production ideas connected to paper documents. Workflows from the past often show straight lines like this:

Figure 2-5. *A linear work flow has no room for the natural back-and-forth of creative work and approvals*

Charts reflective of DAMs more often are depicted in this manner:

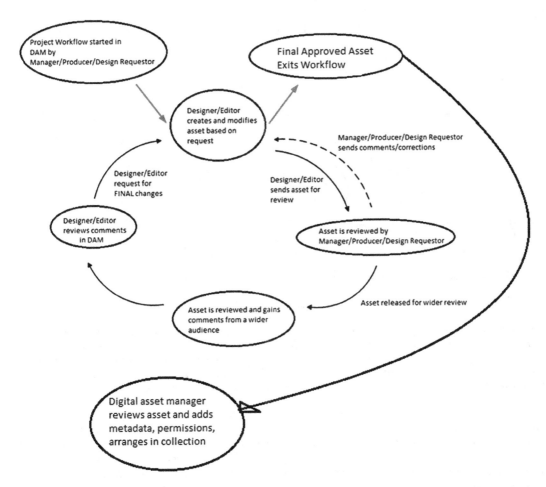

Figure 2-6. *This chart of interactions is a simplification of DAM workflows; for more on workflows, see chapter 12*

As you can see, the interactions with DAM systems are much more reflective of the modern workplace, where many different people may work on one project thousands of miles apart and asynchronously (composing different elements at different times).

To use our clock analogy again, DAMs allow all the separate moving parts of an organization to work together to produce a unified face minute-by-minute. But figuring out how all the springs and gears of your organization will fit together to present the time will take some doing–and not a few false starts. Do your best when interviewing your colleagues to explain that a DAM will break down information silos and that your system, when implemented, will strive to make their work better and easier, not more difficult and onerous.

Costs: Time = Money

Going back to our example earlier in the chapter of three departments with information silos, here is what the same assets, storage, and final destinations might look like with a DAM.

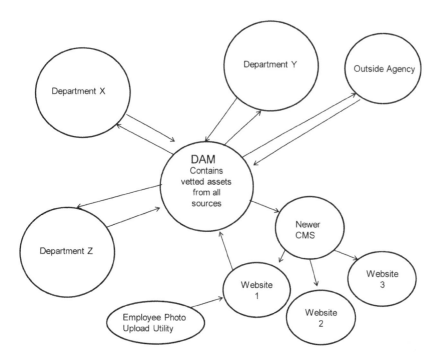

Figure 2-7. *Remember that when you visualize interactions between DAMs and groups of people and web sites that the macro-level workflows will almost never be able to be expressed in a linear fashion. The interactions among people and sources of information are continuous, not deterministic. This graphic only represents how a DAM might interact with a few systems and groups; if we were to overlay the interactions of people using this same graph, those in the X, Y, and Z circles would touch all other spheres*

As you can see in this figure, the DAM sits at the center of all information resources, both receiving and granting access to people in different departments. An effective DAM deployment using our examples from earlier in the chapter would sunset the older content management system (CMS), eliminating that expense from the organization, and set up a relationship with the newer CMS in order to feed web sites. Because DAM takes a centralized role in the arrangement and description of images, an Employee Photo Upload Utility is added on to web site 1 in order to help manage assets that come in from events.

How Is a DAM Different from a CMS?

Because many DAMs include features that integrate with web sites or CMSs, some confusion about what is a DAM and what is a CMS exists. This confusion is often perpetuated by vendors eager to sell a product; in fact, some DAMs currently on the market, such as Adobe CQ5, started as CMS products that have been "realigned" in their updates to match up with DAM needs. In reality, all DAMs need to connect to a CMS in order to effectively manage assets displayed on web sites. The systems that try to have it both ways–to effectively manage assets while also delivering them to the web–rarely do both tasks well, and they more often give lesser experiences in both utilities.

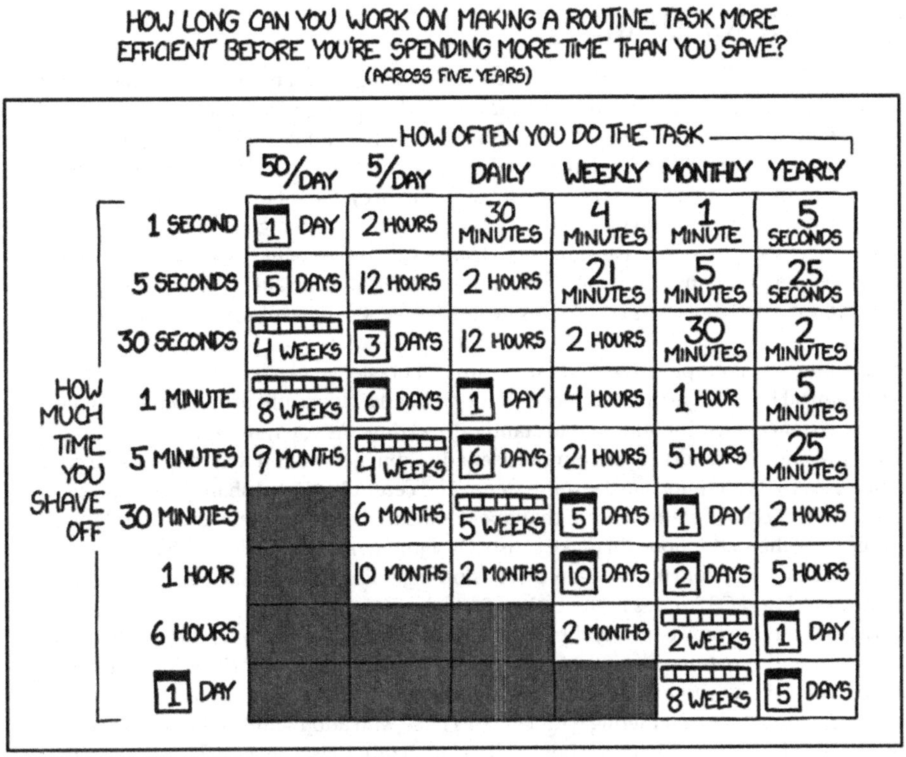
HOW LONG CAN YOU WORK ON MAKING A ROUTINE TASK MORE EFFICIENT BEFORE YOU'RE SPENDING MORE TIME THAN YOU SAVE?
(ACROSS FIVE YEARS)
HOW OFTEN YOU DO THE TASK
50/DAY
5/DAY
DAILY
WEEKLY
MONTHLY
YEARLY
HOW MUCH TIME YOU SHAVE OFF
1 SECOND
1 DAY
2 HOURS
30 MINUTES
4 MINUTES
1 MINUTE
5 SECONDS
5 SECONDS
5 DAYS
12 HOURS
2 HOURS
21 MINUTES
5 MINUTES
25 SECONDS
30 SECONDS
4 WEEKS
3 DAYS
12 HOURS
2 HOURS
30 MINUTES
2 MINUTES
1 MINUTE
8 WEEKS
6 DAYS
1 DAY
4 HOURS
1 HOUR
5 MINUTES
5 MINUTES
9 MONTHS
4 WEEKS
6 DAYS
21 HOURS
5 HOURS
25 MINUTES
30 MINUTES
6 MONTHS
5 WEEKS
5 DAYS
1 DAY
2 HOURS
1 HOUR
10 MONTHS
2 MONTHS
10 DAYS
2 DAYS
5 HOURS
6 HOURS
2 MONTHS
2 WEEKS
1 DAY
1 DAY
8 WEEKS
5 DAYS

Figure 2-8. *Setting up and taking care of a DAM is time-intensive enough that you'll wonder if you're spending more time than you save. While the chart above may not show you the return you're hoping for in time, the savings to your company in ROI may be substantial enough to offset this. See Chapter 10 for more information on calculating ROI. Source:* `http://xkcd.com/1205/` *(retrieved 8/10/2013, CC-BY-NC 2.5,* `http://xkcd.com/license.html`*)*

The cost to a company for failing to implement a DAM will ultimately be more than the time and money spent in setting up a solid foundation for the curated arrangement, description, preservation, and access of digital assets. Included in this chapter is a handy chart for showing how to calculate time savings, but a more in-depth analysis on calculating ROI can be found in Chapter 10.

Costs: Bad User Experience

Items that are difficult to quantify when justifying the effort of a DAM include not only the potential loss of past work, but also the cost to your organization when competitors implement a system and your department or company fails to do so. When given the choice, patrons or customers will always choose the information source easiest to use over a process that takes a long time or is difficult. Because a DAM allows for a more satisfying information/asset retrieval experience, those without a clear DAM strategy in the coming decade will fall behind those that have their house in order.

Building Your Argument for DAM

Large or small, your organization likely has legal counsel that will have some strong ideas about rights management and workflows. The potential cost to the company in fees stemming from poorly managed image licenses is just the tip of the iceberg in legal costs that can accrue from poor asset management. It's important in making your case for a DAM to talk to your legal counsel and get their perspective on what they perceive as the administrative needs in your company relating to asset management. Further, your counsel may have a system of their own (such as a document management system) with which you would like your DAM to interact. An investigation of any existing legal document management system is warranted to make sure your DAM is set up to eventually allow contributions from one area of the business to the other. To many, the main selling point of a DAM is the ability to allow this flow of information across the organization with tight access controls as necessary for sensitive information and legal compliance.

In the introduction to this chapter, it was emphasized that the technical knowledge needed to interact with a DAM was not dissimilar to the technical knowledge once needed in order to read a clock, and the resistance to the use of a DAM was not unlike the resistance once encountered to standardized time. As you move forward in the justification of the expense of a DAM and your efforts to encourage user adoption, be mindful that the learning curve both for the use of a new technology and its adoption can be quite steep. The centralization of shared information assets is as inevitable as the standardization of time zones, but that doesn't mean that as the systems are implemented and grow that every decision regarding their adoption will make sense. Disagreements on specifics will occur, and holdouts on specific standardizations will hold out (see any discussion regarding daylight savings time, or the irregularities of the line that divides EST and CST zones in the United States).

While the chapter on metrics will outline how to justify the initial cost of a DAM, a more compelling argument in the eyes of those with a more competitive nature will be that of "survival of the fittest." If your rivals implement effective DAM strategies first, they will have a distinct edge in the marketplace. Increasingly, large corporations require their outsourced work and vendors to be interacting with DAMs. Those who adopt and champion this new critical technology will survive the next few decades in much better shape than otherwise. Successful businesses strike a balance between short-term operational stability and longer-term growth potential. Those who adopt and champion this new critical technology are recognizing that need for balance and are likely to survive the coming years in much better shape than those who do not.

Conclusion

In the next chapter, assets to manage will be outlined. Often the strongest argument for DAM implementation is simply a lack of easy access to items in the work environment. With increasing file sizes and the desire for a more flexible asset search space, the final trump card in any DAM implementation argument may be the need for a digital strategy where none existed before.

Before jumping into buying a new system, it's helpful to have all your requirements thought through. Once you've outlined your current processes (or lack thereof), it will be time to gather up ideas about how you'd like assets to get into your system, what those assets will look like when they are there, and who and how will the system will be structured. Again, don't get frustrated or overwhelmed, and don't let those who resist standardization shut your project down. Centralization of digital assets, cataloged in a standardized way, is as inevitable as railroad time.

CHAPTER 3

Choosing the Right DAM Solution

Chapter Goal: This chapter will examine the choices that are available in the digital asset management (DAM) marketplace for those who are either seeking a new system or looking to acquire or license a new DAM for the first time.

Why There Is No One Best DAM

There are many different options in the DAM marketplace; what sort of DAM to launch can be confusing. Every DAM conference includes a vendor area with an array of options that can be bewildering to anyone encountering them for the first time. Going online to gather information at first can also be intimidating; when the first-time digital asset manager for a state university innocently asked for information on DAMs from a LinkedIn group in 2011, he was swamped with emails and calls from salespeople. Two years later, he still receives cold calls from vendors. This chapter hopes to help you avoid that type of vendor attention by giving a good overview of the different types of DAMs and what sort of support you would need for implementing each.

The DAM solution that a company or organization chooses should not be a system that can act in an isolated bubble; in order to be effective, the DAM must be connected to many different systems. For example, email alerts used in a workflow mean that the DAM must be connected to an email server, and distributing assets to a website necessitates the use of a content management system (CMS). The ability to stream video to a large number of users effectively will require integration with a streaming video player, and turning that video content into several available formats will require the use of a transcode engine. The DAM itself is a system that allows for the upload, arrangement, description, preservation, and controlled access of digital assets so that they may be downloaded through a variety of means and other programs.

Because a DAM's successful adoption and operation depend on its integration with existing systems and workflows, there is no "one best DAM" for everyone. All of the solutions described here come with customizable user interface options and are available for a myriad of programming languages and hosting environments. Due to the wide variety of solutions available, this chapter will discuss at a high level the DAM types and their support levels for implementation.

Types of DAMs

For the purposes of this chapter, we will break down DAM systems into three types: commercial solutions, open source, and home brew. However, one of the truths about DAM systems is that they very rarely are any of these options used "alone"—every commercial and open source solution that is deployed will need home-brewed customizations, and every home-brewed solution will co-opt open source solutions and license a few commercial extensions. Still, each of these system types deserves its own examination, as a decision on the base code of your DAM will influence every other action an organization takes regarding digital asset management.

Commercially Available DAMs

Commercial solutions are the most common and easiest DAMs to implement, making it important that they should be thoroughly considered. Because most commercial solutions offer support contracts, the DAMs that are available on the commercial market are the best option for those who are launching a new system without a dedicated team that includes IT members.

SaaS, SaS, ASP, PaaS, and Other Acronyms

When discussing the benefits of commercially available DAMs, the biggest advantage these systems have is the availability of help on demand. When licensing a DAM, you will hear these service agreements referred to variously as SaaS (software as a service), SaS (service and support), SLA (service-level agreement), ASP (application-service providers), or PaaS (platform as a service). The most common terms in North America are SaaS and SaS (both pronounced "sass"), so this book will refer to those kinds of agreements with DAM vendors that allow for various levels of system support. Typically these agreements will connect DAM customers to a service center and include a set number of service hours per year that can be used as the DAM team needs them. Outside of the yearly SaS, there will be a set hourly rate for special projects like the one outlined in the case study at the end of this chapter. Be sure to do your due diligence with research on vendors claiming to offer full-service SaaS packages, particularly if you plan to build your DAM team without in-house technical support. Such things as business hours, which time zone the DAM office hours use, holiday schedules, and the like may seem trivial points when setting up a highly technical support agreement, but in a pinch these details can be crucial. As discussed in more detail below, what the DAM vendors represent in their sales materials and what is actually available from their products may vary. Many digital asset managers have been surprised in an emergency to find the fixes needed for their systems have an additional cost or are outside the normal hours and/or services provided.

DAM Caveat Emptor

When comparing commercial DAM vendors, organizations should be aware that often they are not comparing apples to apples; the DAM solutions commercially available vary widely in their capabilities, dependencies, and their abilities to handle differing types of media. Add to this the major name brands that have entered the market in the past few years by re-branding their CMSs, storage solutions, secure FTP options, or other products as DAMs or as having DAM capabilities, and you quickly see how the marketplace can be confusing to those researching for the first time. It is strongly suggested by the DAM Foundation (http://damfoundation.org) that first-time buyers and those learning about DAMs take the time to talk with a consultant who can help an organization sum up its DAM needs and offer best matches for solutions. The Real Story (http://realstorygroup.com/research/dam/), an international consulting firm, offers up a publication each year that serves as a sort of *Consumer Reports* for DAMs. The DAM List, curated by Leala Abbot, is an open-access spreadsheet of all available DAMs with information that is input from digital asset managers across many different disciplines and implementations (http://goo.gl/vltq9H). David Diamond at Picturepark has put together comparisons from DAM vendor websites (http://goo.gl/ZRiKNA), but as with all sales materials, the claims should be taken with a grain of salt. As Diamond himself notes in a blog post titled "Why No One Trusts Your Content":

> *It seems that for 99.9% of vendors, content's main focus is to generate leads, not educate. They don't care whether what they offer is valuable because once the download form has been submitted, they have what they want. Worse, their main audience is the GoogleBot, not the reader. So they stuff blog posts with keyword terms designed to get them ranking higher in search engine results placement (SERP). (Source:* http://damsurvivalguide.com/2013/09/20/why-no-one-trusts-your-content/; retrieved 09/20/2013)

The same blog post by Diamond notes that only 9 percent of those surveyed trusted vendor-generated content. Let that number sink in as your organization shops for a DAM; the sales environment for DAMs is very much "buyer beware." Further, be aware that demonstrations of products can often be overcontrolled. If at all possible, ask your colleagues or peers in other organizations for demonstrations of their systems, and ask for their off-the-record, personal experiences and feelings regarding the systems with which they have had contact.

Open Source DAMs

Open source DAMs are those that are built by online communities and are free of licensing fees. A good list with reviews of available DAMs in this category has been put together by DAM News (http://digitalassetmanagementnews.org/) and can be found at http://opensourcedigitalassetmanagement.org/. New open source DAMs are constantly emerging, changing, and improving themselves. Sometimes DAM vendors can even be hired to assist with the building and support of open source DAMs, but be aware that the fees for this may be higher than for commercial solutions.

One of the great advantages of open source DAMs is that they often come with active, vocal online communities where those who are implementing systems problem-solve in a collaborative environment. When one person solves a coding problem or builds an extension, it is uploaded and made available to everyone using the same DAM. The downside to this open problem-solving environment is that in order to make an open source DAM work, your team must employ one or more persons with a programming background to make the DAM work. IT support is absolutely critical to the function of an open source DAM.

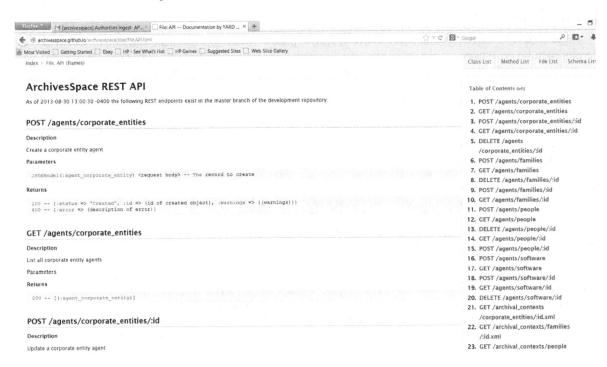

Figure 3-1. *This screenshot from the ArchivesSpace online community shows how documentation and help are available for open source DAMs. Source: http://archivesspace.github.io/archivesspace/doc/fileAPI.html (retrieved 10/5/2013)*

Anyone interested in open source DAMs should listen to an interview of Joe Bachana by Henrik de Gyor on "Another DAM Podcast" (`http://anotherdampodcast.com/2012/06/28/joe-bachana/`). In the interview, Bachana, a twenty-year veteran of DAM implementations, speaks candidly about the history of asset delivery systems, and he gives his opinion that "the open source DAMs are approaching, in general, the workgroup functionalities of products out there, in the marketplace." Bachana also points out that in terms of affordable flexibility, open source DAMs allow for extensions and customizations much more affordably than commercially licensed DAMs:

> The other thing that I find really exciting is that the whole promise of open source, to me, is you don't have to say, "Mother, May I?" The whole idea of innovate and ingenuity in software, the open source software world is the ability to just step up and say, "I want to create something of value that's available or that I need for the context I need it." Without saying, "Hey, may I please do that?" And then somebody saying, "Yeah sure. But pay $20,000 for an SDK [software development kit] and sign this agreement that you won't do this or that." With open source, you can do it. A couple of the open source products have robust web services and published APIs [application programming interfaces] that, essentially, allow you to do anything you want, ranging from connecting the DAM to a product like Drupal or WordPress, or connecting it to your CRM [customer relationship management], if that's what you needed, and so on. That, to me, is the most exciting aspect.

Home-Brew DAMs

This is the least common of DAM solutions, as it is typically expensive to develop, maintain, and support a system developed in-house. However, it may be an appropriate option for organizations that have specific needs that are not met by other available solutions. Some notably successful home-brew DAMs are those employed by the Cartoon Network, iTunes, and Getty Images. That some of the most successful home-brew DAMs are deployed by digital content providers should come as no surprise; when the distribution of digital assets is your main business, it doesn't make sense to lean your business model on anything but in-house expertise.

When you develop a home-grown DAM, documentation is particularly important for digital preservation reasons regarding the assets, metadata, and the system itself. The world of academia is, as of this writing, littered with home-grown DAMs written and produced by individuals who will one day retire or move on without leaving legible technical documentation on their work. If you have inherited such a DAM, do not despair. Check first to see if the retired DAM home brewer started his or her system off an open source platform; if so, with any luck, the tangle of code can be unknotted. If the DAM was home-brewed from scratch and the brewer left suddenly (hopefully with lottery winnings), there may not be much that can be done other than to export the assets and metadata over a metadata crosswalk into an entirely new system. Needless to say, the new system should be one that can be interpreted and maintained by future digital asset managers.

As the previous paragraphs illustrate, coding your own DAM from the bottom up is not for the faint of heart or the shy of resources. That so many academic institutions have home-brew systems is indicative of both the expertise (professors) and low-cost labor (students/interns/adjuncts) that a campus tends to have on hand. The other common environment for fully custom solutions (for those who deliver digital media) sees the cost of expertise and lots of labor as simply part of doing business. Either way, at least one expert—and more (usually two or three)—and lots of hands on deck are needed to make home-grown DAMs work. To those with the resources, this author says Godspeed.

Type of DAM	Scalability (Ease of Growth)	Documentation and Support Available	Coding Knowledge Level Needed
Commercial	Highly scalable	Check with the vendor; a good one will have extensive documentation available; SaS available.	Low coding knowledge needed; a SaS will cover coding.
Home brew	Usually not easy to scale	Usually poorly documented; SaS by outside sources unavailable.	High level of coding knowledge needed.
Open source	Can be moderately difficult to scale	Documentation kept by online community; quality varied; a SaS may be available from some vendor sources.	Moderate level of coding knowledge needed; can be used with a SaS.

Figure 3-2. *Comparison of the Three Types of DAMs*

DAM Support Determines the DAM Software

Before deciding which kind of DAM is right for your organization, it is important to decide whether the DAM will rely on in-house resources for technical support or if a SaS agreement is more appropriate for your work environment. In-house support and SaS agreements need not be an either-or situation; it's possible to use these two solutions for problem solving together, and usually that's the way technical problem solving in DAM works. The more a system is regularly used, the more support both from those in house and from vendors will be needed. The two main support options are outlined below, followed by a case study showing how the issues would be resolved with each, and with the two working together.

In-House Support

Dedicated full-time, in-house technical support for DAMs are commonly found in organizations in these situations:

1. The DAM is central to the business model, as in advertising, video/film production, or broadcast.

2. The DAM is "home brew" or open source, built and maintained by staff, as in large universities, software companies, or large museums.

3. The DAM is so large as to produce a significant return on investment (ROI), and it can support full-time, dedicated in-house tech support.

SaS Agreements

Digital asset managers use SaS agreements with their DAM vendors in these situations:

1. The DAM team cannot afford full-time, in-house support, as in any smaller organization.

2. The DAM is licensed from a vendor with an excellent proven SaaS record, as proven by client testimonials and wide user adoption of the vendor's SaaS model.

3. The DAM is so small or new as to not have proven a ROI that justifies full-time, dedicated in-house tech support.

4. The digital asset managers and in-house support need frequent help with a highly trafficked system that experiences uploads and downloads frequently enough to need highly sophisticated "bug" hunting (log reviews for hung threads, etc.).

The majority of DAM deployments as of the writing of this book rely on SaS agreements with vendors. The primary reasons for the reliance on SaS is that the full-time cost of experienced, qualified individuals for this type of work outstrips the ROI of smaller systems. At present, the field is also full of systems that have yet to mature into stable, proven work environments for their companies. As a DAM matures as a tool for media workflows, storage, and delivery, the proven ROI of these systems will justify more companies hiring full-time support. At that time, truly qualified, competent tech-support persons in the DAM field will be able to command very nice compensation packages indeed.

Case Study: A Photographer Needs VPN Access to a Secure DAM
Problem

Due to security concerns, an organization has its new DAM hosted inside a very secure firewall. For the first year of the DAM's life, archivists have done a great job filling the system with older materials, working out the metadata modeling and search interface, and improving access to their historical collections. The archivists' hard work has now been recognized by the marketing department, who would like the DAM to allow uploads directly from a professional photographer. The archivists understand the Extensible Metadata Platform (XMP) technology and are excited to see their system gain new materials from the source of creation. However, they are stymied by the technical issues surrounding the ingestion of XMP and remote access to the new DAM. The photographer is tech savvy and willing to preprogram cameras to allow for the XMP needed, but he does not have tech support for this type of project.

Solution with In-House Support

The archivists who own the DAM make it clear to marketing that they will need IT support in order to allow system access through the firewall. Together, the archives and marketing staffs appeal to the organization's IT department for help establishing VPN (virtual private network) access to the DAM for the photographer. Though it takes many calls and emails to walk the photographer, archivists, and IT through testing, VPN access is established to the DAM for just this one image source. Progress is slow with uploads, however, as the archivists work through issues regarding the ingestion of XMP data to their metadata model. While the organization's IT department understands the firewalls and servers, they aren't digital asset managers and know little about metadata modeling, XMP, or the indexing of assets by search engines. A happy ending to this solution would include the archivists using their experience linking one photographer into the system to justify a full-time IT person on their DAM team, one with some design experience who can work with them on an everyday basis to allow access for advertising agencies, designers, and photographers who work outside the firewall.

Solution with a SaaS

The archivists email their DAM service providers and open a ticket for a conference call discussing outside access to the DAM. On the conference call, the service providers ask questions about the photographer's ability to connect, and they give a list of questions they will need answered before a solution to the issue can be outlined. After questions regarding the photographer, the organization's firewall, and the desired XMP metadata outcomes are answered via email, the SaaS providers offer estimates of the hours it will take to solve for VPN access and to ensure that the XMP gets into the DAM's metadata model as requested. This prospective bill is then presented by the archivists to marketing; in order to fulfill the request for photographer access to the system, the monies for connection must come from the requesting department. If marketing is then willing to pay for the hours needed for support, the project moves forward, and the photographer is able to deposit images directly to the DAM, where the images are checked for quality control in the metadata by the digital asset manager before being released to the proper access control list. The SaaS providers end up in long discussions with the organization's IT department during this process, as allowing access through the firewall can be a contentious issue for a security-minded company. If the SaaS representatives are flexible and the encounters with IT not too painful, no extra charges are incurred for the IT wrangling. If the SaaS representatives are closely monitored for billings, and IT is resentful of the DAM system or team, extra charges for delays in the project may occur before the problem is solved.

Solution with In-House Support and a SaaS

The archivists talk first with their in-house support (an IT manager assigned to their team) and several others. Once permission to build a connection through the firewall is confirmed, the archivists then open a ticket with their SaaS partners to work out how XMP from the photographer will get into their metadata model. After many conference calls that include the archivists, photographer, IT manager, and SaaS representatives, all together and in various combinations as needed, VPN access is established and the testing of metadata transfer begins. If the DAM team can absorb the cost of the SaaS hours into their budget of support hours for the year, they do so; if not, the billing must be approved with marketing up front. After the connection is complete and starts showing products of success, the IT manager and archivists document the process, work hours, and SaaS costs for the next time a VPN connection is proposed. Moving forward, this documentation can provide the budget to marketing or the archives for additional access to the DAM by outside agencies.

Solutions Summary

In all the solutions above, the organization's IT department must be involved in some way in order for a VPN connection to the DAM to be allowed through the firewall. Having a full-time person on staff or working with someone from IT on a regular basis will serve to build trust between those distributing digital content and those in charge of cybersecurity. Without regular communication and support from IT, the archivists are doomed to stressful interactions whenever the DAM needs to connect with other systems or organizations. At the same time, a good SaaS is worth its weight in gold. Unless your DAM is a home-brew system, no one will know the ins and outs of its code like the people who licensed it to you. Having a set number of SaS hours each year to draw from will allow you access to problem solving for your DAM from experienced experts. How billing for such expenses in your organization is handled will affect your ability to draw down those service and support hours; if you are coming to DAM from a non-IT background, make it clear to your organization that a healthy SaS is needed for a good working relationship.

Conclusions

Staffing concerns will play a large role in what type of DAM is the right fit for your company. While no DAM will succeed without full-time, dedicated staff, it is possible to launch a very small DAM (fewer than five thousand assets) with just one full-time person or with an archivist/librarian or two as in the case study above. If a smaller DAM is a commercial solution backed by a robust SaS, or is an open source solution with an amazingly good technical/organizational mind behind it, a system launch can be successful with just one digital asset manager. However, as that DAM grows, more staffing will be required due to the labor-intensive tasks surrounding the acquisition, appraisal, arrangement, description, preservation, and access of assets. A DAM can set up and launch with just one staffer, but it cannot grow or continue without additional resources. To justify the cost of this staffing, use projections like those found in chapter ten to help sway those cynical of the DAM's worth. No matter how your organization chooses to staff its DAM, remember that digital asset management is never a temporary task: it requires commitment over the long term. Once setup of the system is done, the real work has just begun.

If your organization chooses to launch a commercially available DAM, the choices available (not to mention the sales material of dubious worth) can be overwhelming and confusing. Be sure to give your company enough time both to investigate the options available to them and to build your organization's willingness to support the new system. Recognize that the initial implementation cost will be followed by licensing fees that must be paid annually with expected increases. In the period between 2000 and 2010, it was common for large American corporations to drop heavy one-time investments on DAMs and then fail to support the systems with appropriate staffing or an adequate budget for system growth. Try to avoid the mistakes of the past by setting your DAM team up for success.

Finally, remember always that the DAM you choose must be able to connect with other systems and people inside and outside of your organization. A digital delivery system that cannot provide access is doomed from the beginning. While DAMs frequently launch with a smaller, controlled audience, scalability and access should always be at the top of any digital asset manager's wish list.

■ ■ ■

CHAPTER 4

Where Your DAM Lives

Chapter Goal: *This chapter will consider the unique and significant storage needs of a digital asset management (DAM) system.*

Servers, Hosting, and Storage

Your server is a program on a computer or network of computers. Storage is just what it sounds like; it's how your assets are stored on servers, and it can also refer to how those assets are backed up. Hosting refers to who hosts the content, how they do so, and where those servers and storage facilities are managed and accessed.

At its most basic, a server is no more and no less than a system where your DAM lives. However, because a DAM can and does deal with extraordinarily large files in very large quantities, the strategies deployed to cope with the storage, access, and preservation of assets are anything but basic. In Peter Krogh's *The DAM Book: Digital Asset Management for Photographers*, published in 2009, Krogh spends two full chapters breaking down everything from the fans inside a computer casing to multiple redundant array of independent disks (RAID) deployments. Here in Chapter 4, I endeavor to approach the topic of storage at a middle ground, assuming that the reader is familiar with the basic parts of their computers but will not be immediately scaling up to multiple RAID deployments.

Since where and how your assets and metadata are stored will speak to the security and dependability of a DAM's ability to access information, this topic deserves some serious consideration. To those coming to a DAM from a non-IT background, discussions of servers, system hosting, active and archival storage, backups, and storage-size needs can be particularly bewildering. There are numerous acronyms and words used in storage-requirement discussions that are never used at any other time in human conversation. So what follows will attempt to break down the most common terms and strategies used in digital asset management for those encountering servers and defining storage requirements for the first time.

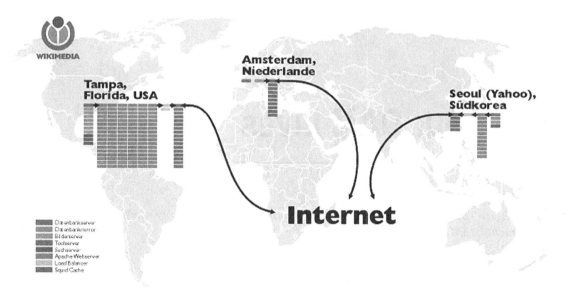

Figure 4-1. *Whenever you see an image on Wikimedia or Wikipedia, that image was saved by someone through the Internet onto one of the web-site servers in Tampa, Amsterdam, or Seoul. When I downloaded this image from its Wikimedia page, my computer retrieved information from the Internet, and the Internet served up that information from one of the locations listed above. The Internet is the open network we all use to share information without actually having our computers call directly to one another, and despite the location of the label on the map, the Internet does not actually reside in South Africa. Source:* `http://commons.wikimedia.org/wiki/File:Wikimedia_server.jpg`, *licensed CC-SA 2.5 (retrieved 10/4/2013)*

Types of DAM Server Environments

Your DAM will live on a server in one of the following ways, and each has its benefits and drawbacks:

- On-site, in a server at your organization

- Hosted by a DAM vendor, in the cloud or off

- Hosted by a server farm/hosting specialist, in the cloud or off

- A mix of any of the three above, with traditional servers for archived assets and cloud storage servers for active assets

On-Site Servers

Traditionally, servers exist in a computer room in an organization. A computer room reserved for servers would be one where a backup power supply exists in case of emergencies, where the intense heat generated from constant server use can be handled without risk of fire, and where special precautions have been put in place to preserve the servers in the event of a flood or other catastrophe. Some of the scariest moments of my life have been stepping into makeshift server rooms where the heat was clearly unmanaged and exposed wiring made me check for fire escape routes. Piling servers into closets may seem like a good idea when space and time are tight, but the fire risk is very real, and even if a fire extinguisher is stashed close by, it seems unwise to pour all one's hard work and thought into a server that may, at the very least, melt itself, if not the whole office.

Figure 4-2. An unsecured and possibly dangerous server environment. It does help to have at least one member of the IT team small enough to do close-range inspections of the hardware. Source: `http://commons.wikimedia.org/wiki/File:Computer-kitten.jpg`, CC-A-SA; photo by Tim Bartel (retrieved 10/5/2013)

By contrast, a well-maintained server room can be a place to experience joy. Often these rooms have raised platform floors in order to provide safe wiring and fiber connection environments. As these raised floors are often composed of metal or lightweight composite platforms, kicking off one's shoes will allow a digital asset manager to feel the subtle hum and vibration produced by spinning hard drives and whirring fans through the soles of one's feet. Listening to and feeling the literal flow of information in a server room while configuring information sources can be transcendent to those who take pride in their work.

However, these moments of transcendent direct connection to a physical server source can come at a high price. Access to the server infrastructure in your organization may mean extra security clearances. For very justifiable reasons, those who take their server security seriously may demand that the DAM team make requests for server access, reboots, and maintenance. While it may seem trivial to get permission to go into a room and hit restart on a DAM server, if the DAM server is sitting right next to the server that hosts your organization's critical sales web site, your IT department may be a little worried that if you hit the reset button on the machine just to the left of yours a major calamity will occur.

Unless you work at a particularly large corporation, scalability can become an issue with on-site servers. It is unlikely that your organization will have loads of unused server memory space available at a moment's notice. However, if you choose to operate out of the cloud or have your servers hosted by a professional service, all the space you wish to purchase is available with very little notice. With the increasing demand for video availability in DAMs, on-site storage is becoming less of a practical choice for systems that need to serve audiences of all but the smallest sizes.

Requirements for on-site hosting include the following:

- A server room (with safety concerns addressed)

- IT support for setup and configuration

- Disaster planning that addresses on-site storage

- Power supply backups

- Security (a locked door, at the very least)

Much has been written about requirements for safe and secure on-site server rooms. Readers may want to consult a few of these resources:

- OSHA: Rules for server-room construction: `https://www.osha.gov/pls/oshaweb/owadisp.show_document?p_table=STANDARDS&p_id=10704`

- Tech Republic: "Setting Up a Server Room": `http://www.techrepublic.com/article/setting-up-a-server-room-part-1-the-basics/`

- University of California at Davis, "Server Room Best Practices": `http://vpiet.ucdavis.edu/bestpractices.cfm`

The last link from the University of California also details a fairly common server-room fire incident, and it is worth reading to those who may be doubters as to the danger of an improperly controlled and cooled server space.

Servers Hosted by a DAM Vendor

Many DAM vendors offer server hosting as part of a service and support (SaS) package. This is a good idea for those launching a DAM without much staff or for whom infrastructure is an issue. If you have a chance to visit the headquarters of a DAM vendor, ask if you can see the server room. If they agree to take you in, what you see should be cold, clean, and busily humming. The vendor should be able to show you documentation of a regular backup schedule (more on backups later in this chapter) and have a brief of a disaster-preparedness plan available. The vendor should be able to speak to the ability to scale up when and if needed.

Advantages to DAM servers hosted by a vendor include having someone else push that server restart button on the rare occasions it is needed and allowing those in on your SaS to have access to the machine, its available storage, and server activity reports whenever needed. You can also get standardized pricing sheets on the costs of scaling up, allowing your DAM team to quickly estimate how much of an increase in budget is needed to take in any surprise video collections. Did department X forget to tell you it wanted to dump an entire television ad campaign into the DAM in Q4? Having a pricing sheet can quickly tell you how much that extra storage space and bandwidth will cost, so that chargebacks can occur.

Drawbacks to vendor hosting include having all your eggs in one basket. Of course, if you are licensing your DAM software from the vendor, they hold the keys to that software and its performance. But if they also host your server, there's a chance for things to go doubly wrong in the same place. Human error, personnel challenges, and the regular buyout cycle in the DAM vendor community mean that you're placing an awful lot of trust in one organization when all your assets and the software used to access them are in the same place.

Hosting Specialists/Server Farms

If you plan to run a DAM that will include web portals with critical access—say, to your Public Relations page, to your crisis manuals/response materials, or to customer web sites that demand 24-hour uptime—you probably want to host your DAM and web sites with a professional hosting company. Names in this business you have probably heard of include Rackspace, EarthLink, and Amazon Cloud, to name just a few, but there are thousands more, including local companies in large cities offering simple colocation plans.

These types of companies live and die by their reputation for security and stability, so any company you sign with should offer you insurance against breaches or downtime. If or when downtime occurs (and this happens to even the best providers every once in a while), the hosting specialists will typically refund you an amount that will be specified in the vendor agreement. If you go with a local company, make sure it is insured and ask for a site visit, just as you would with a DAM vendor.

Commercial hosting specialists should offer you several levels of monitoring and service agreements, so you can pay for as much or as little hand-holding as you like. The service reps at the hosting company should be ready and willing to work with your DAM vendors. When licensing a DAM, you can ask your DAM vendors who their favorite hosting companies are, and they will readily share their opinions, even if they are trying to sell their own services.

Figure 4-3. *This overhead shot of servers at CERN in Switzerland shows an ideal server-farm setup. The servers are located in a spotless room in cooled racks within numbered and lettered rows. The floor is raised to allow for fiber connections. The ceiling is high, is configured to allow for proper ventilation, and contains waterless fire suppression systems. Source: http://commons.wikimedia.org/wiki/File:CERN_Server_02.jpg, photo by Florian Hirzinger CC-BY-SA-3.0 (retrieved 10/6/2013)*

Hosting Defined

Hosting refers to how and where your servers and storage facilities are located and accessed. There are many different kinds and combinations of servers, storage, and hosting. Here are a few of the most common terms associated with hosting in alphabetical order.

Colocation Hosting

Colocation (sometimes referred to as colo) is a hosting strategy primarily used by smaller businesses that lack secure server rooms of their own or that need space in a building that can provide high-speed access. If you choose to colocate your servers, you'll contract with a provider that offers space for your servers and devices on a rack in a server farm, which will usually be a very cold building with high-end fire suppression, security, and blocked-off windows. In this hosting arrangement, you're responsible for everything—purchasing, configuring, deploying, and maintaining the physical hardware (servers, firewalls, etc.), software, and operating system. While this is not a simple solution, and will require you to have your own IT folks to set up and run the server, this option is used by many businesses, such as law firms, web developers, and other businesses that may have great offices in buildings that are unsuited for safe server environments.

Dedicated Hosting

Dedicated hosting is another way of saying that your DAM and web sites don't share their server computer with any other departments, teams, or organizations. Because one computer can run many different servers for many different web sites and departments, your business may not give you a dedicated server (at least not at first—once you start streaming video, the bandwidth needs will quickly change things). Dedicated hosting with a DAM vendor or commercial hosting environment allows organizations to lease preconfigured, dedicated equipment and connectivity from the provider. With dedicated hosting, the customer usually retains control over the hosting environment and choice of operating system. However, the hosting provider remains responsible for hardware and network administration. The vendor or commercial hosting solution will also generally offer agreements with SaS packages, and it may provide usage statistics pages for traffic monitoring. How your organization handles dedicated hosting if you have your own server on-site will vary with the internal IT rules of your company.

Managed Hosting

In this server environment, a commercial provider (either your DAM vendor or a company specializing in server hosting) owns the data centers, the network, the server, and other devices. The managed hosting vendor is responsible for deploying, maintaining, and monitoring the servers, storage, and backup routines. While you would retain full control of the operating systems and applications, this type of hosting agreement allows for levels of security, scalability, and uptime that can exceed basic dedicated hosting and other hosting options for larger DAM systems. While this type of hosting may seem expensive, for mission-critical web sites and applications that need network uptime 100 percent of the time, your DAM and web portals may need managed hosting in order to be reliable.

Shared Hosting

Shared hosting is the most inexpensive of hosting alternatives, whether you have on-site or off-site servers. With shared hosting, many customers or departments host their web sites or applications on the same machine, sharing the cost of an Internet connection that's generally faster and more secure than the regular connection you have at your desk. If there's fiber running to your business office in 2014, you either work for a very large business or that fiber runs exclusively to your server room. However, because the server is shared with others, server performance may be affected and security is easier to compromise if everyone on the same machine doesn't manage or update their firewalls. While inexpensive, shared hosting typically cannot handle large amounts of storage or traffic, and you won't have the authority to hit the server reset button without contacting everyone else who works on your shared machine. Especially with the increasing demand for video in DAMs, no one will want to share a server with your team anyway, so this solution is only recommended for very small library DAMs or archival DAMs.

Cloud vs. Traditional Hosting and Storage

All of the server environments, storage, and vendor option scenarios will present your DAM team with the question of whether you want your system to live in the cloud, in a traditional storage environment, or in a hybrid of the two.

The cloud is a type of hosting architecture that connects many hundreds of thousands of servers to the Internet, allowing them to share computing resources. Because all the computers linked to a cloud environment are able to add or remove resources like CPU cycles, memory, and network storage, servers can scale memory and bandwidth up and down via the Internet service. Infrastructure services like load balancing and traffic shaping, security, and intelligent caching can move up and down with the traffic to and from your DAM or access web sites.

Whether you choose to use cloud hosting, traditional storage, or a hybrid solution, you'll likely have security questions about your provider, and rightly so. In my opinion, cloud hosting is just as secure as any in-house dedicated server option, which is to say that as long as you're paying attention to security and acting responsibly, you likely won't have a problem. On the other hand, if someone is really determined to hack your boxes, there's not too much you can do to stop top-notch talent. Luckily for everyone on the Internet, top-notch talent is very rare or too busy making loads of money to mess with DAM services.

Figure 4-4. *Security risks will always be brought up when discussing cloud services and storage. Unless someone trips over the cord in this comic, the service should be perfectly fine. Source:* http://imgs.xkcd.com/comics/the_cloud.png, *licensed CC-A-NC 2.5 (retrieved 10/3/2013)*

Storage

Storage requirements for your DAM will change as technology and system uses change. Therefore, a storage system and infrastructure that are flexible is required for long-term preservation and access to digital assets. Just as with servers and hosting agreements, this chapter will attempt to break down some common terms digital asset managers encounter when discussing the storage needs of their DAMs.

Active and Inactive Storage

In some cases, organizations may need to separate their storage needs into active and archival (or inactive) storage. Even if you don't start your DAM with these two storage divisions, once you climb past 50,000 assets, it will be time to consider moving assets you don't want active into archival storage so you can make more room for active assets.

Active storage is exactly what it sounds like. It is server space that stores assets that you plan to have returned in search results and want everyone to access on the fly, and it is measured in the amount of active memory space you have on your server. This kind of storage is more expensive due to the need for high reliability and support, and it will need to be backed up regularly and have limited downtime, both planned and unplanned. I am old enough to remember when talking about having 1 terabyte of active storage was a bragging right; today's DAMs that handle video would never start with anything less.

Inactive storage refers to the storing of materials that do not need to be accessed regularly but are kept for infrequent access. Such materials may include previous versions of active documents or documents related to a project or other task where documents are only needed for reference and not on a regular basis.

Professional archivists resent the hijacking of the term "archival storage" by the information age to mean things that are put in separate storage not to be seen or maybe not even returned in search results, as archivists care just as much about arrangement, description, and access as they do about preservation. Still, the vocabulary damage has been done; the words "archival storage" are now synonymous in meaning with inactive storage in IT speak. So often when you hear of storage plans that move assets from active storage to inactive storage, this process might be called archiving or moving to archival storage. Try not to use these terms yourself, as the process of archiving is much more than just moving things around, and it involves digital preservation planning (see Chapter 11). It is more accurate to say that these materials have been removed from circulation, segregated, put into dark storage in the DAM, or are now inactive.

Backups, or the process of backing up information, should be done every night for your DAM. This process of saving information off the active server is often part of a vendor SaS, but it can also be baked in to your hosting agreement. The sheer relief of being able to call for a system restore from backups when you've made a terrible error

31

must unfortunately be felt to be believed. Because the size of a backup can be significant, be sure to factor in the needs of backup storage in your server and hosting plans. Backups are a form of inactive storage that can become active when needed.

It may be desirable to store system backups offline on a regular schedule. These system backups should be stored securely in an off-site location for disaster response if necessary. In the next figure, you can see how offline storage tapes might be retrieved by using robots or other automated tools to appear as online storage through the use of a storage area network (SAN).

Figure 4-5. *These types of backup tapes may be stored at a special facility and are sometimes hooked up to a robotic retrieval system. Source:* `http://en.wikipedia.org/wiki/File:Super_DLTtape_I.jpg`*; CC-BY-SA-2.0 User:Austinmurphy (retrieved 10/5/2013)*

DAS, NAS, SAN, and RAID

Direct attached storage, or DAS, is storage that is directly attached to your server, typically used for backups, and is often just a hard drive that lives on the same computer as your server. However, it should be noted that all hard drives will eventually fail, and digital asset managers should always keep in mind that the failure of a drive is a matter of "when," not "if."

Network-attached storage, or NAS, is a storage strategy that should be considered if you plan to have a DAM with very large amounts of assets or videos. While most readers will have DAS on their work computers in the form of an extra hard drive, readers will recognize NAS as a shared drive accessible to all or some in their work groups. Just as with your shared drive at work, the speed of the NAS is likely greater than any individual computer accessing it, but it will slow with more and more user traffic. When you map an individual computer to a shared drive, you are directing your computer to recognize a specific path within a NAS.

A SAN is a storage architecture that attaches remote devices like off-line tape storage to servers in such a way that the devices appear locally attached to the servers. NAS, by contrast, uses file-based protocols that make it clear that the storage is remote, and computers request a portion of an abstract file rather than a disk block. A SAN is faster than NAS but is much more expensive. If your DAM has a connection to a shared drive, that's a NAS connection. If your DAM deals with a lot of video, you're probably going to want a SAN to deal with that.

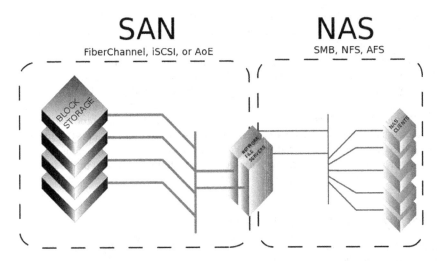

Figure 4-6. *The blue box shows how a DAM server might be connected to both a SAN and NAS storage. Source:* `http://en.wikipedia.org/wiki/File:SANvsNAS.svg`, *photo by Wikimedia user Mennis CC-A-SA-2.5 (retrieved 10/5/2013)*

A RAID is common in video production environments, but it may become more used in everyday DAMs as both the demand for and production of video grow. RAIDs are an example of virtual storage in that the information may physically be stored on several different drives, but the file itself will appear as one whole. If you're serious about providing access to many videos, you'll want to get more information on RAIDs and look into server storage environments that have already deployed this type of storage strategy before. RAIDs are not without fault or failure, and they require their own kind of regular maintenance. A big question with RAIDS are their speeds or latency (the time it takes to access a particular item in storage). Advanced RAID systems have quite a bit of redundancy built in to them, with assets backed up more than once to ensure survival of data even if one drive fails.

How Much Storage Does Your DAM Need?

In all of the discussions of servers, hosting, and storage, you'll be asked to provide estimates on system requirements and use. In all discussions of file size and use, the following table is often helpful.

Name	Symbol	Binary Measurement	Decimal Measurement	Number of Bytes	Equal to
Kilobyte	KB	2^{10}	10^3	1,024	1,024 B
Megabyte	MB	2^{20}	10^6	1,048,576	1,024 KB
Gigabyte	GB	2^{30}	10^9	1,073,741,824	1,024 MB
Terabyte	TB	2^{40}	10^{12}	1,099,511,627,776	1,024 GB
Petabyte	PB	2^{50}	10^{15}	1,125,899,906,842,624	1,024 TB
Exabyte	EB	2^{60}	10^{18}	1,152,921,504,606,846,976	1,024 PB
Zettabyte	ZB	2^{70}	10^{21}	1,180,591,620,717,411,303,424	1,024 EB
Yottabyte	YB	2^{80}	10^{24}	1,208,925,819,614,629,174,706,176	1,024 ZB

It is often helpful to compare file sizes to known quantities. For instance, a typical episode of the television series *Doctor Who* at standard definition, or SD (720p), comes in at around 1 GB per episode. The same series in high definition, or HD (1080p), comes in at a little over 3 GB per episode. Because 1 TB of server space is equal to a little over 1,000 GB, it would take 1,000 SD episodes of *Doctor Who* to fill a 1-TB drive but just 333 HD files to fill that same drive. That's just file size; you haven't yet accounted for the room needed for metadata, access, your DAM software, and memory to account for the actions of users. Increasingly digital asset managers are dealing in petabytes; a good discussion of storage can be read in an article by Vincent LaForet titled "To Delete or Not to Delete: 'THAT' Is the Question" (`http://blog.vincentlaforet.com/2008/08/28/to-delete-or-not-to-delete-that-is-the-the-question/`).

You can get a rough estimate of the storage size you need for your servers by asking your DAM vendors for their space requirements and estimating file sizes from your asset inventories. When thinking ahead and budgeting, be sure to allow your DAM annual room for growth in memory, backups, and storage, along with the increase in prices for such that will go up each year.

Addressing Common Storage and Hosting Concerns

When designing the storage and hosting solution for your organization's DAM, there will undoubtedly be conflicts over the direction your system should take in the following categories:

- Speed versus safety

- Flexibility versus reliability

- Flexibility versus consistency

- Usability versus quality

- Accessibility versus security

In each instance of these dueling needs, an organization has to find its own balance on the continuum of server and hosting performance. This list of common storage and hosting concerns owes much to the work of Henrik De Gyor from both his blog (Another DAM Blog) and his podcast interviews of digital asset managers. When addressing these concerns, it's worthwhile to speak to peers and ask them how they came down on each side of these difficult decisions. Just as with DAM systems, there is no one good fit that will sit well with everybody, especially with situations where you may face internal differences of opinion, answers don't come easy, or decisions may not remain static.

> *One of the main [concerns] is accessibility versus security. For daily workflow, we really want assets to be as accessible as possible. We want people to be able to get whatever they might need to get their job done, but in the long-term, you generally want to carefully want to manage your permission structure and make sure that people only get access to the stuff that they should have access to and prevent people from doing things that might be bad like accidentally deleting assets or changing metadata when they shouldn't.* (Source: *David Klee, Media Asset Management, NBC, Another DAM Podcast Transcribed, p. 243*)

Conclusions

When planning your DAM's server environment, hosting, and storage needs, there is much to consider. Access to your server, backups, the expected numbers and sizes of assets, and the needed service and support for all these things will go into determining how and where your DAM lives. Staffing as always will play a large role in these decisions, as the availability of in-house expertise will go a long way toward making all of these decisions. When in doubt, don't be afraid to ask questions of your DAM vendor or hosting company. Often, efficiencies and/or service improvements may be available that you are unaware of; these topics are so broad and ever-changing that new information and options are always becoming available.

While some of your decisions regarding hosting and hardware may be ones that your DAM lies with for years at a time, other decisions regarding trade-offs in performance, security, accessibility, flexibility, and usability may be contentious and require adjustments over time. Just as every DAM system deployment is different, so too are the tough calls on where your DAM lives.

CHAPTER 5

■ ■ ■

Staffing for a DAM

Chapter Goal: *This chapter will outline who digital asset managers are, what they do, and how to hire them.*

Finding Successful Digital Asset Managers

When digital asset management systems (DAMs) fail, they often do so due to inadequate or misaligned staffing. If a company does not assign the right full-time employees to run a DAM after spending great amounts of time and money on finding the right system and vendor agreement, the DAM is doomed. User adoption of a DAM hinges on both the usability of the system and the availability of training and reference resources, all of which require full-time attention. When a company launches a DAM with little or no dedicated staff to attend to user needs, it has set itself up for failure, no matter the particular DAM vendor or access platform that is used. Some companies try to implement DAM with the strategy that "DAM is everyone's responsibility," and this simply means that once the job belongs to everyone, it de facto belongs to no one, and the DAM ends up unloved and unused. Assets don't arrange, describe, preserve, and provide access for themselves. In order for a DAM to succeed, a full-time manager must be in charge of the system. Regardless of whether it is a cloud or in-house installation, regardless of the type of DAM, regardless of what the salesperson tells you—there must be a full-time manager behind the scenes in order for a DAM to work.

Because staffing is so critical to a successful DAM implementation, in 2012 the DAM Foundation (www.damfoundation.org) launched its first demographic survey of the profession. This chapter will focus heavily on the findings of that survey, as it is the only one that is published in a peer-reviewed journal and that is available at the writing of this book (see *Journal of Digital Media Management*, volume 2, issue 1, September 2013). DAM is still emerging as a profession, and so the data captured from that survey reflect the work environment of its time.

What Do Digital Asset Managers Do?

When selling their systems, DAM vendors often like to give the impression that their DAM is so advanced that designers, advertising agencies, writers, and everyone else will be uploading, downloading, and searching the system with little to no assistance. Needless to say, *they are selling you something*; DAMs are inherently labor-intensive. No DAM operates well without someone (or, for larger systems, several someones) paying close attention to the everyday workings of the system and the metadata governance.

In the DAM Foundation survey, participants were asked to identify many aspects of their work, including their primary tasks, how they were organized in their institutions, and the types of records with which they work. The authors of the study thought that the types of assets in a DAM and where the system was housed would inform the type of work done by the digital asset managers. It was anticipated that strong differences would be shown between those who worked primarily with documents and those who worked mostly with videos, for instance, or that those working in marketing would have very different tasks than those working in archives environments. However, the results came as a surprise. The type of asset or type of system in which one worked did not matter: all digital asset managers do basically the same tasks everyday. It did not even matter where the DAM was housed or how it was organized. DAM work is DAM work, and it's mostly made up of the following nine tasks, which are listed in order of commonality.

Primary Functions of Digital Asset Managers in the Last Twelve Months

Figure 5-1. *Primary reported tasks of digital asset managers showed a high uniformity of tasks. No matter the system or organization, digital asset managers primary do the same type of work*

Arrangement and Description

Creating inventories, forming collections, and creating metadata for materials in the DAM were reported by digital asset managers in the greatest number as primary functions of the job. By cataloging and grouping items in ways that allow for optimal search engine discovery, digital asset managers fulfill a key role for those creating, using, and repurposing items in a DAM. The group least likely to report this as a primary function were those who identified themselves as directors. When we talk about managing assets, these are the core tasks related to that phrase.

Reference Services

Answering calls for assistance and research related to the DAM was the second most-reported function for digital asset managers. Helping internal and external audiences use the new technology a DAM represents is often itself a full-time job. While many businesses dream of buying a DAM and using it as a self-serve library, experienced digital asset managers know that providing reference services are key to the adoption, growth, and maintenance of a system.

Maintaining Access

Creating and auditing access control lists (ACLs), testing and responding to feedback from user portals, monitoring registration, and dealing with login issues are daily activities within an active, healthy, and secure DAM. Without a person to take care of these tasks, users will quickly become frustrated with their lack of access and will abandon the DAM or find ways to work around the system. As well-used DAMs grow, they often develop custom user portals for various audiences, including custom uploaded application programming interfaces (APIs) that must be monitored.

Outreach and Advocacy

Internally advocating for input/upload to a DAM, promoting the DAM as an access and workflow solution, and publicizing DAM holdings to the user base are all part of creating an environment for successful system adoption. In larger organizations, it may take years for separate information silos to become aware of each other, and part of advocacy and outreach is simply communicating that the DAM is available to all as a centralized repository.

Managing Long-Term Projects

Consolidating libraries, running scanning projects, developing APIs, sunsetting redundant systems, and linking to other systems are long-term projects that involve digital asset managers. It's not surprising that 67 percent of those surveyed reported that managing long-term projects was a primary task.

Selection, Appraisal, or Acquisition

Someone has to go through all those hard drives stacked in the closet, not to mention the older files on the shared drive once it gets full. Remember when so-and-so retired and you found that drawer full of old photo DVDs? You should probably hire someone to go through all those things, determine what are duplicates, what images are of value, and what belongs in the DAM and at what access level it should be cataloged. There has never been, nor will there ever be, a machine or program that can accomplish this task for you due to the amount of institutional knowledge and decision making that is needed.

Professional Development

Highly successful digital asset managers attend conferences and continuing education programs, read professional literature, and participate in professional associations. The DAM field is growing and changing so quickly that participation in professional development activities is absolutely necessary in order to keep up with the technology and new processes. Constant professional development is not optional for a digital asset manager; it's part of the job.

Teaching DAM-Related Courses

Critical to the successful adoption and integration of a DAM into the workplace is the availability and frequency of courses on how to use a DAM, how to upload and download assets, and how to get help with these tasks. It is not unusual for someone to need in-person instruction from the digital asset manager. While ideally everyone could learn from prerecorded lessons, there will always be times when live instruction is best. As the DAM grows and custom user interfaces are developed, this task becomes even more critical to the users of the system. Often those who are on the most hesitant about using a DAM can be won over by personalized user education. This effort can be continued by sharing experiences outside of your organization and by enriching others with your knowledge gained at conferences and events.

Digital Preservation Activities

Developing and playing a key role in digital preservation strategies such as migration, server backups, and security-risk assessments are all part of a digital asset manager's job in keeping the DAM safe and accessible. As these same tasks are critical to any organization's long-term digital health, those working in a DAM should also seek to involve themselves in the organization's overall digital preservation planning.

How Are Digital Asset Managers Paid?

According to the DAM Foundation's first salary survey, **the average pay for a digital asset manager in 2011 was $81,403 (USD)**, and the median pay was $65,000 (USD). However, it should be noted that this was the first survey of its kind, and the sample set was only 100 participants. Because the first survey drew its sample set from those involved with DAM professional groups and social media, extremes were present, reflecting those at the tops of their careers speaking at events, and those on the Internet looking to further their early careers. The top 22 percent of respondents earned more than $100,000 (USD), while the bottom 41 percent earned less than $60,000 (USD).

Digital Asset Managers by Reported Salary in 2011

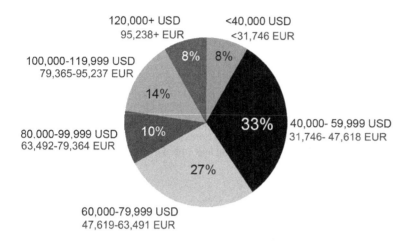

Figure 5-2. *The net income reported by digital asset managers for the calendar year of 2011*

Who Earned the Most?

In the 2011 survey, digital asset managers earned more when they were working for publishers or when the DAM was organized within a creative or design team. The publisher pay rate is likely related to location though—most large publishing concerns are located in regions where the average pay is naturally higher, such as New York City and London. The earning numbers correlated with creative/design teams stand independent of location though and can be seen as true indicators of earning power. Because creatives understand the value of findability and re-use rather than re-creation of assets, they value their digital asset managers more highly and compensate them along those lines.

In the top 20 percent of earners, 57 percent were male and six individuals reported a title containing "director." The time with a current employer or the amount of time in the current profession seemed to have no effect on the pay of the top 20 percent. This is not surprising as none were at the start of their careers; these high earners were seasoned professionals who had come into the DAM field already demonstrating an ability to learn and adapt to new technology.

Who Earned the Least?

Those digital asset managers who earned smaller salaries were younger (25 to 34 years of age), worked in academia, or were organized within an archives or special collections department. Educational background had no effect on these workers: those under 35 were more likely to have an advanced degree than their peers, but they still made less. This is indicative of overall demographic trends in the U.S. workforce at the time of the survey. Those who were over 45 reported less education but more earnings, reflecting the market pressures that kept younger workers in school longer.

Gender and Digital Asset Management

That a little more than half of these highest earners were male should not be interpreted as industry bias; rather, the gender imbalance at the top reflects society as a whole. The longer one has been in the workforce, the higher the earning potential in DAM. More men over the age of 50 have been lifelong workers than women, who achieved workplace representation (if not pay parity) on par with their male counterparts in the 1990s. As more women age into eligibility for director status during their careers, more women will be represented at that level.

Digital Asset Managers
by Gender

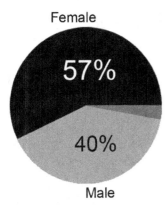

Figure 5-3. *Gender in digital asset management in 2001*

Gender will become more of an issue in this field if current trends continue, but in quite another way. In the lowest 41 percent of earners, 75 percent of them were female. This was reflective of age, as previously mentioned, but this group shared another disturbing statistic: the strong likelihood of possessing a master's degree in Library Science. Wages for librarians have been depressed for decades in the United States, leading the American Library Association to pass a minimum wage resolution in 2007, asking that professional librarians be paid no less than $40,000 (USD) per year (http://ala-apa.org/improving-salariesstatus). In 2011, this suggested minimum was raised to $42,485 (USD). Low wages in the library field are reflective of how American society values a traditionally female-dominated field of public service. DAM as a profession runs a real risk of facing lowered wage averages if the work is lumped under Library Sciences, even if the work remains as technically challenging, detail-oriented, and labor-intensive as it is today. Librarians did not face the lowering and shrinking of their wages over the last 50 years because their jobs became less technically demanding or less skilled; it was the perception of the profession as "women's work" and the devaluing of their role in society that sunk their collective professional ship.

While the arrangement, description, preservation, access, and, above all, findability of information has fell to librarians in the twentieth century, DAM professionals would do well to keep the term "digital asset managers" and not call themselves "librarians" or "archivists." While the jobs are very much the same, and my background in library science gave me an excellent grounding in the techniques and processes that help in the understanding and implementation of a DAM, labeling the job as "digital librarian" or "digital archivist" may be the path to low earning potential over a lifetime.

Racial and Class Diversity

In the DAM Foundation survey, participants had the option to identify themselves racially for demographic purposes. Forty-three percent of respondents chose not to identify themselves by race, either out of personal choice or for fear of being identified in the survey results. It is therefore difficult to draw any conclusions about the racial makeup of the profession, but participation at DAM conferences closely mirrors the racial makeup of tech professionals in the United States as a whole, which is to say it's about 80 percent white/Caucasian (http://www.bls.gov/cps/cpsaat11.pdf). Just as within the tech industry as a whole, digital asset management should make more of an effort through internships, mentoring programs, and scholarships to continue to recruit a more racially diverse workforce.

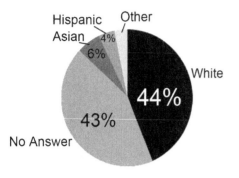

Figure 5-4. Race in digital asset management in 2011

At the very first-ever meeting of the DAM Foundation (at Createasphere, LA, winter 2011), a debate regarding education and class background broke out. The contention around education and class in the emerging profession cuts to the heart of who digital asset managers are and what they do: is it a blue-collar or white-collar profession? Are years of education in information science strictly necessary, or will certification and experience suffice? As of the writing of this book, none of these questions or debates have been decided, and as society as a whole deals with the imbalance of education to pay reflected not only for digital asset managers but for other professions, no easy answers are available. Line up a row of the most talented digital asset managers in 2014 and you are likely to see those with advanced degrees next to those with none at all, as well as a wide range of backgrounds and life experiences.

Educational Background

Despite the information in the above paragraph, Human Resource departments would like a standard educational background to use when writing a job description or when filtering through applicants to determine who would be best suited to run a newly installed DAM. Due to the newness of DAM as a profession, there is no current educational standard. Plans for a certificate program from the DAM Foundation and the University of British Columbia are under way, but the program will not be available until late 2014 at the earliest. Still, your most likely indicator for a successful digital asset manager is hiring someone who has worked with a DAM before. Experience really counts in the DAM profession, but for the HR professionals reading this book, who absolutely must have an educational standard for their résumé filtering programs, the three most common educational backgrounds reported in the DAM Foundation survey are listed here.

The Four-Year Degree: BA/BS/BFA

While the difference between the three types of degrees lumped together here can be vast, all three degrees traditionally take about four years each to complete. In this most commonly reported form of education, the resulting statistics mirror those of the overall survey. Slightly more likely to be female and slightly less likely to be white, we can safely generalize that most of those working today in a DAM have a four-year degree. Surprisingly, participants who had four-year degrees but who did not hold an MLS/MLIS (the second most commonly reported educational background) made more than those who had attained a higher degree. That more education did not translate into better pay may be a reflection of the age of respondents: those with an MLS tended to be younger than those who possessed just a four-year degree.

Master's of Library Science: MLS/MLIS

As mentioned above, having more education did not correlate with higher wages for those with an MLS or MLIS. The mean and median wages for those working in a DAM who possessed an MLS or MLIS were lower than those with just a four-year degree, although this may be a result of age and experience. Those reporting this second most-common degree in the DAM study were the most likely to be in the 25- to 34-year-old age bracket, and most had been with their current employers for three years or less. This group was the most likely to respond that they planned to pursue additional education: a PhD, MBA, or other advanced degree. Unsurprisingly, those whose degree requires a cataloging class reported arrangement and description as their most common function, with reference services following close behind.

Another Master's Degree: MA/MS/MFA

Those listing a master's degree were also the most likely to simply list "other" as both their employer and primary function and the least likely to list arrangement and description among their duties. With 91 percent finding DAM as a second or third career, 63 percent within this group reported joining the profession after having the DAM-related duties assigned to them by their employers.

Who Manages the Digital Asset Managers?

In 2011, the most common employers of digital asset managers were producers of consumer products, publishers, academic/educational institutions, and companies in the broad category of "other for-profit organizations," which covers everything from UPS (the delivery service provider) to Atlanta Metadata Authority (a cataloging outsourcer). The employers of digital asset managers affected pay and position, but not their overall job duties; as previously written, DAM work is DAM work, no matter who is paying or in what system it occurs.

The visibility and status of digital asset managers, however, strongly depended on where the employers organized the DAM. The DAM's location in an organization can affect who is hired to work with the system, how that person is compensated for work, and an enterprisewide effect on how the DAM is used. The four most-common functional units for a DAM were creative/design, marketing, media library (including production teams), and archives/special collections.

Functional Units Employing Digital Asset Managers

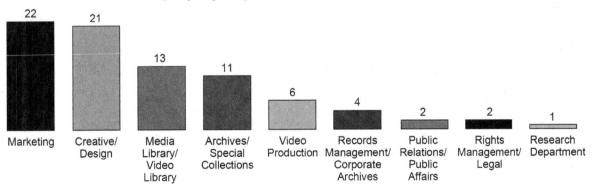

Figure 5-5. *Departments where DAMs lived in 2011*

Interestingly, despite the wide variance in pay among these groups (those in creative/design units earn significantly more than those in archives/special collection departments), the reported work remained relatively uniform, with a few notable differences. While those on creative/design teams listed providing reference services more frequently than any other duty, those in marketing had other priorities—although both groups reported being very involved in outreach and advocacy for their DAMs. A large gap between the mean and median pay of those on creative/design teams reflects the diverse titles of those participants in the study; a number of directors were in this group, and, reflecting a wish not to be identified, 29 percent chose not to describe their current employers.

Survey participants in marketing departments had many similar results to those on creative/design teams, with notable deviations in pay and primary functions. Reference services came after five other duties for those in marketing, and those in marketing were much more likely to be involved in teaching others how to use the DAM. *Mean and median salaries reported for DAM workers in marketing were very close, reflecting a true average—between $75,000 and 76,000 (USD) (59,524 and 60,317 [EUR]) for 2011, which also squarely covers the midrange for the median and mean overall reported salaries for all DAM worker*s. Proving they are adept at marketing themselves, those working in this industry had the highest median salary, if not the highest mean, of the functional units.

Those working in media libraries were more likely to work on long-term DAM projects than their peers organized elsewhere. Both the long hours and long-term projects are possibly the result of the high percentage of those in media libraries who noted they were employed by publishers.

DAM systems housed in archives and special collections existed among the widest range of employers reported for any functional unit. Despite this wide range of employers, those in archives/special collections reported making less on average than their peers. Unlike other DAM workers, those under an archives/special collections umbrella were just as concerned with digital preservation activities as they were with arrangement and description, reflecting an archives mentality. The specialized knowledge and skill sets associated with digital preservation are compatible with some MLS/MLIS degree programs in the United States, and so that degree was represented highly in this group, along with its correlation to lower pay.

Main Roles in Daily Work

When attending DAM conferences, it's clear that those working in the DAM field fall loosely into one of four groups: directors/VPs, managers, supervisors (midlevel or low-level managers), and specialists. Three of these four roles are outlined in the brief sample job descriptions here; the supervisor/low-level manager has been left out, as the description would simply be some combination of manager and specialist, depending on the organization. Readers should feel free to copy and adapt these job descriptions as they need for their own hiring and other HR purposes. These descriptions were put together by using job postings for various positions from many different companies, and they should be adapted by organizations to fit their own hiring needs.

Director or Vice President
Compensation Average: $110,000 (USD)
Job Description

A paragraph or two about your company/organization should be at the top of each job description, so that potential employees know who you are and what they might be getting into. If you work at an established organization with a Human Resources department, they probably already have this text canned and you can just copy and paste it here before describing the position. The author put this paragraph at the top of each form just as a placeholder for your own text.

The **Your Organization or Company (YOC)** is seeking a **Director or VP**, Digital Asset Management. This position reports to [VP or C-Level person] and is responsible for all other DAM employees and contractors.

The Director/VP of Digital Asset Management is responsible for the development, oversight, and management of YOC's enterprise digital asset management strategy. This strategy will support the use of a diverse matrix of digital assets within the enterprise in today's workflows but will also shape the long-term infrastructure for tomorrow's digital asset needs. Successful management of this strategy requires this role to identify, implement, and support systems and processes. This role must also be able to connect with a range of business units, determining each business's unique need, allowing areas of customized support to be supported while also influencing the adoption of enterprise DAM solutions where they make sense.

As part of the enterprise digital asset management strategy, the VP/Director will also develop YOC's digital preservation program. This program addresses the most cost-effective methods for storing digital assets in today's infrastructure and also identifies key digital assets to support tomorrow's content use and distribution needs.

This position will recognize and mandate the necessity of accurate digital asset cataloging and metadata standards programs, making efficient use of company master data, cataloging captured during a workflow with tailored cataloging programs that ensure digital asset metadata that ensures proper storage and efficient search and retrieval of assets. Additionally, this role will establish budgets to launch and support related digital asset management initiatives.

The Digital Asset Management VP/Director is responsible for all digital asset types, covering a wide range of business domains with an equally wide range of business functions [list the functions, like Public Relations, Creative Services, IT, C-level offices, Publishing, Production, Usability, Marketing and any others here]. This role not only supports the needs of the YOC businesses, but also develops programs supporting the complex versioning of digital assets and connection to DAMs at other companies/organizations.

Key Qualifications

- Demonstrated success **implementing** digital asset management solutions and workflows in a complex enterprise creative environment

- Proven success as a key member of a matrixed, cross-functional team. Able to **communicate and direct** equally well with people in business, creative, and technical positions

- Able to apply sound judgment and **demonstrated leadership ability**

- Outstanding attention to detail and commitment to excellence

- Excellent oral and written communicator, with great interpersonal skills. **Able to forge trusting relationships within a diverse team**

- Familiarity with **the issues surrounding copyright, rights of image, and rights relating to the creation and distribution of information, imagery, and other licensed materials (audio, video, text, CAD, etc.)**

- Solid technical background, **experience managing technical projects**, and/or hands-on technical experience

- Understands software development **requirement gathering, methodologies, implementations, and timelines**

Responsibilities

- Establish [or maintain, if you're re-hiring] an enterprise digital asset management strategy; communicate and validate this strategy to appropriate stakeholders, successfully implementing this strategy and monitoring its progress across all business lines

- Establish [or maintain] an enterprise "digital asset life cycle"; mapping and identifying key digital asset stages from raw asset, work-in-progress asset, final asset to archive asset as a key component of efficient digital asset management workflows and applications use

- Identify and implement both digital asset management efficiencies within business units and opportunities for shared services across business units, which optimize workflows and applications in an effort to maximize cost savings

- Develop regular monitoring of DAM system statistics and ROI for regular YOC reporting, measurement, and analysis

- Identify new lines of businesses for enterprise digital asset management programs and successfully incorporate these businesses into the appropriate programs; successfully foster adoption/use of DAM across YOC's departments [production, distribution, operations, marketing, etc.]

- Establish an enterprise digital asset cataloging and metadata standards strategy; communicate and validate this strategy to appropriate stakeholders, successfully implementing this strategy and monitoring its progress across all business lines

- Develop project schedule with digital asset managers; estimate, negotiate, and obtain resources to meet project requirements; maintain, adjust, and update program and project plans and identify and communicate project risks as needed

- Develop support teams, user guides, a DAM help desk, and training programs to provide user application support that ensures a large user community is able to use digital asset management tools efficiently, minimizing any potential loss of productivity from user inexperience, user error, or any other user issue that may prevent them from working with digital assets in the enterprise

- Establish digital asset management storage and retention programs that store the appropriate digital assets at the appropriate times, not only supporting the needs of the business today, but also anticipating the future needs of the business by enabling future programming and future sales by enabling efficient search, use, reuse, and repurposing as needed

- Establish enterprise digital asset management strategies that enable the effective monetization of content, understanding the requirements of Sales, Business Development, and Marketing groups

- Work with YOC's IT organization to build buy-in for strategies and planning

- Define and drive YOC's Master Digital Asset Management strategy

- Establish and maintain budgets

Digital Asset Manager
Compensation Average: $75,000 (USD)
Job Description

A paragraph or two about your company/organization should be at the top of each job description, so that potential employees know who you are and what they might be getting into. If you work at an established organization with a Human Resources department, they probably already have this text canned and you can just copy and paste it here before describing the position. The author put this paragraph at the top of each form just as a placeholder for your own text.

The **Your Organization or Company (YOC)** is seeking a Digital Asset Manager. This position reports to the Digital Asset Management VP or Director and is responsible for Digital Asset Management Supervisors/lower-level managers and Digital Asset Specialists.

Key Qualifications

- Demonstrated success **working with** digital asset management solutions and workflows in a complex enterprise creative environment

- Proven success as a key member of a matrixed, cross-functional team; able **to work equally well** with people in business, creative, and technical positions

- Able to apply sound judgment while **working independently within tight timelines**

- Outstanding attention to detail and commitment to excellence

- Excellent oral and written communicator, with great interpersonal skills; **able to forge trusting relationships within a diverse team**

- **Fanatical about creating order from disorder**; understands **the "correct" level of process** to apply to different projects

- Solid technical background, experience managing technical projects, and/or **hands-on technical experience**

- Understands software development methodologies and timeline

- Proficient in Adobe Creative Cloud products

- Demonstrated **commitment going above and beyond to help** customers, system users, or patrons in solving problems or locating information

Responsibilities

- Become immersed in the [Department Organization] environment to gain a thorough understanding of YOC's needs

- Monitor, report, and analyze on DAM system statistics and ROI

- Identify unique ways to organize and manage the entire digital asset life cycle from creation to distribution, production, and archiving

- Demonstrate an understanding of legal issues around asset use and create solutions that serve both creative and legal requirements

- Find elegant and creative solutions to regular system issues in the everyday use and access to YOC's DAM

- Create clear and detailed case studies/user stories and reporting/acceptance criteria to identify and prioritize requirements and workflow

- Participate in the development and maintenance of asset metadata models incorporating industry standards and YOC's unique requirements

- Schedule and conduct regular meetings with vendors, contractors, and third parties using YOC's DAM in order to manage input and meet user needs

- Understand tools available internally and externally to devise solutions that are flexible for our organization's use while making our process more efficient

- Develop a thorough understanding of user needs and how these differ to create solutions that work for individual audiences

- Develop, schedule, and conduct DAM user training for different audiences both internal and external to YOC

- Participate and influence YOC's larger DAM enterprise direction and solutions

- Clearly present proposals, status, and solutions to other departments and management

- Manage relationships with outside vendors and contractors working with YOC's DAM; accept invoices and manage payments

- Marshal resources from a matrix functional group to get things done, and use resources effectively and efficiently

Digital Asset Management Specialist
Compensation Average: $50,000 (USD)
Job Description

A paragraph or two about your company/organization should be at the top of each job description, so that potential employees know who you are and what they might be getting into. If you work at an established organization with a Human Resources department, they probably already have this text canned and you can just copy and paste it here before describing the position. The author put this paragraph at the top of each form just as a placeholder for your own text.

The **Your Organization or Company (YOC)** is seeking a Digital Asset Management Specialist. This position reports to the Digital Asset Manager or Digital Asset Management Supervisor and isn't responsible for anyone else. This is an entry-level position.

Key Qualifications

- Demonstrated success **working with** digital assets

- Demonstrated commitment **going above and beyond to help customers, system users, or patrons**

- Proven success as a key **member of a team**

- Able to apply sound judgment while **working independently within tight timelines**

- Outstanding **attention to detail** and commitment to excellence

- In possession of articulate communication skills; **able to forge trusting relationships within a diverse team**

- **Fanatical about creating order from disorder**

- **Hands-on technical experience** with library systems, content management systems (CMSs), or other large searchable databases used in the creation of web pages, media, or research

- Understands the critical importance of timelines

- Knowledge of Adobe Creative Cloud products

- Familiarity with YOC's email or standard office software

Responsibilities

- Become immersed in the [Department Organization] environment to gain a thorough understanding of YOC's needs

- Identify unique ways to organize and manage the entire digital asset life cycle from creation to distribution, production, and archiving

- Demonstrate understanding of legal issues around asset use and create solutions that serve business, creative, and legal requirements

- Assist with the creation of case studies/user stories and reporting/user acceptance testing (UAT) to identify and prioritize requirements and workflow

- Participate in the development and maintenance of asset metadata models incorporating industry standards and YOC's unique requirements

- Understand tools available internally and externally to devise solutions that are flexible for our organization's use while making our process more efficient

- Develop a thorough understanding of user needs and how these differ to suggest solutions that work for individual audiences

- Conduct DAM user training for different audiences both internal and external to YOC

- Participate in YOC's larger DAM enterprise direction and solutions

- Clearly present products of work and reporting to Digital Asset Manager or Supervisor

- Support outside vendors and contractors working with YOC's DAM

- Provide excellent service and support to those using YOC's DAM, going above and beyond to arrange, describe, preserve, and provide access to digital assets

Where to Find Great Contractors

Due to the detail-oriented and labor-intensive nature of metadata creation and governance, sizable DAMs will employ contractors to help out when large batches of assets need to be organized in the DAM quickly. Cataloging outsourcing companies, such as Archive Media Partners, started out servicing archives and libraries, but they now include corporate DAMs in their client bases. It is also increasingly common to find individuals, usually former librarians, archivists, or those in the video industry, who are now contract workers helping to create metadata for one or more client DAMs. Operating mainly by word of mouth or meeting new clients at DAM conventions, an independent contractor who generates uniformly quality metadata is worth his or her weight in gold. Some well-known contractor firms as of the writing of this book include IO Integration, Marlabs, HintTech, and Cognizant; there are many others and the trend toward outsourcing continues to grow. Whomever your organization employs, make sure that the contractor documents all processes for continued consistency.

In order to outsource metadata creation, your contractors may need access to your DAM at an admin level, depending on how your system allows for mass uploads of metadata or assets. For organizations or corporations behind industrial-strength firewalls, this may require steps such as creating a custom virtual private network (VPN) connection or issuing security tokens or credentials. While setting up a contractor to work remotely in your DAM may seem like a pain, the reward of having off-site staff that can be tapped when needed to arrange and describe large sets of material is usually worthwhile to a DAM in its first few years. and if your organization is shy of hiring, it is possible that your DAM team may rely on contractors throughout its life.

To find great contractors, ask other successful digital asset managers if they know of any who are currently looking for new clients, or ask around at DAM conventions. Usually there will be someone who knows someone, and even a contractor who has his or her hands full can pass on a name or a contact who can be of help. While job postings for this type of work are currently rare, if the DAM field continues to grow at its present rate, it's likely we'll see these in the future.

Conclusions

It is clear from the results of the DAM Foundation survey that digital asset management is a profession where tasks overlap those traditionally assigned to librarians and archivists. However, other tasks critical to DAM, such as maintaining access to user portals, implementing new technology, training staff, managing long-term projects, and problem solving in new technologies, are usually assigned to those in roles as diverse as system administrators, instructors, records managers, and other information technology professionals. That all these tasks have now combined in digital asset management to form one new profession is evident by the very existence of the DAM Foundation. The snapshot of the profession provided by the information from 2011 should be regarded as a picture of an emerging profession. It is likely that as job postings for experienced digital asset managers increase that market demand will change the average and median salaries.

Whether your DAM succeeds or fails will depend on your organization's commitment to staffing the DAM with enough people to meet its goals. The successful adoption of workflows and the socialization of a DAM are highly dependent on the employees and leadership of a DAM team. When hiring for these positions, it's critical to employ people who are dedicated to self-development and who are highly engaged with their professional community. While some IT functions can be outsourced through a service and support (SaS) agreement with a DAM vendor, and bulk arrangement and description can be handed over to metadata contractors, much of the everyday work in a DAM can be handled only by full-time employees dedicated solely to the DAM. As mentioned previously in this chapter, anyone who tells you otherwise is likely selling you something.

■ ■ ■

CHAPTER 6

Assets to Manage—You Can't Drink the Ocean

Chapter Goal: *Explanation of different types of assets to manage and why the types of assets must be identified early. Information on workflows, versioning, and expiration utilities.*

It's very easy to become overwhelmed when you start a digital asset management (DAM) project. Your organization may have years or decades of content that needs organization or consolidation. All or none of this content may have been organized in different ways over the years. It can be difficult to know where to start, so it's helpful when finding your beginning in DAM to think of your project in terms of moving from a macro (very high level) to a micro (very detailed level) organization. To that end, we'll start this chapter discussing the types of assets that will go into a DAM, and we'll end with versioning (the variations of each asset). All the points discussed in this chapter should be thought out *before* your organization purchases a DAM, as systems vary widely in their treatment of different kinds of assets, their organization ability, and the management of workflows.

Asset Types

In DAMs, digital assets are broken down by item type. When discussing assets in a DAM, the *file type* (i.e., .jpg, .docx, .flv) is not discussed, as these are far too numerous to list, and standards regarding the files can vary. Instead assets are grouped as listed below, and it will be helpful for you to determine early on what your primary item types are. Most DAMs will need to deal with all of these item types, even if in your primary deployment you choose to focus on only one. Some DAMs are better at handling documents, while others excel at video; knowing your organization's priorities will help you choose a system to implement. Below each item type are listed considerations for the handling of that item type. Not all features are needed to build a great DAM, but some common elements are listed here to give those deciding between vendors for the first time some things to think about. While some features like color-based search or full-text searchability are must-haves for one organization, they might be rarely used at another. Base your DAM requirements on just a few core elements your company needs, and consider vendors who might offer a new tool not listed here that is a good fit for the way your audience will search.

Item Type: Image

This item type is usually the most important to those setting up a DAM, as the application of search terms to imagery is DAM's primary reason for being. If your organization creates a large amount of visual content (more than a thousand graphics per year plus thousands of photographs), you may wish to split the image item type into two—one for photographs, and one for illustrations/graphics. For most smaller DAMs (with fewer than 50,000 assets), one item type is enough to give search results for photos, with graphics/illustrations picked out in the keyword field or a subtype heading.

For a company that designs web sites, a separate type for graphics may be critical for the handling of banners and such. Different versions of images (touched-up versus original versions) can also be quite a problem, but because this is actually an issue for *all* item types, we'll discuss it at the end of the chapter, along with item expirations.

One major difference in DAMs occurs in the way they handle the conflict between CMYK and RGB item types during display. For those not acquainted with design and printing, CMYK (Cyan, Magenta, Yellow, and Black), or four-color, printing items do not display accurately when authentically rendered on a computer screen. This is because all television and computer screens run on a different color scale of RGB (Red Green Blue). For example, when a photograph of a child with rosy cheeks rendered in CMYK is displayed on an RGB screen, the rosy cheeks will appear flushed—as if the child has a fever. This is because the color scale of the computer monitor isn't as sophisticated as the process that originally rendered the image. If your DAM audience is narrow enough—say, just a few dozen photographers and designers—they'll know and understand that the CMYK images displayed in the DAM on RGB screens aren't true: that the child really doesn't look as if she has a fever in the downloadable CMYK asset. However, if your DAM audience includes lots of people who aren't familiar with the ways and hows of color scales, they may be put off by the disappointing appearance of CMYK images in their searches. As many DAMs are meant to be the connection point between designers and a wider audience, the CMYK/RGB color conflict will have to be corrected for thumbnail displays. How a DAM handles this will then be a big consideration in your system choice. Talk to your potential DAM users about their expectations of the DAM; if photography is really all they expect, focus your vendor search on those that offer the best in photo-handling capability, including, but not limited to these characteristics:

- Ability to manage the CMYK/RGB conflict in display—Are RGB thumbnails generated to accurately reflect the CMYK files that can be downloaded, or will CMYK images appear off-color within searches?

- Integration points with common design software like Adobe products—How well does the DAM do with add-ons like Adobe Drive or PDF editing tools?

- Facial recognition software—Some DAMs tout the ability for their systems to recognize faces for help in tagging/keywording. Does your organization really need this feature, and, if so, how well does it really work?

- Handling of releases and other legal documentation—How are releases and shoot documentation attached to images in the system?

- Automatic resizing and/or generation of preset sizes on asset uploads—Can standardized sizes be generated from images on upload? When resizing, how does scaling work? Can the standardized resizes be pulled into your organization's content management system (CMS)?

- Lightboxes/personal collections for users—Does the DAM offer the ability for users to form their own collections as they search around? Can users save personal collections to access at a later time?

- Color-based search functions—Does the DAM recognize color and allow for searches based on color percentage in the image? Does your organization need this feature?

Item Type: Document

This item type includes everything that one would think of as a document in your organization—memos, letters, mailings, releases, and so on. Remember not to get hung up on the file extension, as the handling of that will be taken care of in your metadata record (see Chapters 8 and 9). Be sure to ask your DAM vendor if there are any document file types that the prospective DAM struggles with; a DAM should be able to store any document file, regardless of its type.

One major difference in the handling of documents in DAMs is the availability of full-text searching of documents. Full-text searching cuts down dramatically on the amount of keywords that must be added to document metadata; it allows the search engine to go through all the words in a document. If you work in a Microsoft Office environment, you've experienced full-text search already on your desktop, as Office has offered full-text searching for a number of years. Be sure to ask your DAM vendor if full-text searching is available and, if so, what types of files can undergo a full-text search. Some very large document DAMs actually allow users to turn off the full-text search option, as the time it takes for the search engine to go through all the documents can substantially slow down the return of search results. Searching through keywords is, of course, much faster, but that requires the time- and labor-intensive work of tagging all the documents. Deciding how you want a system to search this item type will be a key decision in your choice of a DAM. Some questions for vendors about the document item type include the following:

- Do you offer full-text searching? If so, can users turn it on and off?

- Are thumbnails of documents displayed, or does the user see only document icons?

- Are quick views of documents available, or must users download them to read?

- Does your system handle multiple alphabets?

- How are document relationships managed between other item types (releases linked to images or video)?

Item Type: Video

In some organizations, this item type actually has its own DAM, separate but connected to the DAM for all other items. This is due to the uniquely complicated workflows and file types utilized in the construction of videos. If you primarily use a DAM system for video, it's strongly advisable to start with a workflow-based approach to DAM deployment rather than an existing asset approach (more on that later in this chapter).

How you treat video items in your DAM will hinge on one crucial question: how is video initially created for your company? If it all happens in custom editing bays at an in-house facility, you're going to need a workflow inside your DAM if one does not already exist in your production units. If the majority of your video is received as finished products from external vendors, or if your organization produces very little video, then you can treat the ingestion of this item type in ways similar to other digital assets for the most part.

Where video and audio both diverge from other assets is the need for time-based metadata. The records for video can be so complex that very lengthy record standards have been developed for them, like PBCore (Public Broadcasting Core), developed out of WGBH in Boston. While your organization's video metadata records need only be as long or short as required to fill your users' search needs, it's important to understand that video metadata records will be very different from the metadata required of other item types. **A key to fulfilling the need for housing video in the same DAM as other items is the digital asset manager's ability to manipulate and maintain separate metadata models for different item types**. This will be discussed more in depth in the metadata chapters 8 and 9. Below are a few questions to ask about a DAM's ability to handle videos:

- How are display thumbnails for video chosen and/or manipulated?

- Does the DAM generate its own proxy files?

- Does the DAM come with its own transcode engine? If not, what are the recommended choices?

- What streaming services have been integrated with existing systems?

- Are there existing deployments where this DAM has been connected to others? If so, what other DAMs have worked well with this one?

- Is video playable with the DAM's out-of-the-box features, or must a separate video player be purchased and installed? What are the preferred players?

Item Type: Audio

Like the video item type, audio will have very different needs for its metadata records due to time-based information. Unlike video, the need for transcode engines and streaming services is nearly nil, unless your organization is in the business of providing primarily audio content (like podcasts or audiobooks). While the file sizes of video get quickly out of control, audio, for obvious reasons, is easier to handle. Those of us old enough to remember Napster will have fond memories of our first DAM experience browsing audio files, even though we did not know we were interacting with an early DAM tool in a peer-to-peer environment at the time. Here are some considerations for DAMs regarding handling audio:

- What is the preferred file type for audio? If assets are ingested in another file type, will the DAM transcode the audio? Are there audio file types with which the DAM struggles to display or play?

- If no transcode engine is built into the DAM, what are the preferred integration partners?

- Does the DAM offer a choice of audio file types for users to download? Can we customize the choice of file types offered?

- Is audio playable during a search, or must the file be downloaded first? If a player must be purchased for this feature, what are the preferred partners?

Item Type: Web Code

It's easy to overlook web code or web items as an item type when setting up a DAM, but this is a mistake. Because most coding is the reuse and adaptation of code that has been previously written, great efficiencies can be realized by the organization and searchability that a DAM can bring to archiving web code. Common to many organizations is the practice of simply saving older web-site construction on stacks of hard drives, causing those who build the sites headaches when searching for previous work. Likely the designers or IT folks faced with searching through such a pile of hard drives have sometimes found it easier to simply re-create their work rather than to try to find what they've already coded once before. If you plan to use your DAM as a major repository for web code, consider the following:

- Will the code be saved as plaintext files or in its native format?

- Will web sites be re-creatable (clickable), or will simple PDFs of the look of each site be attached to a zipped archive of the code files?

- Does your organization plan to store web sites in the DAM simply to preserve the past or to use the code on an ongoing basis?

How Complex Multimedia Files Are Handled Within Item Types

Complex multimedia files are increasingly standard for presentations and e-books. A single presentation may include a PowerPoint file, a video file, an audio file, and several dozen graphics and photographs. After reading the earlier breakout of item types, you may wonder how a complex file with all of these elements would be handled in a DAM, where assets are broken out by item type. The answer to this is simply that it depends on the DAM owners.

There are several methods for approaching complex file types. We'll briefly outline just three here, and more will be discussed later in the book. When faced with a complex file, DAMs may do the following:

1. Treat the file as one single asset with no linking files.

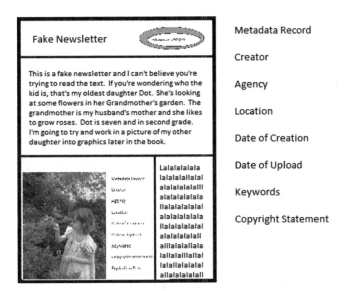

2. Treat the file as one single asset but create links or relationships to sources (links to high-res copies of images, original graphics, videos, etc.).

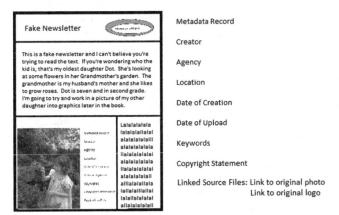

3. Have the asset be a parent file with child assets as they appear in the parent. In the example here, the child files are listed separately, but they could also be rolled into a zipped file.

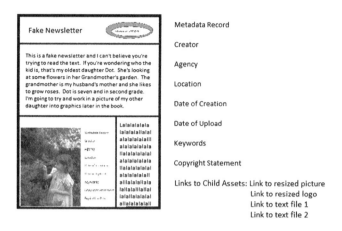

Obviously the choices your organization makes regarding complex items will depend on both user expectations and the amount of man-hours available for the arrangement and description of items in the DAM.

Deciding How to Manage Assets and Expectations

In Chapter 2, it was mentioned that the process of ascertaining the storage, use, and final destination of digital assets was virtually identical to the appraisal and acquisition processes that archivists and records managers have employed for decades. The similarities between the work of digital asset managers and traditional archivists don't end there. For the last 100 years, the branch of Information Science concerned with the retrieval of information was called Library Science; the subset of Library Science concerned with past records was called Archival Science; related practices to both Library Science and Archival Science became Records Management, a discipline that boomed as laws were formulated to govern the amazing explosion of records generated in the last half of the twentieth century. As long as humans have produced recorded information, we have struggled to agree on the best way to store and access that information. That Library Science became sophisticated enough to become a postgraduate level of study in the United States and elsewhere should indicate the millions of hours of thought and writing that have gone into the study and argument around how we arrange, describe, preserve, and provide access to information materials.

You don't need to have a degree in Library Science, Archival Science, or Records Management to be a good digital asset manager, but understanding that all the problems you face in organizing and providing access to massive amounts of information are not new issues—just old problems dressed up in new technology—can go a long way in helping you understand how to approach DAMs in everyday practice.

When John Cutter published his first overview of the Cutter Number system (which became the basis for the Library of Congress in 1882), debates on the best way to organize information were already well established. The Dewey system was first published in 1876, and the idea of indexing library materials on cards was seen as a revolutionary step forward in organization and speed of research. By the time I was gently walking genealogists through their first encounters with computer catalogs in 1995, most universities and major cities had already moved to cataloging through the centralized system of WorldCat. Created in 1971, WorldCat freed librarians from constantly re-cataloging books or magazines with wide circulations. The ability to just download already available records to local online search systems was a major efficiency for libraries. By the time this book prints, WorldCat will house something like 300 million records pointing to 2 billion physical and digital assets. As we move into the new century, online catalogs of electronic books and records are common, providing not just the catalog information for locating a resource, but the actual resource itself. This leap forward in written information delivery is in many ways just as responsible for the need for DAMs as the complicated process of photograph and video delivery.

Frequently, digital asset managers face a large volume of information to organize in a new DAM, and they are asked to formulate a date by when the project will be "done." In her 2012 presentation at the Henry Stewart DAM conference, Stacey McKeever addressed "the myth of done" as it relates to DAM. As she stated, *"Part of Digital Asset Management is managing expectations and explaining that while phases of the DAM (such as launch and sets) are done, the DAM itself is a viable entity with no end."* Thus DAMs have a starting point, but never a day or time when they are finished. You may choose to transfer digital assets from a current DAM to a new DAM – but even then, the assets live on. DAMs are only done after your organization is folded into another and your DAM's assets are absorbed into a different digital archive.

There is no finish line for a DAM, but there is a starting point. Once your sources, storage, and final destinations for assets have been charted for your organization's present workflows (see Chapter 2), it's time to start discussing how different types of assets might be organized. In order to do this, decide which collections you plan to ingest first. There are two paths that digital asset managers can take when building up their first blocks of content: the path of **existing content**, and the path of **workflows**. While both methods of content ingestion/upload are important to building a successful DAM, they differ substantially in their approaches. We will explore both below, starting with existing content. In an ideal world, DAM teams would begin with enough staff to tackle both existing content and workflows simultaneously, and they could launch their systems with both an archive of useful assets and the tools to walk them through the blending of old and new content when they must add a new asset. (The actual process of creating and accessing assets will be discussed in Chapter 7, while search strategies are further discussed in Chapters 8 and 9.)

Before you buy a DAM, it's critical to decide which approach to a DAM launch you wish to take: workflows or existing content. Often products excel at one or the other, and while you'll need a system that provides good options for both, determining your organization's emphasis in system use will go a long way in determining which system you purchase.

Starting a DAM with Existing Content

When you start a DAM with existing content, you'll benefit from the applications of several tenets of archival acquisition theory. The first is the approach of moving from a macro (high level) to a micro (lower level) organization. When thinking about the information you wish to move in to the DAM, think about it in large groups first. Don't move from department to department cherry-picking the most in-demand assets; take in blocks of assets, warts and all, and sort through them once you've decided to take them in. Before beginning the actual upload and metadata processes (which are outlined in Chapters 8 and 9), you should decide on the storage strategy you want.

Do you want content stored and searchable in large containers, or stored and searchable as individual assets? This question is one that archivists struggle with daily. In 1987, Henry J. Gwiazda published the method of accessioning collections at the Kennedy Library in Boston, and this process can be very useful for digital asset managers when discussing their collections today. The Kennedy Levels are as follows:

> **Level A:** Processing at the **item** level. In the DAM context, this means uploading each item as an individual asset and putting some unique metadata on each individual asset. In search results, single thumbnails and documents will be represented.

> **Level B:** Processing at the **folder** level. In the DAM context, this means loading assets as folders or zipped files in small related groups (e.g., all photos of one model from one particular photo shoot). In search results, you could show either a representative thumbnail of the folder or just an icon of a folder for documents. Because metadata will only be applied once to the folder as a group, searching for individual assets will require users to open the folder. Level B processing in DAMs often means breaking out campaigns or projects by item types.

> **Level C:** Processing at the **box** level. In the DAM context, this means loading folders or zipped files in large groups (e.g., all products of one campaign or project). In search results, no representative image will be shown, as level C processing will lump all images, videos, and documents together under one metadata record.

Most DAM users expect level A processing from the search results of their DAM. However, the process of arrangement, description, and search management to produce level A results is very **time- and labor-intensive**. While stock houses like Getty or Associated Press may have the resources to hire dozens of catalogers to continually create and tweak metadata on individual records, not everyone does. Examples of level A processing in DAMs occur where businesses, such as MLB (Major League Baseball), Disney, and Hasbro, have made substantial investments in DAM staffing. Examples of level C processing are very common in the advertising world, where the emphasis on quick turnaround of new product and little reuse of older assets means that dumping mixed items into one folder with a campaign name is good enough.

Most DAMs choose to deploy a mixed strategy of arrangement and description, with highly desirable assets getting the level A treatment and the archived content of little reuse value getting the B or C level of attention.

Starting a DAM with Workflows

If you choose to start your DAM with a workflow approach instead of an asset approach, you will likely buy a very different DAM than otherwise. In fact, there has been a recent trend in large corporations to run two parallel DAM systems: one for production workflows, and one for distribution and storage. As most organizations struggle to launch just one system, or to come up with a solution to unify several different DAMs and CMSs that have all been bought separately from each other, you're likely going to try to find a DAM that can do it all: run workflows and then distribute the end products to your users. For most companies, finding a DAM that runs both ways will not be a challenge: most publishing DAMs accomplish both tasks. However, if your business produces a substantial amount of video in dedicated video editing bays, the current recommendation by many would be to run two DAMs. During the writing of this book, we found that the needs of video editors are just too different from the needs of those in print production, graphic design, web coding, public relations, or any other field to mix intensive video workflows with distribution. If, however, your video content is primarily produced by vendors in their own DAMs, you won't have to worry about video workflows, so by all means charge ahead with one system for both needs.

When discussing workflows, it is too simplistic to think of them in the sense that assets need to be checked in and out for editing. Organizations buying a DAM due to costly mistakes regarding the versioning of documents or graphics will often focus too heavily on the edit history of an item, and thus center their ideas of workflows around interaction with an asset, rather than interaction with coworkers and the workflow itself. The mistake of centering your DAM workflows around versioning is a common one, and it leads to forcing people to work around the DAM, rather than adapting the DAM to work around your people.

The workflows in your DAM should be adaptable to the way your organization works, and changes to the flow and authentication of information should be possible. Don't make the mistake of learning how your DAM handles workflows and pushing your ideas of how checks and comments should be made into the existing framework. Make flowcharts with your team members regarding how assets should be acquired, described, and passed around for comments and editing *before* talking to your DAM vendor or consultant. Then you can buy a tool to match your task, rather than trying to match the task to your tool. Minor adaptations to match affordable system requirements are acceptable, but you should not overhaul your company to match system requirements that employees will ultimately reject. Chapter 12 will outline the processes involved in building efficient workflows, but before establishing these processes, you need to determine how your organization will handle static versus living assets, versioning, expirations, and watermarking. Each of these elements will be used in the day-to-day operating of any DAM, but they are especially critical when discussing workflows.

Static Versus Living Assets

When outlining your existing and desired workflows for DAM, it will be helpful to define what are **static** versus **living** assets in the system you hope to build. A static asset is one that is unchanging; while it is available to users, it should maintain a unique identifier or file name once in the DAM. If a static asset is to be reversioned—cropped or altered or edited—it should be downloaded and, once changes are made, submitted to the DAM again as a new asset with a relationship of some sort to the original. Here are some examples of static assets and their children and relations:

Example 1: The master file for a logo is a static asset that never changes, but it can be downloaded and incorporated into a print ad—which is then an entirely new static asset.

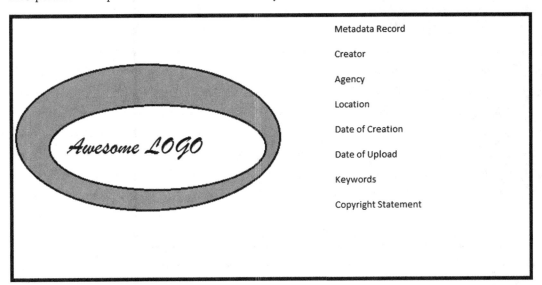

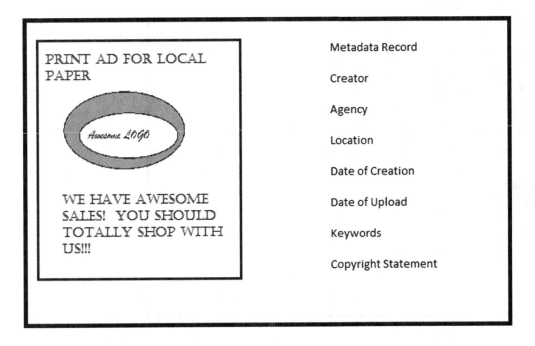

Example 2: An original photograph where the derivative files (cropped selections) are listed as children, and the files using the asset are listed as related files.

Metadata Record

Creator

Agency

Location

Date of Creation

Date of Upload

Keywords

Copyright Statement

Expiration Date

Child Assets: Link to cropped asset

Related Files: Link to Newsletter asset

Metadata Record

Creator

Agency

Location

Date of Creation

Date of Upload

Keywords

Copyright Statement

Expiration Date

Parent File: Link to original asset

Related Files: Link to cropped use

In the examples above, the first two assets—the logo and the print ad—are two distinct assets. The last example is what is known as a **derivative.** Derivative assets are those that are not new on their own in any way. While the newsletter took our examples and made something entirely new by using both the logo and photo to illustrate the newsletter content, the cropped image has no new content on its own. It will be up to your organization to decide if derivative files are listed in search results on their own, with their own metadata, or if they are simply linked as associated files on the original photos' records.

How your company handles derivatives in DAM should be part of the discussion regarding static versus living documents. Remember that any file can become a child asset or a relation *after* going through a workflow—the metadata and organization of a record can always change at any point in an asset's life, and the final steps of a workflow may include arranging the asset with its parent, child, and related files.

Whether an asset is considered to be static or living will determine how it should be managed. In the examples so far in this chapter, we see finished products—a logo, a photograph, and a compound asset—that are now static. It is likely that the logo and photograph came into the DAM as static items, fixed as originals from their upload. But the compound object might have had its origins as a **living asset**, one that needed approvals, data manipulation, or updating over time. There are two main ways in which living assets are active: through versioning and through workflows. This book will detail how workflows operate in depth in Chapter 12, but when you facilitate a discussion about setting up a DAM that will start with a workflow approach, you need to determine both how your organization deals with static and living assets, as well as the approach to versioning and expirations.

Versioning

In versioning, an asset has one unique identifier or file name *always*, even though the document may have many versions over time. New versions, when uploaded to the system, appear to users in search and display, while older versions are archived in the DAM and are usually inaccessible to everyone except the system administrators. Depending on the capabilities of the DAM in use, documents can be versioned within the DAM or uploaded over the older version.

The capability of the DAM you choose to track and archive differing versions of assets may be affected by legal considerations. Publicly held corporations and charitable organizations with strict reporting requirements will have obligations to stockholders and reporting boards that may require access to versioned assets. Talk to your legal counsel while assessing your needs for a DAM in order to determine their requirements. Making sure you get versioning right may be as simple as granting admin permissions for the DAM to compliance officers or as complex as limiting your choices in systems to just a few. The shifting laws regarding privacy and accountability in the information age mean that any detailed discussion of legal requirements put forward in this book would surely be dated by the time of its publication. Your best bet in any situation regarding digital law to date is simply to treat others the way you would like to be treated; if you think accessing earlier versions would make your job easier or more confusing, then it likely would be for others in your organization too. Design your access accordingly.

Expiration Utilities and Visible Watermarks

Of course, no discussion of living versus static assets, or of versioning and workflows, would be complete without mentioning both the watermarking and expiration utilities of DAMs. In organizations where the expiration of image rights has become a costly issue, the ability to hold photographs in a centralized library with clearly marked expiration dates or stamps may be the entire reason you are now reading this book. While watermarks are helpful when sending sample images for placement and proposed uses, the principal use for visible watermarking by digital asset managers is to alert system users of an asset's expiration.

Examples of visible watermarking, L-R: Traditional logo watermarking, Expiration stamping, For Placement Only (FPO) marking. Digital watermarks are not visible.

Some systems will be able to apply watermarks and expiration stamps automatically by putting the assets in expiration workflows that will apply the required marks on the selected date. Other systems will require you to generate new thumbnail parts one by one. When thinking about how watermarks and expiration dates will be used in your system, remember that it is likely that keeping up with these duties will require someone whose full-time job is the care and keeping of the DAM. If your organization does not plan to have at least one full-time DAM staff member, it's best to let people know that watermarking and expiration utilities will have to wait. Even if every DAM vendor you speak with pitches their expiration and watermark utilities as effortless, the governing of these systems is rarely without growing pains and will require support.

Bringing It All Together

At the beginning of this chapter, it was stressed that thoughts regarding assets to manage should be laid out for the organization before buying a DAM. If, however, you find yourself in the position of dealing with a DAM that has already been bought and handed to you to manage with little or ill-informed ideas regarding any or all of the points then covered, try not to panic. While your situation isn't ideal, no DAM is perfect, and you can still use the concepts outlined both in this chapter and this book to help your organization bring what they have into line and to focus on what a better DAM for the future might include.

If you're feeling overwhelmed by the assets you have to manage after reading this chapter, remember, you don't have to take everything on all at once. No one expects you to drink the ocean, and you can use the strategies outlined in Chapter 2 to build a priority list for the collections you plan to put into the DAM, and you can apply the discussions of file types here in Chapter 6 to help your audience decide how they would like those files treated. While discussions of workflows and versioning may seem dense at first, the more you work with assets in DAM, the more comfortable you'll be visualizing the concepts and file structures used to arrange and describe your content. Keep in mind as well the quote from Stacy McKeever about the "myth of done," and set expectations with your management about what a DAM really can do with the budget and employee hours provided.

Most digital asset managers choose to start their DAMs with an asset-based approach rather than to tackle workflows first, and it's easy to see why: setting goals for taking in X number of assets per month, or sunsetting an older CMS by taking on its critical assets are easy wins for a DAM. However, if you choose this path for your fledgling DAM, be careful in your presentation of its abilities. It's critical for the long-term adoption of your system that users understand the workflow capabilities of DAM, as well as how the system can help them work with people in other groups. If your DAM is seen as only a library or archive without the ability to help with living assets, you run the risk of becoming isolated from the generation of new content, and thus ever behind the real needs of your users. Your DAM should be perceived as a living system with no end, a central part of all communication with employees and those outside the organization.

CHAPTER 7

■ ■ ■

Creating and Accessing Assets

Chapter Goal: An overview of access considerations, including access methods for users, user/ system interaction, and discoverability.

Making DAM Usable

In Chapter 2, a needs assessment process for identifying where assets are and what should be prioritized for digital asset management (DAM) ingestion was outlined. In the chapters about asset types and DAM launch strategies, surveys of existing assets and system-launch approaches were considered. Once all these things come together, and you're sitting in front of your shiny new DAM, it's time to start uploading and creating assets and granting access to them. Creating and providing access to assets in a DAM involves many different daily tasks for a digital asset manager, which include but are not limited to the following:

Creating and maintaining access control lists (ACLs)

Uploading assets

Arranging and describing assets, via either a mass upload or one-by-one

Maintaining access to the DAM and its portals

Providing reference services to users who need help

Educating users about DAM asset creation and access

Before this chapter begins to discuss how assets are created, it will be helpful to discuss the DAM user audience and ACLs. After all, an organized collection of digital assets isn't worth anything if those assets aren't used, and in order to make a usable DAM, a digital asset manager must know his or her audience and what that audience would wish to access.

Identifying DAM Users

In the needs assessment for your DAM, you likely identified more than one group and subgroup that have assets that will be preserved and maintained in the system. Each group of users brings challenges and different requirements that must be considered early in the evaluation process. In this chapter we will use three different common departments as examples of user groups: a creative/design team, a public relations (PR) department, and a marketing department. All three of these functional units need to access materials from each other, but their working-day needs can be very different. Let us pretend in our example that, for human resource reasons, our three groups of users don't always get along; there's a history of mistrust and a lack of sharing between the three divisions. For this reason, each group wants to participate in the DAM because it wants to gain access to the others' materials, but each group also wants to protect its working files from the others. Going in with this scenario, let's now explore how a DAM might allow for both sharing and controlled access for all three groups.

Creating Access Control Lists

ACLs in DAMs are the lists that control access to assets. In very basic off-the-shelf DAMs, the DAM may come with just three ACLs or user groups to start with: an Admin group that allows those on the DAM team to see everything in the DAM, a DAM user group for those with registered access, and an ACL that allows for some of the assets to be seen publicly on the web. A graph of these three basic ACLs would look like the following figure.

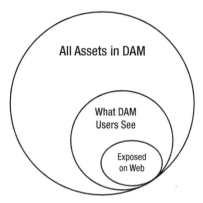

Figure 7-1. *An example of a simple access control list*

Administrators can see everything, DAM users can see objects that are relevant for their work, and the public can see what is posted from the DAM on the web. However, these three ACLs from an off-the-shelf DAM aren't going to satisfy our three user groups who distrust one another and have different needs. When collecting assets from the three departments in our example, let's start with creative/design first. When the creative/design team members are approached for DAM participation, they agree to put all past assets into the DAM at first, but they make it clear that a large portion of these uploaded assets should be viewable by only them. So a new ACL is created, wherein the admins and creative/design see more assets than the normal registered user would. This would alter our ACL graph to look like the next figure.

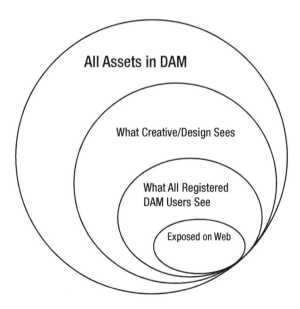

Figure 7-2. *The revised access control list*

The creative/design team members are so happy with their DAM access that the marketing and PR groups are eager to join the new DAM. All three groups realize that creating a hot folder on their servers or shared drives would be the most efficient way to upload materials to the DAM, so the creative/design server and the shared drives of the departments are linked in to the DAM, although only assets they wish to share are moved into the system. Further, each department wishes to have its own special access area, just like the one outlined for creative services. The groups would also like exclusive ACLs between the three of them: there are some assets that PR only wants to share with marketing, and some assets that PR only wants to share with creative/design. This very quickly creates even more ACLs.

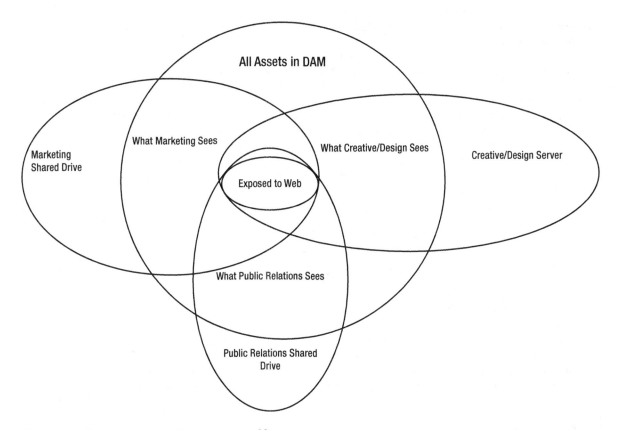

Figure 7-3. The next version of the access control list

Once these ACLs are created, and the number of assets in the system starts to grow, members from each of the three departments come to you and ask for special subgroups. Marketing and creative/design are testing some new advertising, and only a few people on each team are allowed to know about the project, leading to the creation of a "secret project" ACL. All three teams have been complaining that the others don't contact them about event planning; this also involves users from several other teams, and some promotion on the web, but some events are a surprise! So an "event planning" ACL is planted inside the general registered user group with some of the assets exposed to the web. Finally, PR has been dealing with some assets so sensitive that only PR management is allowed to see them. They want these documents in the DAM for legal reasons, but only a few special persons should have access. This leads to the "sensitive materials" ACL.

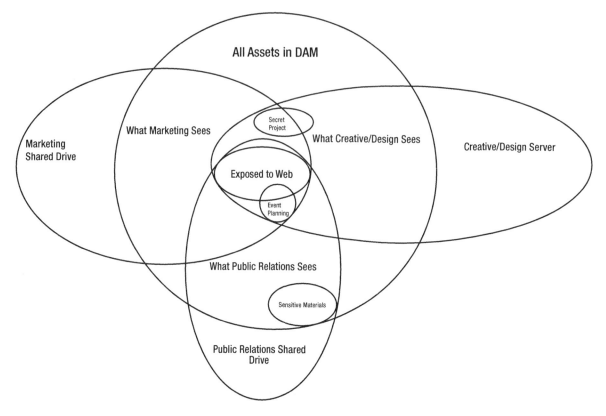

Figure 7-4. ACLs for special subgroups

In active DAMs, the number of ACLs can quickly grow to more than two dozen, making those who wish to chart them cross their eyes. Still, as you chart out the ACLs for your DAM, make the visualizations part of your user training. The number of ACLs and the complexity of their management are key to helping others understand the work of a digital asset manager and how the DAM can assist with content security, sharing, and planning.

Uploading Assets

The ingestion of assets to the DAM can be broken down into two forms of uploading and metadata creation: those very large sets that require mass actions, and the one-by-one uploads by those who are either not trained in digital asset management or just loading an asset or two.

Really Big Sets Uploaded by Digital Asset Managers

In 2005, Greene and Meissner published "More Product, Less Process: Revamping Traditional Archives Processing," which successfully argued that the process of indexing individual items unnecessarily slowed materials from being accessed by researchers. Now referred to as MPLP, the More Product, Less Process way of taking in large amounts of records is the accepted norm in many government archives. If you choose to start your DAM with an emphasis on workflows, you may want to take in a few blocks of content from shared drives under the MPLP idea, adding metadata to only large folders of content. However, most users of DAMs reject MPLP as a means of organization, preferring item-level descriptions. With this in mind, below we'll outline a process that takes in a mass amount of assets and then applies item-level descriptions. This method avoids the time wasted by individually uploading and describing assets one at a time, while still providing A- or B-level descriptions (see Chapter 6).

This process can be especially helpful if you are starting your DAM with a legacy collection from an earlier system, and all those assets will be uploaded to the new system and cataloged by your DAM team. Here are the steps to uploading and cataloging items by mass action in most DAMs:

1. Upload a large set of assets (this will take a while).

2. Export a comma-separated values (CSV) sheet of the assets. A CSV sheet is a spreadsheet of assets with the metadata in separate columns for each metadata field (see the figure).

3. Fill out the missing fields with the appropriate metadata.

4. Upload the CSV sheet.

	A	B	C	D	E	F	G	H	I	J	K	L	M	N	O
1	ID Code	Agency	Contributor	Date of Creation	Description	Expiration	File Name	Format	Keywords	Location	OriginalAltered	Person			
2	10000001	International Agency	Marketing	10/1/2014	Image used in print ads, Q1 2015	10/1/2015	WK239537	tiff	loads of keywords from the pre-loaded controlled list here	City, State, Country	O	Names of models here			
3	10000002	International Agency	Marketing	10/1/2014	Image used in gate signage, Q1 2015	10/1/2015	WK239537	tiff	loads of keywords from the pre-loaded controlled list here	City, State, Country	O	Names of models here			
4	10000003	Photographer Smith Studios	Sponsorships	3/1/2014	Specific sporting event sponsored by Big Corp, teams are the Reds and the Blues. Contact John Doe in Sponsorships for information on use. Altered image to blur other brandnames.	6/1/2014	Smith0301	tiff	loads of keywords from the pre-loaded controlled list here	City, State, Country	A	Names of athletes here			
5	10000004	Internal Creation	Employee Comm	1/1/2014	Image from Employee Contest. Winner in cute puppy division	NA	MVC2485.	jpg	loads of keywords from the pre-loaded controlled list here	City, State, Country	O	Names of Big Corp employees here			

Figure 7-5. *Sample CSV sheet. Digital asset managers regularly work with sets of assets that are in the hundreds or thousands, so it is easier to add metadata via CSV sheets en masse rather than one-by-one. See Chapter 8 for more on metadata creation with a CSV file and how to teach your DAM to pick up automatic metadata from XMP*

Self-Service Uploads to DAM

If you allow users to upload assets, it's usually better to have them load their images or documents one-by-one in a customized upload utility. An upload utility that is specially designed for people that are not digital asset managers can be as simple as a desktop hot folder where designers drag and drop assets or as complicated as a custom-coded pop-up on a departmental web site. There are several good reasons to have custom upload utilities outside the DAM for those not working directly with the digital asset managers:

1. If the upload utility is added to the creator's desktop or departmental web page, you aren't asking the DAM users to go anyplace new to upload. The custom upload utility becomes part of the audience's already-in-use workspace.

2. Your DAM users may lack the level of computer literacy to use the upload function within the DAM, which will likely include extra steps like assigning ACLs. In addition, a custom upload utility can drop assets from different departments into fixed ACLs that keep the items quarantined until a digital asset manager can review them for wider release.

3. A custom DAM upload utility keeps interaction with the DAM simple. With a custom upload utility, necessary metadata can be pushed down to radio buttons or fixed fields. A custom upload utility on a departmental web site can preassign metadata to that department and region.

4. A legal release (a click-wrap document, or Terms of Service) can be added for users of the custom upload utility, granting your organization rights to use the uploaded content as needed. When you deal with employee-submitting photography, this capture of legal release information during upload can often be critical for image reuse.

A custom DAM upload utility can allow for user-created assets to appear directly in the DAM, or it can automatically assign the new assets to an ACL that DAM team members can access for review only. It is highly recommended for metadata governance purposes that user uploads be screened by a dedicated DAM team member. For more on metadata and uploads, see Chapters 8 and 9; for more information on workflows in the DAM, see Chapter 11.

Arranging and Describing Assets

Most DAMs come out of the box with the ability to upload and edit assets one-by-one inside the system, but as reviewed above, the inside-the-DAM approach to building a meaningful library of assets will only get a digital asset manager so far. Mass upload and editing capabilities are a must, and how assets are manipulated will depend on the type of system with which you work. CSV sheets have been the de facto standard for the past decade, with tab delimited and cURL scripts mostly left in the past. If you are working in a system that requires tabbed or cURL uploading, do what you can to upgrade the DAM or push to purchase a new one. Due to the stability of CSV editing in Extensible Markup Language (XML), preservation archivists prefer CSV data, as it allows for the easier movement of metadata from system to system. Once you've mass-migrated several thousand assets out of a legacy system in CSV data as opposed to cURL, you'll never want to work with anything other than the preservation standard of XML again.

User System Requirements: XMP and XML

A few systems lean on the Extensible Metadata Platform (XMP) editing tools inherent to Adobe products in order to edit the metadata of assets. While XMP is strongly pushed as a metadata standard by photographers, the Society of American Archivists and the American Library Association only recognize XML as a metadata preservation standard; these two ideas stand not in opposition to each other but are rather derived from separate points of view. From a photographer's viewpoint, having XMP metadata embedded in an image or video means that the data will travel with that asset forever. From an archivist's or librarian's point of view, XML is a standard code base that allows data to move from platform to platform, even when the digital asset itself may no longer be readable. The best systems find a happy medium between both XMP and XML standards, with photographers and video teams embedding standard metadata in their XMP files, which are read by the DAM at upload and translated into XML-based metadata models. This crosswalk of XMP data into XML fields means that the data remain both embedded *and* readable. Further, implementing both XML and XMP as data storage (http://www.olc.org/ore/2intro.htm) means that the records are future-proofed by both standards. In the event of calamity, at least one set of data should survive to be read by systems of the future.

User Access Methods

Before uploading assets to a DAM, digital asset managers should consider their target audience and users, specifically their needs and technology skill levels. As discussed earlier in this chapter and in others, within just one organization there are likely several groups with different needs that all want to access the DAM. If the digital asset manager tries to serve all groups with just one interface, there is a high likelihood of only pleasing one group or none at all. For instance, designers often wish to see all the products of a photo shoot, while those in PR would rather skip the dozens of repetitive shots for a selection of just a few. While some access preference issues can be solved with the judicious use of ACLs, once an organization and DAM then hit a certain size, custom web portals are a must. Allowing the PR team to search a small ACL in the DAM through its own departmental web page would be an ideal solution, but what if a department doesn't have its own web page?

Building an Access Web Page

For reasons of both security as well as meeting user needs, it is often desirable not to let anyone outside of the DAM log in to the DAM itself at all. In these cases, a web site is constructed that pulls information and search results from the DAM. This is very preferable to a direct DAM access solution, as the HTML of the access web page can be altered quickly without affecting the performance of the DAM itself. Remember this image from Chapter 2?

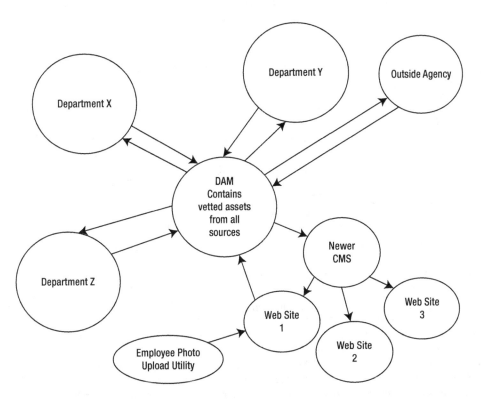

Figure 7-6. *A DAM interface with three departments, an agency, a content management system (CMS), and an upload utility on a web site. This graphic also occurs earlier in the text*

With a web-site access layer, the image can then look like this:

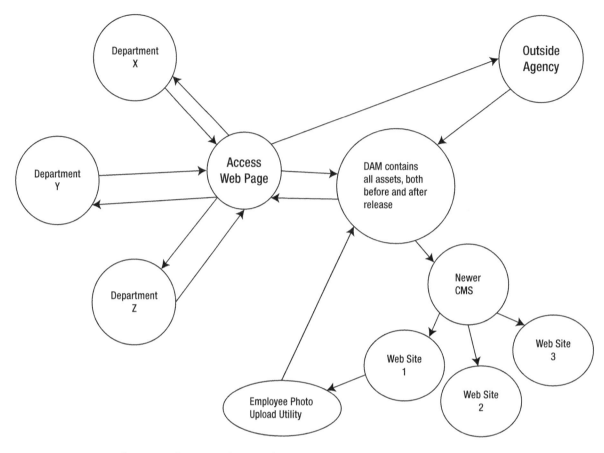

Figure 7-7. *Access web page used to secure the DAM from uploading parties*

As you can see in this new example, everyone in agencies and departments is now touching the access web page to upload and download items. These users may also be touching the CMS, which is a separate utility from the DAM, though fed by it just as the access web site may be. When employees upload photographs through web site 1, these items go into the DAM but are again accessed through the CMS or access web page.

Keeping DAM access limited to digital asset managers both internally and at agencies ensures that users in departments X, Y, or Z don't accidentally move or delete critical collections. It also ensures that they only get the search results they want, instead of search results cluttered by *all* items in the DAM. While too many search results returned isn't a problem for DAMs starting out, once the asset count climbs above 50,000, your DAM users will beg you for fewer, more relevant returns to their searches. This is often best controlled by redesigning the search interface of an access web page.

Who Approves Users?

Another argument for a full-time digital asset management staff is the availability of a person who can both walk users through registration and approve users for the different levels of access. If it is desirable to your DAM users to have existing credentials from their internal web-site controls passed through to the DAM, remember that there will likely be a cost and effort to integrating a single sign-on system between the existing security infrastructure of your organization and the new DAM. No one likes to continually update and remember multiple passwords and sign-ons, so if it's affordable, try to keep the security as simple as possible. Again, the advantages of an access web site are that the digital asset managers can keep the access web site open to all those within your organization's security system, while locking down the DAM to those with separate credentials.

Finding Specific Assets

One of the most important aspects of a DAM is how specific assets are found. By separating your user access interface from the DAM, items can become more easily found through custom search tools. Further, items such as model releases, legal documents, and archived items can be kept for search by only those with full DAM access, while everything else is searchable through the web portal.

This book will go into the specifics of how search and metadata work together in the chapters on search strategies and metadata modeling, but while access is being discussed it is helpful to have a brief discussion on private collections, kits, and custom access points.

Kits (or Public Collections)

When promoting a group of assets for use together, digital asset managers may find it desirable to form a kit to make asset retrieval easy for their users. For example, if your organization has a new marketing campaign centered on Mother's Day, multiple departments and teams may have generated graphics, photos, documents, canned text, and promotional emails to associate with the campaign. Rather than forcing your users to either search on a new key term or search for each item individually, it is more desirable to form a public collection within your DAM that may be accessed via a link on the web portal or in a folder on the DAM. Different systems have different ways of naming or calling out public collections, but to avoid confusion, many find it handy simply to call these items grouped in a way everyone can access readily a kit.

Private Collections (or Lightboxes, Saved Items, My Items)

Private collections–sometimes called lightboxes in reference to the old method of sorting through slides and negatives–are collections that users can form for themselves, whether working directly on the DAM or on a portal. The ability to form private collections–and to share those collections by permission granting and/or email notification–is highly desirable for designers. Once your DAM has tens of thousands of pieces of media, the ability to form and share multiple collections of items for later review, decision making, and group work will help keep your users sane and happy. If you wish to make your DAM part of a workflow or the everyday work of your users, private collections are critical to the findability of assets in the system. With shareable private collections, a designer can simply pull up what he or she wants and then direct others to the newly formed grouping of assets, so no duplicate searching work is required.

Even More Custom Access Points

While earlier in the chapter the creation of web pages for access was discussed, it is possible to put links to kits and individual items or even a "search the DAM" utility on departmental web sites. Granting access to a specific kit of training materials on the internal web page relating to a relevant topic, for instance, is a great way to grant easy access to materials without asking users to search the DAM. Just as the custom upload point for employee photos was diagrammed earlier in the chapter, custom download utilities may be used as needed.

Access for Brand Management

Once your DAM is up and running, your branding team may wish to use the system to approve and control use of your organization's branded assets (i.e., photography, logos for use on customer web sites and catalogs, etc.). This is an excellent case for a web site with customized HTML5 utilities that allow for assets and workflow run by the DAM to be partially exposed to the public. The following simplified graph shows how a brand approval web site might work with a DAM, an email provider, an e-sign utility, and legal resources.

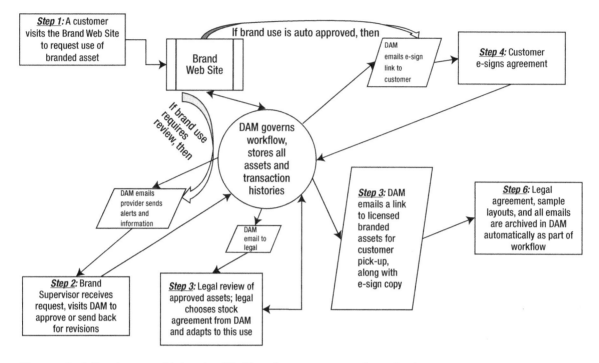

Figure 7-8. *Believe it or not, this is a simplified brand-review process. The author has seen brand approval processes that spanned five pages of flow charts and took more than six months to complete*

Providing Reference Services

Reference services are essential for providing access to a DAM. There is no DAM in existence that does not need a full-time digital asset manager available for reference assistance. Your company could build the most beautiful, user-friendly DAM in the world, and fill it with immaculate metadata records, all the required legal releases, and the best ACLs, but without a live support person to call, chat, or visit with, your DAM users will become frustrated. Until artificial intelligence makes substantial leaps forward, someone will always need to be available for reference services. According to a DAM Foundation demographic study of digital asset managers (discussed at length in Chapter 5), providing reference services was the second most common duty reported by those working with DAMs.

Providing reference services doesn't mean that you just find things for users; rather, reference services help users frustrated by not finding the answers to the questions they didn't know they needed to ask. A good digital asset manager is focused on the accessibility of their system and the needs of their users, and so customer service plays a large role in providing help in using the DAM. Listening closely and taking the time to find out what your users really need can be just as instructive to the digital asset manager as the person seeking an asset.

The key role that reference services plays in digital asset management is one of the reasons librarians are often drawn to DAM work; helping users find assets is much like working the information desk of a very private library (and no one dumps their unruly children in your workplace to play). If you come to DAM not from a library background, it may be useful to read up on materials relating to what library schools call "the reference interview." This interview is considered so critical to information science that the American Library Association actually runs workshops several times a year on the topic (http://www.ala.org/rusa/development/referenceinterview). While a formalized class on answering information/asset requests may at first seem like overkill, a century of library science backs the refined art of answering and asking questions in ways that meet user needs.

Here are a few links about reference interviews:

"The Reference Interview: Theories and Practice," by Stephanie Willen Brown (originally published in *Library Philosophy and Practice* in 2008): `http://www.webpages.uidaho.edu/~mbolin/willenbrown.htm`

"The Steps of a Reference Interview," by State Library of Iowa: `http://www.statelibraryofiowa.org/ld/i-j/infolit/toolkit/geninfo/refinterview`

"Mock Reference Interviews" by Jimmy Ghaphery: `http://www.people.vcu.edu/~jghapher/interview/index.html`

"Ohio Reference Excellence": `http://www.olc.org/ore/2intro.htm`

Training for DAM Users

With all the complexity of the images presented in this chapter, it should come as no surprise that training plays an important role in the use and adoption of successful DAMs. It's a good idea to make a short video available to first-time users to help them get started. Make the link to the training video direct, findable without searching, and available to those without access. After your users have logged in, you can offer additional short videos on specific search or sharing strategies. At the end of every training video, make it clear that reference services are available, and give information on how a digital asset manager may be contacted for assistance.

Publicizing your reference services during training will lead those experiencing real difficulties to call your team for help, and that call for help should be welcomed. Every reference request is a chance for a personal training session, and you'll often find that a user's frustration is not really with the DAM (which he or she may have been bad-mouthing all around) but with an obscure browser setting or true computer problem that needs an IT fix. Many times those providing reference services will be able to fix a frustrated user's search difficulty with a simple demonstration or by routine maintenance (clearing a browser cache or defragging, for example).

The more DAM users associate your system with someone who can help them, the more positively they will feel about submitting their own assets to the DAM. To this end, even once the training videos are loaded, it's important to schedule both in-person and live web training at least a few times a year. You'll be surprised at how much your users will learn from you and how much you'll learn from them in face-to-face training. Often new projects, opportunities for integrations, and workflow improvements can arise out of training sessions, so be sure to have someone on your DAM team who likes training and excels at adult instruction. Providing good training sessions is critical to providing access to your system and to performing the kind of outreach that will encourage the upload of assets.

Conclusions

The creation and access of assets in a DAM is a complex subject formed both by the technology the DAM is based on and the people who interact with the system. As seen above, the information in the system–the metadata, ACLs, and workflows–is shaped by that technology and its users. In a day of the life of the theoretical DAM we've constructed for this chapter, you might have a digital asset manager uploading large sets of assets and then cataloging them via a CSV file; at the same time, an employee might be uploading pictures of her dog for a contest on an internal web site, designers may be forming and sharing collections with others in three different departments, while a brand manager approves use of your organization's logo on an external customer web site. All this while users have questions to be answered, training to be scheduled, and new users need access approved.

The continual upload and download of assets from an easily accessible centralized source is what DAMs were designed to do. Never forget though that the most important idea behind a DAM is making the machine you build serve the users, not the other way around. A successful DAM is one where the system and digital asset managers adapt to the needs of the organization. That isn't to say that meeting those needs is always popular or painless; making a DAM work will depend on the adopting departments meeting the DAM team halfway, and this often requires a push from upper management toward compliancez and accountability, if only for the sake of digital preservation. But if you can manage to make accessing assets in the DAM easier than a department's current system, the battle for DAM user adoption will be halfway won.

CHAPTER 8

■ ■ ■

Finding Assets

Chapter Goal: Outlines how search works, and describes the relationship between a search and metadata.

Basic Metadata and Search Strategies

When you construct a digital asset management (DAM) system, the inevitability of hours spent poring over metadata modeling and search strategies may loom over new digital asset managers. If, however, those new to the field can learn to enjoy and even look forward to this task, they can expect a long and rewarding career working with DAMs. The findability of assets speaks to the ultimate usefulness of a DAM for designers, marketers, and legal staff.

This book will not endeavor to compress the more than 100 years of library and information science findings about controlled vocabularies, metadata modeling, and searching strategies, but I hope to provide a good overview of the terminology, theory, and practice behind the tasks related to these concepts in DAMs. This chapter will cover the fundamentals of metadata and searches. The next chapter will discuss the same topics for very large sets of assets and how digital asset managers may deal with advanced description and search issues. First, however, we will cover the basics.

Types of Searches

Inside every DAM is an indexing tool that enables a search; the indexing tool may be referred to as a search engine or an information retrieval tool. At the time of this writing, the most popular indexing tool for DAMs is Solr (`http://db-engines.com/en/ranking/search+engine`, retrieved 10/11/2013). Older systems using Lucene, the predecessor of Solr, are still around, but Lucene is gradually being phased out in favor of Solr, which offers superior performance in faceted searching. In order to explain facets, we will first have to examine more traditional search strategies. Most of those reading will be familiar with two types of traditional search: **navigational search** and **direct search**.

Navigational Search

Navigational search uses a hierarchy structure (taxonomy) to enable users to browse the information space by iteratively narrowing the scope of their quest in a predetermined order, as exemplified by Yahoo! Directory, DMOZ, and others (`https://sites.google.com/site/facetedsearch/`).

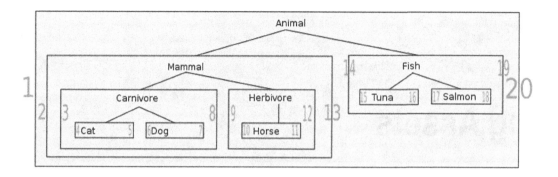

Navigational search by nature contains nested sets, as shown in the illustration. Mammals and Fish are two nested sets here within a hierarchical taxonomy. At each step, users must decide: I am looking for an animal. A mammal, not a fish. A tuna, not a salmon. Navigational search necessarily relies on those searching to know what they are searching for, and it may not provide options that allow for more nuanced searching. In the example, typing in "American Shorthair" would not return the result "Cat," and metadata beyond the level of "Cat" have not been provided. Likewise, it would not be possible to view all the animals of the American Northwest, as location has not been made a subset of Animals. Navigational search, due to its limitations, is no longer preferred as a search strategy. Source: http://commons.wikimedia.org/wiki/File:Nestedsets.svg, image by Wikimedia user Daf-de. CC-A-AS 2.5 (retrieved 10/11/2013).

Direct Search and Full-Text Search

Direct search occurs as users simply type words in a box. Google and Bing both use direct search as a method of web-site retrieval, so direct search has become the expected norm for most who wish to find what they would like in any indexing system. A **full-text search** is a type of direct search where files, metadata, and documents are returned as search results when the words typed in the direct search box match up exactly with words in the searched assets.

The technical considerations for full-text searches in images, documents, and video are very different. In order for full-text searches to effectively return documents in results, the documents must be machine-readable. This simply means that the search engine must be able to read the words inside your document files in order to tell searchers what is there. There are extensions that allow for search engines to read Microsoft Word, Calligra, and many other types of word processing files, but all digital asset managers should be aware that Adobe PDFs must be saved in an **optical character recognition (OCR)** format in order to be machine-readable. This is because PDFs are essentially pictures of a document, rather than word processing files; saving the PDF with OCR capability renders the characters as letters, not just as black-and-white images.

Metadata Types: XMP vs. XML

In order for full-text searches to return any type of graphic content (content without OCR words, such as photographs, illustrations, or videos) the direct search engine must be programmed to include Extensible Metadata Platform (XMP) metadata as well as the descriptive DAM metadata in its search parameters. XMP is a form of metadata that resides on an image or video file in its native state, and it automatically will include such specifications as dimensions, creation date, and other information that allows the file to be displayed on a computer. As mentioned in the chapter on creating and accessing assets, XMP is one metadata code standard, while Extensible Markup Language (XML) is another, and the best systems work with both. This is exemplified in a full-text search when the search engine returns results for images that use both XMP metadata and metadata put into XML fields.

Here is a sample of how metadata can look (a) in a DAM's HTML search layer, (b) in XML, as in a DAM's programming layer, and (c) in automatic XMP for the same image.

> This image with metadata looks as it might be displayed in a DAM. These metadata may sometimes be referred to as **guide metadata, display metadata**, or **descriptive metadata**.

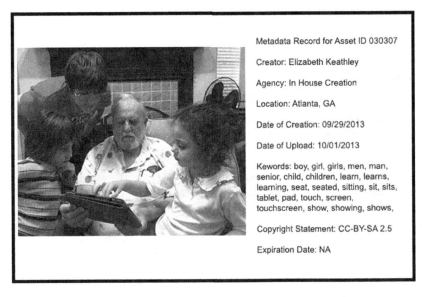

Metadata Record for Asset ID 030307

Creator: Elizabeth Keathley

Agency: In House Creation

Location: Atlanta, GA

Date of Creation: 09/29/2013

Date of Upload: 10/01/2013

Kewords: boy, girl, girls, men, man, senior, child, children, learn, learns, learning, seat, seated, sitting, sit, sits, tablet, pad, touch, screen, touchscreen, show, showing, shows,

Copyright Statement: CC-BY-SA 2.5

Expiration Date: NA

Figure 8-1. *An image with the metadata as it might appear in a search*

> The following XML is for the same image, and it might appear in a DAM's code layer. These metadata may be referred to as descriptive metadata as well, as the information is meant to simply describe the object.

```
<Asset ID>030307</Asset ID>
<File Name>IMG216.tiff</File Name>
<File Size>2,643KB</File Size>
<Creator>Elizabeth Keathley</Creator>
<Agency>In House Creation</Agency>
<Location>Atlanta, Georgia, GA, USA</Location>
<Date of Creation>09292013</Date of Creation>
<Ingest Date>10012013</Ingest Date><Keywords> boy, girl, girls, men, man, senior, child,
children, learn, learns, learning, seat, seated, sitting, sit, sits, tablet, pad, touch,
screen, touchscreen, show, showing, shows</Keywords>
<Model Names LR>Dot Keathley, Ruel Brown, Wayne Robert Brown, Diana Keathley</Model Names LR>
<Copyright Statement>CC-BY-SA-2.5</Copyright Statement>
<Expiration Date>NA</Expiration Date>
```

> The XMP for the same image, which can be read in the background of the image file, is shown next. Don't be intimidated by how long this record is; all the different tags are meant to provide interactive tools for various kinds of DAM systems. Because so much of the information in XMP is meant to provide specific machine-readable instructions, XMP records will sometimes be referred to as **process metadata, administrative metadata,** or **structural metadata**. The record actually includes all these types of information; examples of all three have been noted below.

```
<?xpacket begin="" id="W5M0MpCehiHzreSzNTczkc9d"?>
<x:xmpmeta xmlns:x="adobe:ns:meta/" x:xmptk="Adobe XMP Core 5.5-c014 79.151481, 2013/03/13-12:09:15 >
    <rdf:RDF xmlns:rdf="http://www.w3.org/1999/02/22-rdf-syntax-ns#">
        <rdf:Description rdf:about=""
            xmlns:xmp="http://ns.adobe.com/xap/1.0/"
            xmlns:photoshop="http://ns.adobe.com/photoshop/1.0/"
            xmlns:xmpMM="http://ns.adobe.com/xap/1.0/mm/"
            xmlns:dc="http://purl.org/dc/elements/1.1/"
            xmlns:tiff="http://ns.adobe.com/tiff/1.0/"
            xmlns:exif="http://ns.adobe.com/exif/1.0/">
        <xmp:CreatorTool>5.1.1</xmp:CreatorTool>
        <xmp:ModifyDate>2013-09-29T16:56:01</xmp:ModifyDate>
        <xmp:CreateDate>2013-09-29T16:56:01</xmp:CreateDate>
        <xmp:MetadataDate>2013-09-29T16:56:01</xmp:MetadataDate>
        <photoshop:DateCreated>2013-09-29T16:56:01</photoshop:DateCreated>
        <photoshop:ColorMode>3</photoshop:ColorMode>
        <photoshop:ICCProfile>sRGB IEC61966-2.1</photoshop:ICCProfile>
        <xmpMM:DocumentID>74CC50E4154DDC66F2D7495C85318122</xmpMM:DocumentID>
        <xmpMM:InstanceID>74CC50E4154DDC66F2D7495C85318122</xmpMM:InstanceID>
        <dc:format>image/jpeg</dc:format>
        <tiff:ImageWidth>2592</tiff:ImageWidth>
        <tiff:ImageLength>1936</tiff:ImageLength>
        <tiff:BitsPerSample>
            <rdf:Seq>
                <rdf:li>8</rdf:li>
                <rdf:li>8</rdf:li>
                <rdf:li>8</rdf:li>
            </rdf:Seq>
        </tiff:BitsPerSample>
        <tiff:PhotometricInterpretation>2</tiff:PhotometricInterpretation>
        <tiff:Orientation>1</tiff:Orientation>
        <tiff:SamplesPerPixel>3</tiff:SamplesPerPixel>
        <tiff:YCbCrPositioning>1</tiff:YCbCrPositioning>
        <tiff:XResolution>72/1</tiff:XResolution>
        <tiff:YResolution>72/1</tiff:YResolution>
        <tiff:ResolutionUnit>2</tiff:ResolutionUnit>
        <tiff:Make>Apple</tiff:Make>
        <tiff:Model>iPhone 4</tiff:Model>
        <exif:ExifVersion>0221</exif:ExifVersion>
        <exif:FlashpixVersion>0100</exif:FlashpixVersion>
        <exif:ColorSpace>1</exif:ColorSpace>
        <exif:ComponentsConfiguration>
            <rdf:Seq>
                <rdf:li>1</rdf:li>
                <rdf:li>2</rdf:li>
                <rdf:li>3</rdf:li>
                <rdf:li>0</rdf:li>
            </rdf:Seq>
        </exif:ComponentsConfiguration>
```

ColorMode, ImageWidth, ImageLength, and BitsPerSample are all examples of structural metadata, which help the computer render the image.

```
            <exif:PixelXDimension>2592</exif:PixelXDimension>
            <exif:PixelYDimension>1936</exif:PixelYDimension>
            <exif:DateTimeOriginal>2013-09-29T16:56:01</exif:DateTimeOriginal>
            <exif:ExposureTime>1/15</exif:ExposureTime>
            <exif:FNumber>14/5</exif:FNumber>
            <exif:ExposureProgram>2</exif:ExposureProgram>
            <exif:ISOSpeedRatings>
                <rdf:Seq>
                    <rdf:li>320</rdf:li>
                </rdf:Seq>
            </exif:ISOSpeedRatings>
            <exif:ShutterSpeedValue>13721/3512</exif:ShutterSpeedValue>
            <exif:ApertureValue>2970854/1000000</exif:ApertureValue>
            <exif:BrightnessValue>2049/2981</exif:BrightnessValue>
            <exif:MeteringMode>5</exif:MeteringMode>
            <exif:Flash rdf:parseType="Resource">
                <exif:Fired>False</exif:Fired>
                <exif:Return>0</exif:Return>
                <exif:Mode>2</exif:Mode>
                <exif:Function>False</exif:Function>
                <exif:RedEyeMode>False</exif:RedEyeMode>
            </exif:Flash>
            <exif:FocalLength>77/20</exif:FocalLength>
            <exif:SubjectArea>
                <rdf:Seq>
                    <rdf:li>1295</rdf:li>
                    <rdf:li>967</rdf:li>
                    <rdf:li>699</rdf:li>
                    <rdf:li>696</rdf:li>
                </rdf:Seq>
            </exif:SubjectArea>
            <exif:SensingMethod>2</exif:SensingMethod>
            <exif:ExposureMode>0</exif:ExposureMode>
            <exif:WhiteBalance>0</exif:WhiteBalance>
            <exif:SceneCaptureType>0</exif:SceneCaptureType>
            <exif:Sharpness>2</exif:Sharpness>
            <exif:GPSLatitude>33,53.92N</exif:GPSLatitude>
            <exif:GPSLongitude>84,35.11W</exif:GPSLongitude>
            <exif:GPSAltitudeRef>0</exif:GPSAltitudeRef>
            <exif:GPSAltitude>291/1</exif:GPSAltitude>
            <exif:GPSTimeStamp>2013-09-29T20:55:58Z</exif:GPSTimeStamp>
        </rdf:Description>
    </rdf:RDF>
</x:xmpmeta>
```

> ShutterSpeedValue, Flash, ExposureMode, and other camera information are part of the process metadata of the XMP record.

> GPSLatitude, GPSLongitude, and GPSTimeStamp are part of the administrative metadata. Cameras can also be programmed to include photographer and model information.

The (a) revealed metadata in the search layer is pulled in this example solely from some (but not all) of the XML sample data (b). However, a full-text search could also be programmed to read though the XMP data (c), returning search results on things such as color mode, shutter speed, the type of camera speed, even GPS coordinates. Further, a DAM can be programmed to have specific fields from XMP translated into the XML metadata model upon ingest.

This method of basic metadata input is increasingly standard: the DAM reads from the XMP the file size, file name, location, and more directly from the background metadata within the image itself. XMP allows for photographers to set up other direct entry fields as well, such as photographer or agency name, model name, and more. Professional photographers are well aware of the power of XMP, and most will use XMP in some form to allow for direct searches of their own catalogs, just as a means of organizing things in their own studios.

Faceted Search

Direct search has distinct drawbacks, however, once users need to sort through many hundreds of thousands of pieces of information, especially visual asset information like photographs and videos. Visual assets do not respond well to the if/then structure of a hierarchal taxonomy, as an image can mean many different things to many different people. Direct search, when applied to visual assets, only goes as far as the details of the metadata record. As a result, large DAMs often limit their hierarchies to just a few levels of subject headings and rely on a combination of direct search with faceting. Users, therefore, will need to limit their search results.

Faceted search allows for navigation of complex asset sets by combining text searches with controlled lists (usually presented in the form of combo boxes/drop-down lists). Users will reflexively recognize faceted search options from their experiences shopping on the web. Amazon.com, for example, first has users type words into a direct search box; once full-text search results are returned, faceted search options appear, asking the searchers to narrow results by item type, size, color, purpose, or other relevant facets. Facets can handle complex sets of interrelated objects, be set within continuous dimensions, and work well with custom controlled vocabularies.

A custom controlled vocabulary is critical to the success of any DAM and is a part of the ingredients that go into the design of a faceted search. When digital asset managers refer to a controlled vocabulary, what they mean is a predetermined list of terms that will be used to describe an asset. These set lists of words are usually governed by the digital asset manager or a team that includes the digital asset manager. A controlled vocabulary is often used to describe both lists of keywords and controlled lists in a faceted search. Keywords are simply the terms used to describe an asset, when those words do not exist within the asset itself, and therefore could not be found using a full-text search.

To better explain controlled vocabularies and keywords, let us examine a set of words common to many controlled vocabularies. Color is something of great importance to those working with imagery, and so the dominant color or color schemes of photos or graphics is something that is important in search results. At the same time, people use different words to describe color; designers especially may differentiate between very slight gradations. This is why designers should not be allowed to set color keywords; to them it may seem natural to refer to different shades of gray as asphalt, aluminum, or gunpowder, but few outside the designer's friends or compatriots would describe that exact shade of gray in that way. The median shades between black and white always present a challenge for controlled vocabularies as the word commonly used to search for them may be spelled either as "grey" or "gray." Therefore, let us use a small drawing of a mouse to illustrate several different metadata and search strategies regarding keywords, facets, and controlled vocabularies.

Figure 8-2. *A shady mouse*

If you were to pass out this image of a mouse to a room of people, and ask them to describe it, you'd come up with many different results. The colors would be described differently, with both spellings of gray present. Some would use the term "rodent," while others would use "rat" or "mouse" or both. In a controlled vocabulary, terms would be fixed; if the keyword "mouse" is used, your controlled vocabulary can dictate that "rat" must be treated as a synonym, or that "rat" and "mouse" must never be used to describe the same object. When cataloging the image of the mouse, the person inputting color (whether color is treated as a facet or keyword) would pick the correct term from a list like the following:

Color Keywords

Red

Orange

Yellow

Green

Blue

Purple

Pink

Your company color name

White

Black

Grey, gray

If this list existed for color descriptions in your controlled vocabulary, those adding metadata would be restricted to cataloging colors with only these words. No choosing magenta or fuchsia or turquoise: just the list of 11 colors above. Of course, this begs the question of black-and-white or grayscale images, and the color mode of an image is different from colors in the image. The facet of color mode would be specified differently; here is a small example.

Color Modes

Four-color, 4C, CMYK

Three-color, 3C, RGB

Black and white

Grayscale

Full-color

While both the colors in the image and the color mode of an image could be used as keywords to search for our mouse image, most DAMs will choose to pick out color or color modes as elements for a faceted search instead. In order for color or color modes to be treated as facets, the **metadata model** for assets must be set up in such a way that the **user interface** can utilize **facet filtering** for searching in a specific way. Chapter 3 covered the basic structure of a metadata record in reference to how complex assets might be handled in an upload. Now that it's time to talk about search strategies, it's time to consider the metadata modeling of process.

CODED COLOR-PICKING OPTIONS

The DAM vendor Media Beacon has addressed the color-naming issue by having a color-matching/color-picking tool that recognizes shades within XMP color spaces and allows for cross-referencing against them. This technology is proprietary, and while a few other systems have attempted other color-matching schemes, the Media Beacon system remains the best—and likely will until its patent is trumped by a newer technology.

Metadata Modeling Standards

In "Seeing Standards: A Visualization of the Metadata Universe," a chart compiled by Jenn Riley and Devin Becker at Indiana University in 2009, 105 different metadata standards were "evaluated on [their] strength of application to defined categories in each of four axes: community, domain, function, and purpose" (http://www.dlib.indiana.edu/~jenlrile/metadatamap/, retrieved 10/15/2013). This invaluable visualization chart could not be reprinted in this book as the standards depicted are so numerous and conflicting. Shortly after Riley and Becker's chart was released, I had a copy of the chart printed and laminated to use in meetings when explaining metadata modeling. Due to the multitude of metadata standards, a print shorter than five feet long diminished some of the details to an unreadable font. I strongly recommend those studying metadata standards to visit the graph online and to print their own copy if possible; it can prove to be an invaluable guide in discussions of modeling. Even if you can't understand all the detail of 105 different metadata standards broken down visually, the print is impressive and explains to people the complexity of metadata and search work more quickly than anything else might.

In her explanation of the metadata map, Jenn Riley wrote, "The sheer number of metadata standards in the cultural heritage sector is overwhelming, and their inter-relationships further complicate the situation." In an article in the Spring 2012 issue of the *Journal of Digital Media Management*, I and my coauthors of the article "The Sorting of Competing Metadata Models in Digital Asset Management" proposed a solution to all the conflicting metadata standards for digital asset managers: throw them out. There is no one true metadata model. Use **Simple Dublin Core** as the base for your DAM's metadata model, but don't treat it as a hard and fast set of rules. Use what you need, add what isn't there—for instance, a field on color modes, as mentioned earlier in this chapter—in order to meet the needs of your users.

Dublin Core

Most metadata models will follow the basic outline of Dublin Core. In the 1995 OCLC metadata workshop in Dublin, Ohio, 15 common elements of metadata were outlined and are now called Simple Dublin Core. These elements are as follows:

Title

Creator

Subject

Description

Publisher

Contributor

Date

Type

Format

Identifier

Source

Language

Relation

Coverage

Rights

Qualified Dublin Core includes three more elements: audience, provenance, and rightsholder (provenance is an archives and museum term indicating the asset's chain of custody). Many DAMs come off the shelf with either Simple or Qualified Dublin Core elements preloaded as the fields in their metadata models. No matter what your organization does or how it operates, you're going to want to modify your list of elements—your metadata model—to fit the needs of your DAM users. For instance, photographs typically don't have titles, and this field is therefore useless for systems solely focused on imagery. Our examples in Chapter 6 listed both Creator and Agency fields: in some organizations they may be two separate facets that need to be listed; in others, the creator and agency may be synonymous; or all creators are agencies, so the name of the field needs to be changed. If you find yourself constantly explaining to DAM users that the field "Contributor" really means "Asset Contact" or "Project Lead," then change the name of the Dublin Core field in your DAM to match what you really mean. A good DAM user interface will be a tool that fits needs, not one that forces people to match their thinking to system limits. Your metadata model should be rigid enough in its controlled vocabulary and upload standards to produce uniform search results, but it should be flexible enough in its changeability of user interface and faceted searches to meet user needs.

More Than One Metadata Model

As you outline your metadata model, don't be afraid to implement more than one model to accommodate faceted filtering. If your system will house videos and photographs, there is a need for videos to have their own model with fields for aspect ratio, time-code notes, closed captioning notes, and many other details necessary to find and use video not needed for photography. Likewise, systems housing both photographs and graphics often have separate models for the two types of images. In our mouse example, would the image be considered a graphic or an illustration? Are those two terms synonymous for your DAM user group? Would they like graphics and illustrations to show up in search results with photographs? These types of questions will inform how many metadata models exist in your DAM as well as what fields will exist in each model. Title, for instance, is a great field for video metadata models, but a poor one for computer graphics. Remember when modeling that less is often more; the fewer fields in a model, the more likely that model is to be completed by those uploading to the system. Likewise, the more fields you can restrict to combo boxes/drop-down lists of controlled vocabulary choices, the more successful your efforts will be for faceted searching.

Building a Metadata Dictionary

In order to avoid confusion regarding how to use your DAM's metadata models once they are set up, it is often desirable to create a metadata dictionary. This document, often kept as a spreadsheet but also available as internal DAM documentation in some systems, outlines the use of all of your fields and delineates your controlled vocabulary. It is my hope that one day spreadsheets can be done away with in the construction of controlled vocabulary, but at present it's the best tool available for those working in older or smaller systems.

One way to organize a metadata dictionary is in a simple document that just outlines the use and choices for each field of the metadata model. Here is a sample metadata dictionary that might be used for the image of Example A earlier in the chapter:

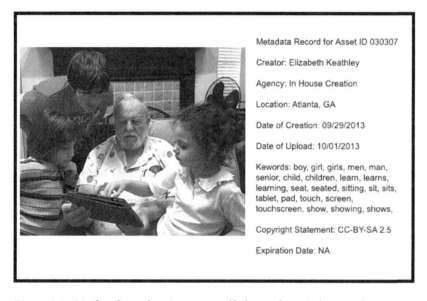

Figure 8-3. *My daughters showing my grandfather and cousin how to play a game*

Sample Simple Metadata Dictionary for No Name Organization
Asset ID—this field is automatically generated on image ingest.
Creator—this field names the photographer.
Agency—this is a combo box field. Choose one of the following from the drop-down menu. If you do not see the agency listed, contact a DAM administrator to add to the list.
List for Agency:

```
Agency YAY!
XCKD
Jimbo's Awesome Pics
In House Creation
```

Location—this field is a combo box field. If you do not see your location listed in the options, you may add it in; please follow the location-listing convention.

Date of Creation—this is the date the image or graphic was created. The date should populate automatically on ingest from XMP, but if not, enter by using the calendar feature. If the date is unknown, round to the first of the known year or month; for example, an image from 2003 with no other information would be 01/01/2003; an image known to be from August of that year but with no specific date would be 08/01/2003. It's critical that this field be uniform for good search results.

Date of Upload: Autogenerated by the DAM on asset ingest.

Keywords: Please use the keyword dictionary in the system to auto-pick keywords. If you have not been trained in this utility, please email damhelp@ourcompany.net. A digital asset manager will assist you.

Copyright Statement: This field is a combo box field; please refer to your copyright training to select the proper option from our list.

Expiration Date: This field allows for a calendar date selection, or you may hit the NA (Not Applicable) button in order to indicate this image never expires.

If you have a more sophisticated DAM, you'll have a function that allows for an internal build of this type of delimited documentation for each field in your metadata model, but for the purposes of being inclusive, let's discuss how to build out this document externally. While a very simple document will work for a very small DAM, once your DAM begins to expand to more than 10,000 items with multiple points of ingest, a more sophisticated document will be needed. **Commonly, a spreadsheet with a tab for each metadata field is used**. Keyword dictionaries are much the same, with tabs broken out for actions, colors, product descriptions, and so on.

Keywording and Keyword Dictionaries (Also Known as Tag Libraries)

Keyword dictionaries provide helpful synonyms and controlled lists to the different teams that may be feeding assets and information into the systems. Individual catalogers (who are well versed in the knowledge of the specific metadata for your products, services, and general terminology) should only add to or take away from the keyword/tag dictionary with approval from a centralized DAM governance person or committee. It may be helpful to hold regular meetings on the topic of metadata governance in general, as search theory and practice are often wildly divergent. However your organization chooses to tag or keyword images for searches, an authority in the area should be appointed and respected, or searches will degrade in quality as time goes on. Unless you want asphalt, aluminum, and gunpowder added to your controlled vocabulary as colors, metadata governance is crucial. Whether your DAM keeps its keywords/tags in a drag-and-drop system, in autopopulating lists, or just on a spreadsheet, access to the ability to add in tags or keywords should be restricted to the digital asset manager and skilled catalogers.

■ **Warning**   Some DAM projects can get bogged down early on with determining and setting up a controlled vocabulary for keywording/tagging. If the digital asset manager sets up the metadata model correctly, the keywords/tags will not be the main facet those searching for assets in the DAM will use. With facets for main subject, date range, contributing team or department, and other fields that can channel a search, users can often experience very successful results without using keywords much at all, especially in smaller systems. Truly useful tag libraries/keyword dictionaries take years to build, and they will grow constantly in the first few years of the system build as new assets dealing with new products and services are added.

Conclusions

The real work of any DAM team lies in its ability to upload, arrange, and describe desirable content for system users. This description is defined by the fields in the DAM's metadata model, and so the system must be able to adapt these models to meet user needs. I contend that there is no one true metadata model; while Dublin Core remains the best base from which to build out fields for DAM metadata modeling, it is worth a look at the work of Jenn Riley and others when adapting schemas for use. For instance, while the dozens of elements listed for PB Core (`http://www.pbcore.org/elements`) may at first seem excessive, the Public Broadcasting Metadata Dictionary is a well-thought-out program that meets the needs of its many users, and a digital asset manager could do worse than to borrow from such sets when modeling his or her own fields for video description.

Your metadata models will change in response to the search needs of your users at least a few times in the first year of your DAM, and they should continue to change over time. The construction of new facets for search, of additions and subtractions to delimited fields and combo boxes/drop-down menus, and the expansion and changes to keywording techniques will assure the full-time employment of digital asset managers for years to come.

■ ■ ■

CHAPTER 9

Describing and Searching Mass Sets

Chapter Goal: To outline how digital asset managers may acquire mass sets of assets and to define the strategies around the design of search tools that allow assets to be findable in large digital asset management systems (DAMs).

Taking in All the Assets

In the previous chapter, we discussed the basics of metadata modeling and search strategies. In this chapter, we're going to cover in more detail the processes that allow digital asset managers to upload large sets of assets, as well as the search strategies that are deployed to help DAM users find what they need. Without an organized process that thinks through the intake of large sets of assets from creation to asset retrieval, both digital asset managers and DAM users can quickly become overwhelmed with sets of assets returned in searches that are unhelpful, and to that end the first part of this chapter will focus on the process of acquisition, while the second half will break down the technical strategies that return best results from mass sets of assets.

Readers should keep in mind when considering mass metadata capture that keywording/tagging–that function critical to granular search results–will still be the job of the digital asset manager. While there are shortcuts and best practices to gaining the upper hand on most metadata, quality keywording for best search results remains labor-intensive and highly skilled work.

Capturing Metadata from Creation Sources

Designers, agencies, and other creative teams commonly get the assets into the DAM in a variety of ways, including, but not limited to, the following:

1. Uploading assets into the DAM directly

2. Uploading assets through an application programming interface (API)/custom upload tool

3. Using a hotfolder/custom tunnel

4. Handing a drive to the digital asset manager

5. Sending the digital asset manager a link to an external image-storage source, such as an FTP site, DropBox, and so on

In the asset acquisition methods listed as 1, 2, and 3, the assets should always push into an access control list (ACL)/upload folder where the digital asset manager can perform quality control on the items before distribution. While the acquisition by the asset methods listed as 4 and 5 should be avoided at all costs when discussing mass sets of assets needing description, they are sadly still very common, as many people do not understand the increased workload and time delays this will likely cause in the availability of materials to the DAM. This is because in the first three methods of mass asset acquisition, the upload functions can be configured to require a few key pieces of metadata that the asset creators likely know off the tops of their heads, but they may take the digital asset manager days to track down. Crucial information, such as location, date of creation, and model names, can be far more easily discovered if the creator's name is at least attached to the upload record, even if the information is left out of the description. Missing information is the reason those first three methods push into a holding area for quality control; by empowering creators to upload their own materials, a relationship is fostered that allows for better search outcomes from assets in the DAM between the digital asset manager and the source of the assets they manage.

Method of Upload	Pro	Con
1. Direct upload	The asset is immediately in the DAM.	The DAM interface may be confusing to inexperienced users. Quality control, number of DAM licensed users, and security may be an issue.
2. API upload	The API may be configured to address the specific needs of the user audience. Digital asset managers can require specific metadata input (but not too much!). It brings metadata entry and upload function to the users on their already visited web sites. It also fosters user input and accountability.	This requires investment in development from the DAM vendor and DAM team.
3. Hotfolder upload	A hotfolder tunnel can be configured to deliver assets into a custom ACL and/or with custom metadata fields. It can be used in combination with the Point-to-Point Tunneling Protocol (PPTP) to transform existing metadata into desired metadata. It brings upload function to the user's desktop, and it fosters user input and accountability.	This requires a substantial investment in development from the DAM vendor and DAM team. Extended troubleshooting may be required in the first six months of use.
4. Drive upload	There is little work for the end user.	It will require investment to deliver assets with the correct metadata. Some metadata may never be discoverable. If drives fail, assets may be lost. It is extremely costly in terms of time and manpower, even more so than hotfolders or APIs over time. Duplicate files and records are often evident.
5. External site upload	There is little work for the end user.	This may require an investment to deliver assets with correct metadata. Some metadata may never be discoverable. It is costly in terms of time and manpower, even more so than hotfolders or APIs over time. Risk of a security breach and the loss of copyright control are possible with third-party Internet file-delivery sources.

Figure 9-1. *Table of pros and cons of the most common upload methods. Not listed as an option here is paying outside contractors to do all the work; if your organization chooses to have a third-party metadata/cataloging company to handle these tasks, these contractors will likely use one of the five methods above*

Whatever process is used to acquire the assets, metadata should come along for the ride. The digital asset manager's goal should be to **try to get as much metadata added to assets before they come into the DAM**. If you choose to build an upload API, or uploading tool, ask for an Extensible Metadata Platform (XMP) crosswalk to be part of the uploader if your DAM does not automatically read XMP into your metadata model. As mentioned in the previous chapter on metadata basics, XMP is the metadata layered into a visual asset at the time of creation or edited into the object at the time of completion. Your uploading tool should be able to pull as much as possible automatically from the assets being uploaded, such as file name, extension, and size, preventing the unnecessary work of adding that information by hand. Further, XMP can be written or programmed into assets at the time of creation.

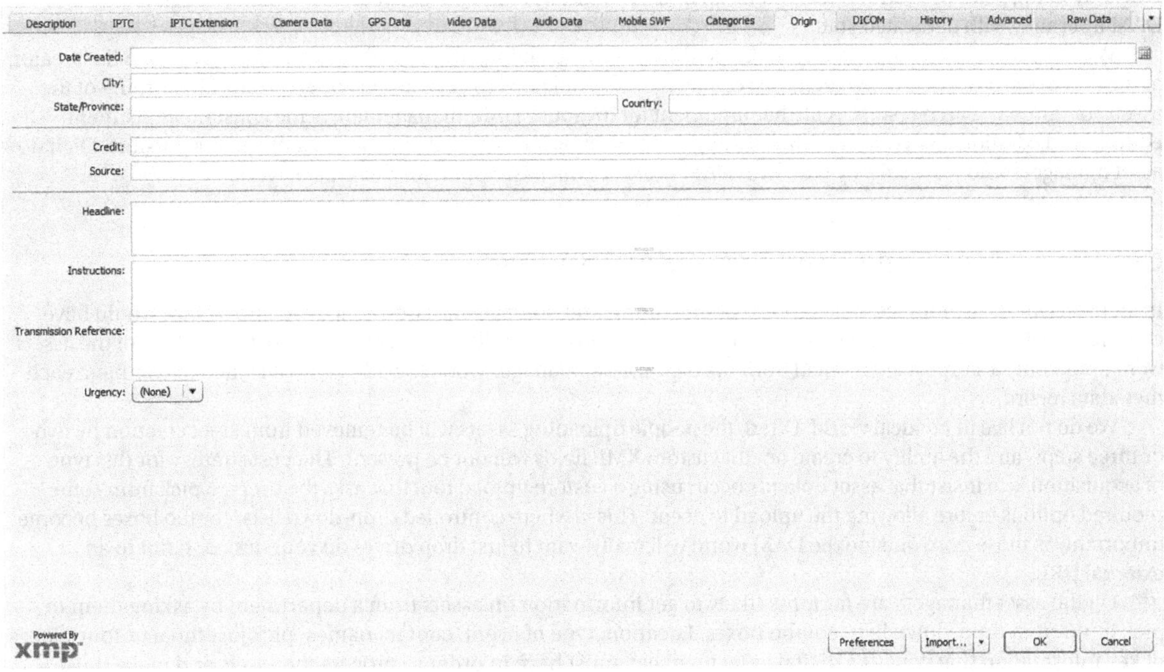

Figure 9-2. *A blank XMP record. All of these fields can be viewed and edited in Adobe products by clicking File, then File Info. Note the IPTC tabs; IPTC is one metadata standard often used by professional photographers*

For photographs, the XMP is created on the camera at the time of capture or is entered afterward in batch actions by the professional photographer. Your DAM can be programmed to take information from specific XMP fields and walk it directly into your metadata model on asset ingest. Some photographers will talk about programming the IPTC extensions in their cameras or for photo shoots; this is simply another format for the metadata within the XMP layer of a digital asset. Talk with your professional photographers, video-camera crew, or audio engineers before the event, and ask them to add in as much information as they possibly can to the files they plan to generate, no matter which file type or standard they plan to use.

Building Tunnels to Agencies and Other Systems

If you are working with a large advertising or publishing agency, odds are they will have their own DAM, with its own metadata models and file-sharing methods. While just picking up the files from the agency's site may seem like a good idea at first, this method means that the metadata for the asset are being entered twice: once in the agency DAM, once in yours. Efficiencies can be realized by connecting DAMs through custom tunnels and/or PPTPs. The building of this type of tunnel will require real programming knowledge and IT support from both DAM owners, but the investment in time and money is well worth the effort to avoid double entries from system to system and to ensure that all work products made by the agency for your company are in a DAM *that your organization owns*.

There has been a major push by advertising agencies to sell digital asset management to their clients in the last decade, often at laughably high prices. The sales pitch is usually that since the agency has a DAM, its staff will organize and tag assets for the client, so the client doesn't have to worry about a DAM. Given that most companies don't use the same agency decade after decade, the author wonders how access to assets is managed after the agency contract ends. Are the assets and metadata handed over? How would you ensure that the metadata were readable by another system? How would the asset owners ensure that everything from the old system was given to them? While it certainly seems tempting to let an agency take this complicated matter of a DAM off your hands for a fee, the fees currently being paid for such services often run into the millions of dollars per year–more than enough to house a DAM internally with dedicated staff.

While nearly all of the metadata relating to the file's construction, origin, and use can be derived from the creator, at the end of the day a dedicated digital asset manager will still need to keyword or supervise the keywording of the assets for optimal search results. A further argument for in-house DAM management is the constant adjustment, editing, and additional keywords pushed through a DAM in order to provide the best search results possible. Digital asset managers who work side-by-side with DAM users are the best option for this type of work.

Capturing Metadata from Secondary Sources

In an ideal world, all graphics, illustrations, photographs, and other visual assets uploaded into a DAM would have complete XMP records when uploaded, every upload would execute flawlessly, and because the creators of the assets were uploading, a simple call or email from the digital asset manager would be all that was needed to complete each metadata record.

We do not live in an ideal world. Often, the people uploading assets will be removed from asset creation by two or three steps, and the ability to create or edit custom XMP fields will not be present. The best strategy for this type of acquisition is to insist that asset uploads occur using a custom upload tool that asks the users to pick from some required options before allowing the upload to occur. This is where controlled drop-down lists/combo boxes become important, as those from outside the DAM world will really want to just drop drives on your desk or point to an external URL.

Digital asset managers are far more likely to get information on assets from a department by asking them to pick input from drop-down lists/combo boxes. Location, type of event, contact names–pick just three or four pieces of key information that you, as a digital asset manager, must have in order to process the assets and make those required for asset upload. Asking for more than three or four fields of input may cause pushback, but when you frame your upload arguments as "three fields of automatic picks isn't too much to ask" you're far more likely to get participation and assets.

Managing Expectations in Mass Asset Ingest

Unfortunately, there will be times when very large sets of assets land in your DAM with little or no metadata, and they will need to be described. Digital asset managers have several options when this occurs.

1. Explain to the person or department handing you the large quantity of assets that these assets will be processed when the budget allows, and let the drive sit until funds appear.

2. Create a reserve in your DAM team budget to absorb these types of metadata creation emergencies, allowing for the outsourcing of metadata creation and/or hiring of contractors.

3. Create an asset-cataloging queue, and let DAM directors/managers prioritize the arrangement and description of large sets that come in with minimal metadata.

None of these three options are ideal, and all boil down to the same answer: someone has to do the metadata entry and/or quality control of digital assets, and that means someone has to pay for the work. Digital asset managers could, of course, choose to dump mass amounts of assets into the DAM with minimal cataloging (see Chapter 6 and the discussion of the Kennedy levels of processing). There are only so many times a DAM can be cheated of its metadata in this way, however, before users become dissatisfied with their search results. In the case study that follows, a common situation is outlined regarding a flood of new assets. After a breakdown of various coping mechanisms or solutions are discussed, ways in which search interfaces and DAM indexing can assist in helping users find assets will be explored.

Case Study: The Importance of the Immediate Event
Problem

An organization has scheduled an event where they plan to take thousands–possibly tens of thousands–of photographs. This event will also generate video, and graphics and promotional materials are generated even before the event. Further, participants of the event are being encouraged to create and submit their own images via social media in order to fully document the spectacle. The digital asset manager has been tasked to capture as many important assets as possible both before and after the event, but no one is yet sure what "important" will mean.

The digital asset manager must determine a way to arrange and describe what will be the most important assets as quickly as possible in a meaningful way. Directly after the event, the organization wishes to use all the materials as positive PR, and several other departments wish to highlight the event afterward in both traditional and social media platforms.

Solution 1: Get Ahead of the Problem

The best way to approach the wave of assets coming at the DAM for an event is to start as early as possible. The designers who put together graphics and collateral for the event should have a way to get those in the system as quickly as possible and before the day of the event itself. Offering to make a kit or collection (see Chapter 7 for a discussion of kits and collections) of "event assets" ahead of time may be useful to all, as the designers can point anyone asking for their work to one link on the DAM or on an accessible web site.

By getting ahead of the event, you will be able to answer pressing questions regarding rights, keywords, and who the media manager for the event will be. More importantly, by adding metadata to the graphics early, and pointing everyone to the DAM, a digital asset manager can make himself or herself the point person for image distribution for the upcoming event. This position of distribution authority is desirable as it helps head off those who may take and use images without ever consulting the DAM. Everyone should understand about which clearinghouse is central for graphics, photos, and media sharing.

Solution 2: Shortcut the Metadata (for Now)

The digital asset manager can come up with short-term coping strategies such as a unique keyword or custom facet for the event that will allow for assets to be grouped together (if not sorted so easily). Since the DAM will be flooded in the first few days after the big event with new assets, admit that these will need to be captured in the DAM for now with minimal metadata and just one or two keywords. Shortcutting the metadata will also have the benefit in this instance of showing those who have a chance to look at the big raw mess of assets under your secret custom keyword what the DAM would look like without active asset management.

Once the immediacy of the event has passed, the best assets can get fully described in the DAM and become part of regular search results.

Solution 3: Create a Holding Pen

The digital asset manager could create or repurpose an upload tool that allows all media from the event to be dumped into a special "holding area." This area could be as simple as a custom ACL in the DAM that displays all unreviewed content related to the event, or as sophisticated as a password-protected web site that displays assets from the DAM that have been uploaded related to the event. Either way, segregating the initial rush of content from normal search activity is probably a good idea until the event is over and people have had time to remove images that might not be in keeping with the company's desired image (is that kid drinking beer in the background?). When cooler heads prevail and everyone has recovered from the event, assets can be ranked and processed with adequate metadata records attached.

Solutions Summary

All of the above solutions are valid responses to a high volume of assets rolling into a DAM in a short amount of time. Deploying one or more of these strategies would be valid in containing a flood of information in an organization where this type of event might happen only once or twice a year. If, however, a digital asset manager deploys these quick fixes too often, the DAM is playing a game of catchup that is destined to end with a system or human resources crash. Operating in constant panic mode is just as unhealthy for information retrieval systems as it is for human beings, and at some point, the labor-intensive work of processing all those assets must be completed. If the cost of proper metadata entry and quality control is protested as too costly or labor-intensive, the digital asset manager must point out how this will ultimately undermine the entire system.

Detailed Searching and Granularity

In archives and other cultural institutions around the world, there are backlogs of fifty years or more of photographs, documents, personal correspondence, and more waiting to be processed by archivists so that the rest of us can discover the information within. The backlog of assets is so extreme and pressing as to make the everyday work of cataloging each individual piece of information seem absurd, and to this end in 2005, Greene and Meissner published the article "More Product, Less Process: Revamping Traditional Archives Processing," in the journal *American Archivist*. Now referred to as MPLP, the More Product, Less Process way of taking in large amounts of records is the accepted norm in many government archives. Greene and Meissner successfully argued that the process of indexing individual items unnecessarily slowed materials from being accessed by researchers.

MPLP is often expressed in the DAM world by systems that add metadata only to large folders of content. Most DAM users reject MPLP as a means of organization, as it forces users to spend long amounts of time browsing through folders and personalized file names in order to (maybe) find an asset. Greene and Meissner's methods of collection-level description work well for governmental bodies drowning in documentation, effectively pushing the burden of time from those curating assets onto those who wish to search through them. To sum up: There is a certain amount of time and effort that it takes to find a digital asset. That time and effort can either be spent on the front end of the DAM process by a digital asset management team who invests in quality metadata, or that time and effort can be spent on the user end of the DAM process by forcing users into long searches. As no DAM with inadequate search results will survive for long, it should be clear to those invested in building a successful system that a high degree of quality control, metadata review, and other asset-management activities will pay off in a usable system.

Programming a Helpful Search Interface

In order to continually adapt DAM metadata models and user interfaces and to provide users with the best search experiences possible, digital asset managers should familiarize themselves with the terms and strategies listed below.

Faceted filtering, **continuous facets**, **hierarchical facets,** and **faceted recommendations** are all tools that online shoppers will automatically recognize, as these are commonly used to help narrow wide ranges of search results. After a user enters a few keywords in a direct search box, the user interface then allows the user to make a few choices using faceted filtering. Continuous facets are those that show just one result from a range and allow for multiple selections (for instance, looking at shoes that are both blue and a size 10). Hierarchical facets narrow results and offer new facets at every step along nested sets (when you want shoes from Italy, you must choose Rome or Milan) and faceted recommendations appear when linked by hierarchical metadata (you were looking for blue shoes, size 10, from Italy–would you like to see men's, women's, or children's styles?). Each of these facets is programmed to respond to input from the metadata model, but they can be "faked" or built around additional query strings coded into a web site that serves as a portal to assets in the DAM. Indeed, this is currently how most consumer shopping web sites provide their faceted search experiences.

Cross-link assets are the **parent/child relationships** between files and were discussed in Chapter 6, but the importance of linking assets in metadata records cannot be underemphasized. For true digital asset management to occur–digital asset management that moves beyond simple search and retrieval and into the ability to analyze, repurpose, and manage the assets in the system into workflows–cross links are vital. These types of metadata can often not be captured on asset ingest, and they must occur as part of a separate metadata creation/quality-control process in the routine work of a digital asset management team.

A **fielded search** is often presented as the "advanced search options" in a user interface, one where those seeking assets may query individual fields of metadata for more precise returns. A **date range search** is the most common of the fielded searches, with nearly every DAM including a date range search as an out-of-the-box feature right next to a keyword or tag search field.

A **search within a search** can include elements of either fielded searches or faceted searches or both. Important to the search within a search strategy is a way **for users to realize that they are again searching within a limited set of results**. Users can become confused when presented with a direct search box on their results page that does not return items from the full DAM.

Highlighted results within search results is a common tool for systems that employ full-text search strategies, with the search term being highlighted everywhere it appears in the results. However, if the indexing engine does not handle **stemming** well–highlighting the second half of the word "Caucasian," for example, when the users are looking for assets that contain the word "Asian"– the limited effectiveness of highlighted results becomes obvious. Highlighting is usually desirable in systems with large amounts of text, but as a tool that is applied after several other search strategies have been offered to the user.

More like this and **find similar** searches allow for users to narrow search results along predefined facets without the bother of clicking boxes or making selections in a sidebar. Both of these search strategies are accomplished by programming the search interface to interact with the metadata model along predefined, faceted search parameters.

Actively Linked Metadata

While the search strategies listed in the paragraphs above will likely be familiar to anyone who does a good deal of online shopping or uses Google, Bing, or Yahoo search engines, there are a variety of search tools common to DAMs that those new to these systems may not have seen before. DAMs often choose to reveal partial or full metadata records to those searching in order to facilitate **relevant searching**. By showing DAM users not just their results, but the information linked to those results, the system offers users different ways to help them sort through hundreds of thousands of images.

Search strategies with exposed metadata may include options such as **rollover metadata**–exposing more cataloging information about an asset when the user clicks on a link or just hovers over a metadata field with a mouse. If keywords in the metadata record are exposed, they may lead to **hyperlinked keyword searches**, which give the users another "more like this" way of discovering content. In terms of coding, the ability to hyperlink keywords is closely related to the ability to create **keyword watch lists**, which allow users to receive alerts when new items with specific terms are added to the DAM. DAM search interfaces capable of creating watch lists are also capable of creating individualized lists of **saved searches**, a particular favorite with user groups who dislike creating private collections.

Predictive searches, sometimes called **autocomplete** and **"did you mean"** tools, can be added to direct search boxes for assistance with those who (like the author) struggle with spelling. While preprogrammed utilities for both these search strategies exist, the best bet for better DAM searching strategies is to link these tools to metadata existing within the system. This way, the predictive search can pick up on the controlled vocabulary specific to your organization's assets, providing the users with terms specific to their needs.

The Guts of Searching

While the search strategies discussed so far have mainly dealt with the end-user experience, there are terms and strategies available to digital asset managers that may or may not be revealed to the general user audience. These search abilities are often available to users but rarely used, as they require a high level of computer literacy and a willingness to spend serious time sorting through assets in the system.

	Data Retrieval	Information Retrieval	Knowledge Retrieval
Match	Boolean match	partial match, best match	partial match, best match
Inference	deductive inference	inductive inference	deductive inference, inductive inference, associative reasoning, analogical reasoning
Model	deterministic model	statistical and probabilistic model	semantic model, inference model
Query	artificial language	natural language	knowledge structure, natural language
Organization	table, index	table, index	knowledge unit, knowledge structure
Representation	number, rule	natural language, markup language	concept graph, predicate logic, production rule, frame, semantic network, ontology
Storage	database	document collections	knowledge base
Retrieved Results	data set	sections or documents	a set of knowledge unit

Figure 9-3. The table breaks down search strategies into three types; while most documents can be found in a DAM through information retrival means, the visual nature of creative assets often means that more complex knowledge retrival tools must be deployed. Source: van Rijsbergen, C.J., Information Retrieval, Butterworths, 1979

Boolean searching will be familiar to those of a certain age who remember when DAMs and library systems were much less sophisticated than they are today. A Boolean search uses the terms AND, OR, and NOT either in all caps or between terms set off by quote marks. So the search "John Smith" AND "Sails to Islands" OR "Boating to Saint Simons" NOT "Genealogy" NOT "History" NOT "Ancestor" would give a user links where John Smith was mentioned with one or both of the phrases about boating but would not return links mentioning any of the historic John Smiths and would exclude the flotilla of genealogists linking themselves with historical John Smiths. Any system that accepts Boolean search operators also allows users to substitute AND with the plus (+) sign and NOT with the minus (-) sign as shortcuts. **Advanced Boolean searching** includes the AND NOT, NEAR, and the ability to conduct **nested searches** using parentheses. Use of advanced Boolean searching is generally confusing to those who do not live and die by researching dense documentation all day, but to those who do, mastering these three commands can be crucial. Frequent users of such commercial research databases such as Lexis-Nexus, Westlaw, and governmental databases still lean on advanced Boolean searching to reveal the contents of millions of documents available through full-text search methods.

Wildcard searches are invaluable to digital asset managers, as they allow for searching by sets of like strings of information. The common wildcard in both Solr and Lucene indexes is the asterisk (*), and use of this with incomplete or missing information is helpful in finding assets that may otherwise be difficult to locate.

Stemming was mentioned earlier in this chapter in connection to highlighted results, and it's worth a bit more discussion to digital asset managers really interested in the guts of a search. The first stemming program was written by Julie Beth Lovins in 1968, and it is still the root of all stemming solutions in use today (Lovins, J. B., "Development of a Stemming Algorithm," *Mechanical Translation and Computational Linguistics* 11 (1968), 22–31). When digital asset managers discuss stemming, they are often moving beyond the Asian/Caucasian issue mentioned earlier and making decisions about how their systems will manage strategies related to **natural language processing (NLP)**. This means not only allowing the search engine to recognize conventional stems and roots of words (such as talk is the root of talks, talking, talked) but to realize that words may be related no matter their spelling (talk, spoke, chat, for instance), and returning results these natural language equivalents in search results, if with a lower search ranking than the original direct search input. NLP searches also filter out words such as "the," "for," and others that are common and extraneous to the search; these terms are referred to as **stop words**.

The practice of using NLP to extend an index engine's stemming capabilities is formally referred to as **morphological segmentation**. Very advanced systems may even be able to use forms of **word sense disambiguation**; this allows the DAM to understand how words of more than one meaning are being deployed in an asset. The more advanced a search engine or DAM becomes in deploying NLP, the closer to an AI (artificial intelligence) it becomes. This is not an exaggeration: NLP is one of the major tenets of AI development (`http://aitopics.org/`).

Weighting Search Results

After your system has taken in mass sets of assets, you will likely have input from DAM users on how they would like to refine their searches. Input on search experience might either be gathered from surveys hosted on the DAM interface site itself or solicited through links that anonymize results. Try to avoid gathering complaints in open meetings, as this can lead to a negative view of the DAM as the loudest critics make their issues (legitimate or not) known. Regardless of method, once you have some feedback, it is time to discuss how search results are ranked on return.

For an example of weighted search results, it is helpful to examine a site where the minimal metadata associated with assets has made the way search results are weighted very important. YouTube, which at the time of this writing, is the world's most popular video-sharing site, relies on ranked weights to return a list of generic videos when a user that is unknown to Google searches. In 2013, when a user types keywords in a direct search box on YouTube, videos related to those keywords are shown in search results this way:

```
Keyword Match + Most Viewed
Keyword Match + Most Liked
Keyword Match + Most Number of Comments
Keyword Match + Most Linked
Keyword Match + Most Recent
```

In this weighting of search results, a video with the keyword "cats" with one million views and 100 likes will appear in search results before a video with the keyword "cats" with one million views and 50 likes. Since comments are weighted after likes, even if the second video gathers three time the comments as the first, the ranking will remain the same. The weights here roll downhill as tiebreakers, forever ranking content by listed weights. At different times YouTube's weights will be adjusted and change, notably with the position of the "Most Recent" weight. However, with the tracking of YouTube users through Google, these weights have become secondary to user profiling. Since 2010, YouTube considers the weights of the elements *after* it considers metadata linked to a logged-in user's account. The weights that are used from tracked data are proprietary but obviously consider such information as videos the user has viewed and liked before, search-term histories, and perhaps even ad-clicking behaviors.

Weighting results for users in DAMs ordinarily favors the most recent items first, allowing those searching the system to see the newest assets right away. A common weighting scheme for a commercial DAM might be the following:

```
Keyword Match + Most Recent (by Creation Date)
Keyword Match + Most Recent (by Upload Date)
Keyword Match + Most Often Downloaded
Keyword Match + Most Often Saved to Private Collections
```

When results are weighted by information in a specific metadata field (such as creation date), this is referred to as field biasing. When results are weighted by their popularity or actions taken, these may be referred to as statistical relevancy (persons who typed X were most likely to click Y) or popularity biasing (people really like sharing asset X). Further, multiple relevancy profiles may be used to weight search results around parameters such as ACLs (see Chapter 7). If you know that, in searching, users from the Public Relations ACL will want images of events to show in their searches before images of staged photo shoots, weighting search results for this ACL may be helpful to end users.

Conclusion

When taking in large sets of assets, DAMs follow a very simple and old rule of computing: garbage in, garbage out. The more detailed and controlled the metadata on assets in the DAM, the better the search results. Refining those results to meet user needs is also a labor-intensive process, one that relies on a continual feedback loop from both the digital asset managers and their high-level users on what search strategies they find effective in the system. When users are complaining about the ranking of results in a DAM, rejoice rather than despair; this means that your users are actively in the system searching and know that better results could be achieved with more sophisticated search strategies. With that same user demand, digital asset managers can push for more resources to refine their search returns.

Every DAM must be regularly audited to eliminate duplicate records and to ensure uniformity in metadata, and never is this more crucial than at times when the system will be pushed to take in large amounts of assets in a short amount of time. When pushed to the limit as in the case study "The Importance of the Immediate Event," digital asset managers can use any or all of the search strategies listed in this chapter to help them clean their system. Searching will reveal variant spellings and missing or incomplete data, and a search will arrange assets in weighted results pages that help in the after-event processing of information.

Comma-separated value (CSV) sheets also provide a crucial way to look at specific metadata fields in large sets of records. Using advanced search strategies in the DAM, digital asset managers can break out sets of assets by using specific parameters, and they can edit those records en masse via the CSV. While working with mass sets of assets is never easy, it is what DAMs were invented to do, and it can often make a digital asset manager look like a hero to those seeking to find one crucial image in a sea of thousands.

■ ■ ■

CHAPTER 10

Big Data and Bigger Control Issues

Chapter Goal: *This chapter discusses strategies for performing a detailed audit of existing content and for developing a forecast to determine growth rate.*

Content Audit and Determining Metrics

Everyday work in a digital asset management (DAM) system includes reviewing metrics and auditing content. As the setup of metrics in a system is in part what enables successful content auditing, this chapter will discuss both tasks. We'll start with metrics and how these numbers can help you prove return on investment (ROI) for the DAM. Once we've examined standard DAM measures, we will then move on to how metrics help digital asset managers pinpoint user interface problems and are used in the routine content audits that are crucial to DAM success. We'll examine the DAM system's relationship to the phrase of the moment, "big data," and how metrics and analytics generated by the system are invaluable to brand management. At the end of the chapter are sample reports generated by the examples used in the discussion of the different types of metrics and ROI.

The first thing many digital asset managers do each morning is to log in to their systems and take a look at their system numbers; a quick look at the daily metrics can help determine if there are issues in the system and if your DAM is meeting user needs. Each DAM system sets up metrics viewability in a different way, but a common denominator in home-brew systems is that the metrics are just one click away from the login screen or even presented as the first thing users see. Likewise, links to reports or metrics are highly visible in systems that have been customized. When you evaluate systems for your organization, ask vendors to show you quickly how the system reporting works. If it takes you more than three clicks to get to basic numbers, like the number of system users or number and type of assets in the system, it's likely the DAM isn't something that can really be used without a great amount of customization.

The topics of metrics, ROI, and big data are favorites at DAM conferences, as measures and valuations for asset ROI are unique to each organization deploying DAM. Whichever DAM conference you attend, you will encounter at least one panel or presentation that includes a breakdown of asset metrics and ROI figures custom-made to the system on display. One great example of just such a panel is the 2011 presentation given at Createasphere NYC by Charlie Gray of Motorola (http://vimeo.com/31506629). In parts two and three of the presentation, Charlie laid out the types of metrics developed for his system and how they showed ROI. While many of his measures wouldn't work for any other system—I can't think of another company that uses his head-count metric—you can clearly see the different types of basic measurements on display in his presentation. If you are in charge of a DAM system, I strongly suggest becoming professionally active and attending DAM conferences like Henry Stewart, or local meet-up groups of digital asset managers. Presentations like the one discussed above are shaping standards and emerging best practices in the field, and they can very much help with the development of your own system measurements.

Determining Metrics and ROI

There are four main types of metrics in a DAM that we'll discuss in this chapter:

- Asset metrics, which show how many assets you have, their item types, metadata linked to assets, and download activity

- User metrics, which show how many system users you have, their access control lists (ACLs), and their activities within the system by users, groups, and lists

- System metrics, which show system activities as a whole, including upload, ingest, server activity, and admin actions

- User interface metrics, which are numbers associated with the HTML pages that the DAM system uses to grant access

As system audit work is deeply connected to metrics, discussion of this work will be included alongside each type of measurement. However, auditing work is so critical that we'll also end the chapter with a look at the staffing requirements for this work, as well as an examination of how digital asset managers can use metrics and auditing to assist with brand management issues and the ideas around big data.

Asset Metrics

You should always be able to see your asset count when logging in to the system, as well as a breakdown of each discrete item type. This basic measurement helps you see at a glance if there have been any big drops or adds to the numbers, helping a digital asset manager meet his or her asset upload goals or simply see if someone's been hard at work deleting a lot of duplicates. The aggregate number of uploads and downloads also should be quickly visible, indicating how active the DAM system is at any time.

Metadata that are linked to assets can be measured as well. By allowing for a keyword search within your metrics tool, you should be able to quickly pull the number of cataloged items associated with a particular campaign or product, as well as keep the number of downloads of these items separate from who downloaded them, or from where they were downloaded.

Counting asset actions in a DAM system is a separate operation from counting user actions, as assets and users are stored very differently. As you visualize how you'd like your asset metrics reports set up or customized within your DAM system, it helps to think about your metadata model. Any information attached to an asset or action taken on that asset can be measured in an asset report: number of assets added to an item type, number of downloads, number of times a certain file type or keyword was searched or downloaded, number of assets added each month, and so forth.

While there are no generally accepted metric standards for asset ROI, there are standard ways to develop your own measurements. As an example, here's the National Archives and Records Administration (NARA) Reproduction Fee Schedule:

Table 10-1. *NARA Reproduction Fee Schedule Source:* `http://archives.gov/research/order/fees.html` *(retrieved 7/6/2013)*

Archival Handling Fees (Add to Vendor Fee)	Fee
Still Photo Item	$9.50 per item
Cartographic Item	$9.00 per item
Motion Picture/Video Item	$17.25 per item
Audio Item	$6.50 per item
Regional Archives Still Photo Item	$8.25 per item

As you can see from the table, NARA charges different fees for the retrieval of different item types. The cost to deliver a photograph is different from the cost to deliver a video, and the same is true for DAM systems. Different item types require different valuations. When setting up your asset metrics, align the numbers to meet your business needs. When proving ROI at the end of each year or quarter, be sure to outline for your directors numbers they can use to impress their own superiors: the number of times items from a hot product line or initiative were downloaded, for instance. Then value those asset downloads by item type. Listed below are some common methods for determining value.

Download Values of Photographs

To determine how much your organization will value each photograph download from the DAM system, you'll need to find out how much your company spends each year searching for images and/or purchasing from stock houses. Stock image valuation varies from image use to image use, and don't forget the cost to your organization in keeping up with the complicated licensing and rights management that can come with the use of stock imagery. There are also the costs your organization has paid when accidentally using images an intern grabbed off the Web or when a designer unknowingly used a photo with expired licensing. A DAM system helps reduce the need for stock imagery and limits the exposure for companies that do by tracking the paperwork that goes along with each image purchase.

For the first part of our measurement, find a handy case study within your organization of an image everyone needed but couldn't locate or was unable to determine the rights of use for due to missing paperwork. Once you find this example, price out the number of people and hours it took to find the photograph and/or its rights. It's not unusual for an image chase like this to involve half a dozen people and maybe even billable attorney hours in the case of missing rights information. You can quickly use this internal case study to illustrate how costly an image search without a DAM system can become. Settle on a price per hour of misspent effort, and try to come up with an average time someone might spend searching for an image. Lowballing for an example, let's say that the time and effort put in to locate the high-resolution original of an image cost your organization $25 per hour and took four hours total to resolve. (In this chapter, unless noted otherwise, all figures are calculated in U.S. dollars.) That's $100 of time and effort to make an image that may be saved on multiple designers' hard drives truly usable. We'll call this measurement T&E (time and effort). While you'll introduce your photograph ROI with your image chase case study, come up with a figure you feel is defensible for a standard image search at your organization: the average time it takes someone to find something, and the cost for that time.

Next, ask your designers how they purchase imagery from photographers, from outside agencies completing contract work, and from stock houses. All three of these methods require a different sort of math that will be rolled into what we'll shorthand here as CLF (creation and licensing fees).

Third-Party Agency Sources

When photographs are created or purchased by a third-party agency, does your company get to download the originals for use, or does the third party retain them, requiring your organization to call back and pay for retrieval? The scenario of calling back to request originals is all too common and costly, and this can be eliminated by loading all items your company paid to have created into the DAM system for later searchability. Likewise, when stock imagery is purchased, a copy with the licensing information should be kept in the DAM system in order to prevent the type of image chase discussed earlier. If your DAM system allows for your company to cut costly calls to third parties for assets they've already paid for at the time of creation, you can factor this cost into your CLF. Take a look at the billing to agencies for each instance of these types of calls. If you were billed $200 for the finding and transfer of a high-resolution image that you already paid for once, that's a CLF that can be cut.

Photographer Sources

When an image is purchased from a photographer, make sure that your organization is purchasing the image outright, with no restrictions, for continued use, in perpetuity. In the past, photographers were able to continue to charge companies for the continued uses of the images that the very same companies paid them to shoot; this type of limited image licensing is no longer used by the majority of buyers, with the notable exception of Getty and image licensing for sports. It's possible that if you're working with a larger or older organization that may not have updated their photographer contracts, they are continuing to pay fees in order to use images they paid someone to create. This is no longer standard practice and can be changed to a fee simple contract for photographers. You should pay your photographers a fair price for their work, but you should only pay them once, and all those products of work should be the buyers' sole property forever. This eliminates ongoing issues of rights management and publication of images in new media. If your update of photographer contracts eliminates ongoing photographer licensing fees, be sure to list this in your photograph download values as CLF.

If you aren't updating contracts to reflect changes with a photographer, the DAM system will likely not cut the cost of image creation. Just because you're managing existing assets more effectively does not mean that you won't need to continue to support new photo shoots. Your goal as a digital asset manager should be to provide your designers and other users with a well-organized and expanded library of items they can use in their daily work, not less. If you can show a savings through better photographer contract management, great! Factor in the amount of fees you pay yearly for ongoing image licensing into your CLF. Otherwise, leave the photography budget alone. Great images don't create themselves, and while times have changed regarding the ongoing payment for art, you still need to pay your photographers a fair wage for their work.

Stock Photography Sources

The costs associated with the purchase and rights management of stock photography have caused many large corporations to severely restrict buying of this type of imagery. An image can cost anywhere from $35 to $5,000, depending on the type and exclusivity of the photograph. It's not unusual for a largish organization to be unaware of its total stock photography spend, as different departments and agencies may have different accounts with several different stock photography vendors. Before calculating the ROI on your DAM system, do your best to find out the account names and purchase records for the stock photography at your company, so that you can determine an average price for an image purchase. It's not unusual for this cost to be somewhere in the neighborhood of $100 per image, or higher if your company relies heavily on purchased images for print publications. In the case of images purchased of celebrities or sports figures, the rates are usually in the thousands of dollars for each image. By managing your licensed image in a DAM system that tracks the numbers of time an image is used, and on what type of publishing platform, better rates may be negotiated. If you're buying a royalty-free image with unlimited use, you can add that image to your DAM with the paperwork, so that others in your organization can benefit from the purchase. You can also keep track of expiration dates and track how an image was used and where, leading to greater control over imagery at your company as a whole.

In an age when a simple right-click can copy an image, without reuse documentation, onto any hard drive for anyone to accidentally use, the ongoing cost of stock photography can quickly inflate a company's planned photography spend. Often those who reuse stock imagery without paying mistakenly believe the company purchased use of the image royalty free, or they don't understand that images on the Internet must be purchased for commercial use. Sadly, it's also true that some who do understand that licensed images must be paid for rest comfortably in the knowledge that they probably won't be caught and forced to pay damages—until, of course, they are caught and get a call from the company lawyer. Some stock houses have lawyers on a contract basis that troll the Internet with image-recognition software, looking for illegal use of imagery, for which they then bill the responsible parties. At the time of writing, a typical fee for this type of use is around $3,000 per image per instance of publishing. Add to this cost your attorney's fees and the time your management spent dealing with the issue and replacing the wrongly used photo, and you can see why each infraction can easily be placed at a cost of $5,000 per instance. The savings you can realize by more effectively managing the tracking and purchase of stock photography will go into the calculation of your creation and licensing fees.

In our examples above, we gave a very modest estimate of $100 for T&E. Every time someone downloads an image from your DAM, you can now claim $100 in cost avoidance. If 3,000 images were downloaded from your DAM in one month, you have avoided $30,000 in potential T&E.

■ **Note**   T&E by Number of Photo Downloads = Photo Cost Avoidance

---

Because the numbers are larger and often nonrecurring, CLFs are usually expressed better as an annualized figure, but they may be broken down monthly or quarterly if that's how your organization would like them. Let's assume in previous years your organization paid $3,000 for a call back to agencies for retrieval of previously produced photography, and your implementation of DAM is able to cut that down to $1,000, for a savings of $2,000. Likewise, your stock photography buying budget is halved from $10,000 per year to $5,000 by encouraging designers to use images already in the DAM, rather than purchasing new ones. In addition, if you're able to stop paying out $1,000 per year in photographer licensing by restricting use of images that require payments and switching to one-time fees for buying photography outright. This gives you a combined CLF of $8,000 annually.

■ **Note**   CLF = Cost Avoidance Annually by Reduction of Legal Exposure and Realized Workflow Efficiencies

---

Let's also pretend that in the past year $4,000 was awarded to a stock house that caught an intern using a picture of his favorite sports hero to promote a product on your social media page. While this might be regarded as a one-time occurrence, the cost of exposure to your organization by failure to police images is potentially very high. You could use an event like this to explain why the ongoing cost of a DAM is justified. ROI for a DAM should include an estimate by your legal counsel for potential damages, whether or not your company experiences a stock house penalty like this one. Adding in our imaginary sports-obsessed intern, we now have a CLF of $12,000 per year, or $1,000 per month.

Download Values of Graphics, Illustrations, and Other Digital Artwork

If designers in your organization often find it easier to completely recreate a graphic rather than search through their hard drives for the existing image, you are sadly far from alone. While re-creating simple banners and logos may only take a few hours of work, the inability to quickly access more complex digital artwork can cost a company lots of wasted designer hours or even the cost to have someone rebuild the file from scratch. Due to the comparative rarity and uniqueness of digital art, the valuation for the T&E as well as CLF on artificially created images should always be higher than that for photography. Again, finding a solid internal case study can be wise here, especially in the case of re-creations of already existing graphics to cover for a lack of digital asset management. Use the same formula for photographs, but value the time spent as billable designer hours.

While graphics and illustrations can be more expensive to license than photographs, the CLF figure should be about the same or lower, due to the lack of model and location releases needed for images that do not contain the likenesses of people or possibly trademarked places. While the initial creation of graphics can be more costly than the creation cost of photographs, the long-term liability of digital artwork is far lower. While it's true that the creators of comic book characters are regularly in court defending their copyrights, no drawn superhero has yet to file an infringement on his or her rights of image with any jurisdiction as of the writing of this book. For the purposes of the examples at the end of this chapter, we are going to report a T&E figure of $200 and a CLF of $8,000.

Download Values of Documents

ROI for documents can often be difficult to calculate, because the types of documents stored by DAMs vary. It may be helpful in your organization to value the tracking of releases and licenses as part of the minimization of risk in tracking imagery. However, valuing documents only as helpful for copyright management ignores the power of your DAM to control and distribute presentations, forms, publications, and other everyday work items that may be currently scattered in many different uncontrolled versions across your organization. You may choose to value each type of document separately or with an average value.

As with all asset metrics, your valuation of these items will depend on your metadata modeling strategy. If you choose to value releases and licenses separately from other documents, you may want to make this type of document its own distinct item type. If you feel that a separate item type is too much for those uploading to your DAM to handle, you can differentiate between different sorts of documents in your metadata model with a drop-down list of document categories (releases, presentations, memos, etc.). When modeling that, these sorts of choices will allow you to more effectively sort data when reporting on system activities. For the purposes of our imaginary reports at the end of the chapter, we're going to assign separate values to legal documents, presentations, and template documents, and then lump all other documents together. Our CLF figure will come primarily from the valuation of brand management, which we'll discuss further in the auditing section of this chapter. Valuation on processes and workflows related to brand management remains a very "squishy" kind of math; no one will blame you if you leave out the CLF on documents altogether, especially if you've already determined that the legal paperwork in your document item type is actually valued with the CLF of other items. For the sample metrics at the end of this chapter, we're going to say that our CLF is around $10,000 annually, chiefly from liability related to presentations (salespeople love to violate copyrights in their presentations).

Download Values of Audio and Video

Video is, hands-down, the most expensive type of digital asset to deliver, but of course it produces the biggest ROI. Consider the following: how much does it cost you each time you have to call your video vendor to create a new physical copy, whether on a drive or disc, of even the smallest video? It is not unusual for an advertising agency to charge $500 for a straight dub—a duplicate with no editing—of video your organization already paid the agency to produce. Even when duplicates are produced in-house, you'll have a fee associated with the staff time and resources spent to produce the copy. If the video you need requires light editing, the process will normally take about a day and will cost you in-house material, such as equipment, editing software, editing suite time, and labor. If you don't happen to have professional-grade editing suites on your premises, Crawford, a video-editing vendor in Atlanta, charges around $4,000 per day for editing time and use of its equipment.

All of the above expenses can be greatly reduced with the implementation of a DAM system. It's also worth noting here that if you're starting your system with videos—but it's advisable for first-time digital asset managers to start with photographs and graphics instead—the delivery of audio and video files is fundamentally different than the delivery of every other type of digital asset. Still, you're going to be asked to store audio and video files and deliver them, so how do you value that process?

If you already have billing with local video vendors in place, you will be able to get access to the number of times and the amount your organization has paid for straight video retrievals. Make sure to ask around your company about creative vendors that may be producing one-off videos for web sites or mobile platforms as well. With the implementation of HTML 5, video in web sites is becoming less of a technical hurdle for display and is more an expected part of the Internet experience. Anyone who produces or uses video will certainly have a story to tell about having to run around to several sources to find or copy a desperately needed file. Use these stories and cumulative costs to find an average for how much your company saves each time someone downloads video from the DAM.

Your user interface should be able to deliver video both as a viewable proxy and as more than one type of downloadable file format. So there are several types of metrics for these assets:

Audio and video viewed

Audio and video downloaded

File types downloaded

You could pull these measurements for any of the item types listed in this valuation section, but most systems don't bother to make viewing or download-type distinctions unless the item type is video. Why? The bandwidth and storage requirements for video and audio make it necessary for digital asset managers to keep an eye on demand. As the chapter on storage illustrates, video and audio are memory and bandwidth hogs. For the purposes of our sample report at the end of this chapter, we're going to say that it saves an average of $25 every time a video is watched by someone searching the system, and $700 every time a video or audio file is downloaded. These figures have T&E as well as our CLF all rolled together, because these fees are inseparable for video and audio. While these valuations may seem high, remember that agencies can charge $500 for a simple copy, and we're averaging that with the cost of the use of a video editing suite for simple edits that can now be accomplished with laptop software after the video is downloaded from the DAM. Figure in your liability for rights management, and then the value of a video downloaded from a DAM that is also tracking all the talent and music releases goes up quickly.

Given the high valuation on video, combined with the great popularity and new ease of using this asset, your DAM will show substantial returns within the first few years.

Download Values of Web Code

DAM vendors tend to undervalue the potential of the DAM to store and retrieve web code. However, never forget that this is an ability that will make the web masters in your organization your friends for life. Much of modern web coding is done by cutting and pasting or slightly altering HTML, SQL, or Java code that has been created. When someone codes something tricky in a way that works, he or she wants to go back and replicate the work again, and it's easy to lose copies of crucial earlier coding. Just as with graphic designers, those in charge of web sites often end up rebuilding previous work from scratch, at a cost in time and efficiency.

Web coding won't be downloaded as much as graphics, but it should be valued in the same way. If your organization is smaller, your graphic designer and webmaster are likely the same employee anyway - so valuing their time is about the same. The real difference in valuing web code versus graphics is in your annualized CLF. The legal exposure on coding is nil. The only cost avoidance to be realized here is if you occasionally have contractors code for you, and your in-house web folks can use that previously externally produced code for other in-house projects. This isn't as likely as you might hope; writing code is much like writing an Apress book, and different authors have styles and subjects distinct from each other so that a paragraph from one book dropped into the file of another would cause problems for the reader or browser. For these reasons, it's best to stick with T&E figures when calculating the web-code value. Ask your web personnel to estimate how many hours they've spent searching for and re-creating previous code over the past year, and come up with a valuation for their time. In our example, we use $200 per code retrieval, the same per-piece value we assigned for graphics, illustrations, and digital art.

Table 10-2. *Sample Report Using Examples from Asset Valuations*

Asset Metrics	Q1	Q2	Q3	Q4	Year	Total Value for ROI
Photographs						
Photograph downloads	3,500	3,000	2,250	3,250	9,750	
Cost avoidance @ $100 per	$350,000	$300,000	$225,000	$325,000	$1,200,000	
CLF for all photographs					$12,000	$1,212,000
Graphics, Illustrations, and Digital Art						
Graphic/illustration downloads	1,000	1,500	1,750	2,000	5,500	
Cost avoidance at $200 per	$200,000	$300,000	$350,000	$400,000	$1,250,000	
CLF for all graphics					$8,000	$1,258,000
Documents						
Document downloads	770	1,075	1,130	1,240		
Legal documents	20	25	30	40	115	
Cost avoidance at $300 per	$6,000	$7,500	$9,000	$12,000	$34,500	
Presentations	250	400	350	450	1450	
Cost avoidance at $100 per	$25,000	$40,000	$35,000	$45,000	$145,000	
Document templates	450	500	650	600	2,200	
Cost avoidance at $50 per	$22,500	$25,000	$32,500	$30,000	$110,000	
All other documents	50	150	100	150	450	
Cost avoidance at $25 per	$1,250	$3,750	$2,500	$3,750	$11,250	
CLF for all documents					$10,000	$310,750
Video and Audio						
Number of views	200	300	250	400	1150	
Cost avoidance at $25	$5,000	$7,500	$6,250	$10,000	$28,750	
Number of downloads	150	150	200	250	750	
Cost avoidance at $700 per	$105,000	$105,000	$140,000	$175,000	$525,000	

(*continued*)

Table 10-2. *(continued)*

Asset Metrics	Q1	Q2	Q3	Q4	Year	Total Value for ROI
No separate CLF for these types of media						$553,750
Web Code						
Number of downloads	3	8	5	4	20	
Cost avoidance at $200 per	$600	$1,600	$1,000	$8,000	$11,200	
No separate CLF for this type of media						$11,200
Total Downloads						
All item types	5,353	5,733	5,385	6, 894	23,365	
Total T&E valuations (all types)	$715,350	$790,350	$801,250	$1,008,750	$3,315,700	
Total CLF (all types)					$30,000	$3,345,700

Why Are the Asset Valuations So High When Compared to the NARA Chart?

You probably noticed on the NARA fee structure at the beginning of this chapter that the archival handling fee for a "still item" was $9.50 per, while the figure I have used to value photograph retrieval is $100 per, with a CLF of $8,000. Why should you show a cost associated with photograph retrieval more than ten times what NARA would? Well, there are several reasons:

1. NARA isn't offering downloads on demand. They take your request at the National Archives after you've done your research, and the speed of return on your items depends on the number of staff on hand and the number of requests that are in front of you. While it's true their free offerings and digital download ability are increasing, much investment is required by the American public to make the content truly accessible, which brings us to the next reason NARA items are valued so low per retrieval or duplication.

2. NARA is subsidized by taxpayers.

3. NARA has decades of work behind it and ahead of it; economy of scale is strongly at work in their retrieval processes. NARA is one of the largest archives of content in the world.

4. NARA has many more staff members than your DAM team. The numbers employed by NARA are still not enough; the volume of documentation produced in the last century alone would require many times the magnitude of NARA's current budget to effectively index, let alone make those materials available for searchability and download.

5. NARA's content is acquired by donation; they do not need to pay creators or licensing fees for any of their items.

6. NARA is not a commercial entity, and therefore under the law it does not carry the same liability as a business for copyright, rights of image, rights of location, or other actionable infringements. NARA simply never has to calculate CLFs for its archival holdings.

User Metrics

At the Henry Stewart DAM conference in New York in May 2013, the company Bunchball gave a presentation that promoted a gamification of user metrics designed to encourage user participation within DAMs. This interface consisted of leaderboards shown to all users logging in to a DAM, encouraging users to compete to be first in uploads, logins, and other selected measures. The enthusiasm that this panel generated in the convention attendees by the enthusiastic response to gamification highlighted the difficulty many digital asset managers experience in encouraging user adoption and use of DAMs. A DAM system will allow your management to see, for the first time, how employees and agencies search for and use creative materials in their everyday work. This new visibility into the creative process will make some users uneasy with the idea of a DAM and therefore reluctant to log in. Part of the job of a digital asset manager is to provide visibility via metrics and to put users at ease by listening and responding to those metrics and making adaptations to the way the DAM arranges, describes, and provides access to the assets they need. User metrics enable digital asset managers to accomplish these tasks, and they should always be used to help and reward users for allowing the visibility that makes the DAM so valuable.

While the previous section concentrated on metrics pulled from assets, which required metadata modeling to formulate, this section will concentrate on metrics that relate to user profiles and ACLs within your system. Because user profiles are handled by a different sort of programming than metadata modeling, reporting on user metrics may be in a different location than asset metrics in your DAM interface, though some products have a centralized reporting tool that generates the numbers you need all in one place. How user information is displayed and manipulated remains a strong difference among DAM systems, so our discussion of user metrics in this chapter will necessarily be much generalized. The one common element to user metrics is that they count the actions of users or groups of users, not the items, tools, or interfaces.

The most basic user metric is a flat count of how many people are registered for access to the system. You should have easy access to the number of accounts and how many have been registered in the past month, quarter, or year. At any time you should be able to look up individual users and see their activity records, including the number of downloads. When users register and set up their profiles, they should be required to indicate how they fit into all the ways you wish to measure DAM participation (by region, by department, by agency, etc.). This will allow you to quickly audit DAM use. By measuring the login activity of agency users versus your organization's users, for instance, you can better evaluate your system audience. Just as asset metadata allow for refined asset metrics, user profile fields set up at registration will allow for refined user metrics.

Reporting on individual users should include not only their registration information (usually referred to as user profile or user lookup), but should also list their date and time of registration, the date and time of their last login, the total number of times a user has logged in, and some sort of user action report. User actions can include uploads, downloads, and number of searches. At the end of this section, I've made a list of metrics on individual users and groups.

Time-based user metrics are critical to the maintenance and upkeep of a DAM. As DAMs are increasingly used to move large files around the globe, a time when your office is dark might be a time when users on the other side of the world are busily uploading and downloading large files. When planning regular updates to the system, it's helpful to know what the most quiet time of activity might be, and plan for any service interruptions for then. Likewise, individual user metrics will allow you to more easily identify those whose regular patterns of use might be interrupted by a system update. If you know someone regularly works on the system on a weekend morning, you can let him know service will be interrupted while you're improving the user experience. Interactions like the one outlined above will also serve to emphasize to your users that the tracking the system provides is there to assist them in their work, not to intrude upon their freedom as productive employees.

User metrics are sensitive both to managers and employees, in part because they highlight how DAMs enable workers to be productive employees away from the traditional office environment. When all materials needed for work are available online, and all work can be submitted to workflows online, why hold your employees hostage to or pay for office space? Issues of control, privacy, management style, and work style will all play out regarding DAM work, but especially in regards to the collecting and use of user metrics.

User audits of the DAM should be required at regularly scheduled intervals: once a year for a DAM with less than a thousand registered users, scaling up with more frequency as you add more users. User audits are part of every digital asset manager's life because, as mentioned in Chapter 7, one of the core functions of DAM is access control. By monitoring how different groups of users interact with the system, you will be able to assess how well your metadata, user interface, and other tools are meeting their needs. Below is a list of user metrics I suggest for all DAM reporting; each system will need to customize its reporting in order to meet the individual organization's needs.

List of Suggested User Metrics

Number of users

Lists and counts of users by group

Number of user logins (different interfaces will be discussed in the "User Interface Metrics" section)

Time-based information on logins

Individual user download records

All downloads listed by user

All uploads listed by user

Most popular downloads by user group

System Metrics

DAM system metrics will be familiar to anyone who has held or managed a system administrator role. System metrics are distinct in that the measures originate from the function of the DAM and related systems, and they measure the performance of those tools.

As outlined previously in this book, a DAM is just one piece of a larger system of programs that work together and allow for the arrangement, description, preservation, and access of assets. Each of these individual programs and the hardware they run on have the potential to encounter hung threads, command conflicts, and occasional crashes. The primary function of a system administrator is always technical problem solving, and this can require a high level of specialized knowledge. For this reason, many organizations deploying DAMs choose to engage their DAM vendors in an extended SAS (service and support) contract, offloading the task of monitoring and analyzing system metrics to specialized IT professionals. However, if your DAM is organized within IT in your organization, you may choose to take care of these tasks in-house. As discussed in the chapter on choosing a DAM, the major argument against building a home-brew system is a lack of access to talent that can perform the following tasks associated with monitoring system metrics:

Server metrics, including bandwidth use

Routine DAM log review

Tracking and reporting of security alerts

Review of each discrete application's logs during troubleshooting

It's not typical to provide detailed reporting on system metrics, and these numbers have little value to ROI, so no sample report is included here.

User Interface Metrics

Sophisticated DAM systems have more than one user interface in order to serve the needs of many different audiences. User interface metrics measure points of user interaction with DAM resources, outside of the DAM itself. It is increasingly considered best practice to develop individual web sites that link back to a central DAM. This way, the DAM interface can be tailored to meet the needs of those who work on metadata, versioning, access control, reporting, and other DAM-specific tasks. Web sites that link functionality back to the DAM can be developed for specific departments or user needs. For instance, both Hewlett-Packard and UPS use streamlined web sites to govern how customers request the use of their brandmarks and branded materials, which are stored in DAMs. By having a DAM govern workflows and store legal documentation while streamlining the brand request process through web pages devoted only to the customer's needs, these companies are making both their legal compliance officers and customers happy. The legal teams see the information they need linked in the DAM, while the customers see their requests managed through a simplified and publicly accessible web page.

Other examples of custom user interfaces might include upload utilities deployed on employee access web sites, or web sites tailored to specific departments. The needs of a public relations department, for instance, are often quite different than the needs of your design team, and asking both these audiences to search and use one interface will cause your DAM team to fail one or both of their audiences.

Standard user metrics are no different than those generated for any web site, and this book won't spend too much time explaining web metrics to an audience likely already well acquainted with the subject. At the time this book was written, Google Analytics continued to dominate all web metric markets and needs, and is easy to set up on any URL your access points might generate. If your custom access points are through an intranet, and won't generate statistics effectively by using Google Analytics, you can count user interactions simply by counting the actions generated in the DAM by how those access points affect the system. For instance, creating a custom public user account associated with each access point will allow you to count each time that access point touches the DAM by how many times the custom user is counted logging in. If you have public upload tools, create a custom ACL for assets coming from that upload tool in order to measure them as they are created.

If you choose to deploy workflows within your DAM (and I hope that you do), the metrics generated by actions within the system relating to workflows are counted as user interface metrics. If your DAM does not generate workflow metrics easily, as cited in the sample report below, you can measure the number of actions on each workflow by counting the email alerts that are sent out that correspond to each workflow action (Chapter 12 will provide more information about workflows and email alerts).

Table 10-3. *Sample user metrics*

Interface Type	Monthly Total
DAM User Interface	
Number of page views	10,000
Average time spent per page	3:05
Number of logins	4,000
Number of uploads	2,000
Number of downloads	3,000
Most common access platform	PC
Journalist Access Point	
Number of page views	6,000

(continued)

Table 10-3. (*continued*)

Interface Type	Monthly Total
Average time spent per page	10:04
Number of downloads	4,000
Number of TOS completed	3,500
Most common access platform	Mobile
Most popular page	Press Releases
Special Employee Access Point	
Number of page views	20,000
Average time spent per page	2:30
Number of logins	15,000
Number of uploads	300
Number of downloads	5,000
Number of workflow actions #1	500
Number of workflow actions #2	300
Number of workflow actions #3	200
Completed workflows	250
Workflows in progress	400

Auditing and Big Data

In the sections on user metrics and user interface metrics, we discussed the sensitive but necessary regular review of how the DAM is used in order to make the system function as a usable tool. While all the metrics mentioned in this chapter may make their way into monthly or quarterly reporting, the gathering of all this data becomes really useful when combined with a system audit or big data initiative.

Big data is a new-enough term that it still needs defining in conversation. Simply put, big data is the aggregation and visualization of more data than most people can meaningfully understand without advanced tools to help them. In the 2009 article "Introduction to Big Data," Roger Magoulas and Ben Lorica defined big data in this way:

■ **Big Data**   when the size and performance requirements for data management become significant design and decision factors for implementing a data management and analysis system. For some organizations, facing hundreds of gigabytes of data for the first time may trigger a need to reconsider data management options. For others, it may take tens or hundreds of terabytes before data size becomes a significant consideration.

The meaning of this term may shift in the next few years as our society becomes more familiar with the practice of using analytics to optimize the return on different systems that work together for a common goal, a movement that was arguably popularized by the book and movie Moneyball. In this work by the writer Michael Lewis, a strategy is deployed by the Oakland A's baseball team to build a winning combination of players from a roster of underrated athletes. By using analytics, the A's were able to value the players' strengths based on their performances in combination, rather than as separately valued parts. Just as the managers of the A's were able to take metrics from many different players and show how these numbers would work together to build a stronger team, so may the metrics from the many tools you use to build your DAM come together and show your organization better ways to store, deliver, and use digital assets.

When discussing big data initiatives within your organization—efforts that may combine information from many different platforms to build a larger picture of your communications as a whole—make sure that your management understands the big data initiative that is already under way with your DAM. While it is often a better measure of internal communications processes and use than external, DAM certainly has its place in analytics, even if it's only to push content to creators that respond to the big data findings of external responses to marketing efforts.

The Emerging Field of Metadata Metrics

While a metric for most frequently used search terms may seem like an obviously desirable measurement, metadata measurement can be deceptively tricky. While metrics on assets or users are set up by defined fields with fixed options, searching to find free-form text entry points that also trigger search-engine operation is not that easy. Further, once we have examined the most frequent search terms in our system, what have we learned? Are the most frequent search terms the result of what our users want, or is it the result of the way users have been trained to find things in the existing system?

If you're interested in really examining metadata metrics, check out the research under way by academics like Jindrich Mynarz at the University of Prague and many, many other academics worldwide. I have specifically mentioned Jindrich here because he has an excellent blog post full of links discussing the topic titled "Towards Usability Metrics for Vocabularies" (`http://blog.mynarz.net/2013/07/towards-usability-metrics-for.html`) that outlines several proposed measurements that may emerge as standards for evaluating metadata and controlled vocabularies in the next decade. While I personally believe that the best work done so far is outlined in the article "Quality Assessment Methodologies for Linked Open Data" (`http://semantic-web-journal.net/system/files/swj414.pdf`), Bernard Vatant of Schema.org believes that analyzing metadata this way is simply too exhaustive, and that evaluating controlled vocabularies is simple: "If it's used, it's usable" (`https://plus.google.com/114406186864069390644/posts/Qx3UKffNETt`). We're not quite to the point where this type of measurement is standard practice, and there's still plenty of room for debate.

The Asset Metric That Solves Big Problems for Brand Management

One asset metric that's critical, but has not yet been discussed, is the download report that can be pulled on each individual asset's activity record. Because this chapter has thus far focused on ROI, you're probably thinking about valuing high-priced photos or videos: if a $6,000 clip of a celebrity endorsing a product was downloaded and used by employees and agencies 50 times, you can now better track the effectiveness of spokespeople for your brand. That's one way to think about metrics on individual assets. However, most digital asset managers use individual asset records to respond to crises.

A common example: Company X loves to use employees in its advertising photography. In one of its ads, an attractive employee is shown interacting with a customer in a way that is particularly appealing, and so this photo is used on several web sites and is a popular download from the DAM.

HR calls you one day with some bad news; the employee in the popular photo showed up for work one day inebriated, loudly quit, and was arrested for drunk driving on the way home from the office. The former employee is now trolling the company on the Internet, and you need to remove all images of this former employee from access immediately.

While you're disabling the user from the DAM, and removing access to images of the former employee, take a good look at the download activity on the assets in which the person is pictured. Copy the information of all users who have downloaded the asset in the last year, and email them a polite take-down notice for the photograph. You don't have to include details; just state that HR has requested a record of all the products in which they may have used the photo. If your company is large and uses images of employees in its communications, you can expect to get this sort of notice about once a year. While there's no solid ROI attached to the DAM's role input for this sort of crisis response, the value to your brand management team is clear.

Staffing for Optimum Return

While reporting on asset metrics and calculating ROI is something that will be done once a month at most, the regular monitoring of all other metrics is something that will likely take place daily in an active DAM. This task is best accomplished by a manager or supervisor closely working with the employees who are connected with metadata creation and governance. (This is discussed more in Chapter 10.)

Determining Return on Investment (ROI)

When calculating ROI, three types of costs determine your company's total spending on the DAM. While other sample reports in this chapter have included numbers to give you a better picture of how reports may appear, I have only used letters to represent the DAM spend. This is due to the wildly changeable nature of the DAM vendor market and costs associated with employees. An employee in New York is simply far more costly to an organization than one in Colorado, due to real estate prices alone in the calculation of office space. In addition, the types and sizes of DAMs heavily impact cost. Regardless, the explanation of spend and the following sample chart will serve as a basic guide to showing ROI for a DAM. Don't forget when projecting these costs forward to include a basic 5% increase yearly for natural system growth needs. If you're planning a phased rollout of features and application programming interfaces (APIs), the costs associated with those should be included in your projections as well.

Total cost of system maintenance: This figure should include the annualized cost of any recurring expense necessary for running your DAM. This will include the fees for licensing your DAM software, your SAS agreements, and any other recurring payments for programs or utilities critical to DAM upkeep. This total annual cost of recurring expenses will be referred to as SM (system maintenance) in the sample report.

Staffing costs: The cost of all employees assigned to full-time DAM care and feeding are an important figure to consider when calculating ROI. If you're in a large organization, HR should be able to provide you with a number for the true cost of all your DAM employees: a cost that includes not only the salaries, but also benefits, office space, and other resources your company provides. If your team chooses to outsource the metadata creation piece of DAM, I would strongly encourage you to include that cost as part of staffing, not as an annual cost of system maintenance or one-time enhancement. While outsourcing the creation of metadata is a great help to digital asset managers, especially during the initial setup of the system, outsourcing this time-intensive cost is simply outsourcing the staffing of a crucial part of digital asset management. It's very likely that once you start outsourcing metadata creation, you will continue to utilize this resource to temporarily staff up your DAM team when consolidating information silos or discovering a new (old) cache of forgotten images. We'll use the letter E (for Employee cost) in our formula when calculating ROI.

One-time upgrade/enhancement costs: In the phased approach to a DAM rollout, systems and applications are added to the DAM slowly, over a period of years. For instance, it may not be necessary to add a streaming video distribution service to your DAM until the second or third year of deployment. When this new plug-in service is added to the DAM, costs associated with its implementation would be recorded as an upgrade/enhancement cost, while the yearly license fee would be rolled into the systems maintenance costs. In the sample report, we'll refer to this type of cost as U.

■ **Note**   Formula for Total DAM Spend when Calculating ROI: SM + E + U

Other Types of Cost Avoidance

The valuation of asset downloads and creation and licensing fees has already been discussed at length in this chapter, but there are other types of savings to be realized from DAM implementation. A common efficiency realized by DAM is the sunsetting of redundant web sites or information silos. Because web sites are quick and easy to create, it's possible that your organization may have several web sites of the "document dump" type—places where assets have been stashed in links for quick access, without thought to versioning or updates. When you take down these web sites and roll their contents into the DAM, you can count the yearly cost of storage and site maintenance for the document dump as a one-time savings for the DAM. Likewise, when phasing out older systems, be sure to credit the costs of those systems back to yours. Part of the job of a DAM is to create efficiencies in asset storage and distribution, so make sure you get the monetary credit that goes along with that work. In my own work, I have found the average savings of sunsetting a departmental web page to be around $40,000 per year, and that's the figure I have plugged into our sample ROI report.

Another type of cost avoidance to be counted in the ROI for DAM can be calculated if your organization works with a large advertising or marketing firm. Over the last decade, agencies like Ogilvy and Edelman have begun offering DAM services to their customers at steep prices (often as much as or more than a quarter million dollars per year). While marketing executives may wish to jump on the offer of outsourcing a complicated administrative system like DAM, it's almost always a bad idea. What happens to your organization's access to the DAM if you choose to switch agencies? How would you handle the archiving of so many digital assets in the hands of another company? How will your organization be able to judge the effectiveness of the assets themselves without access to metrics? Asking the creators of media to judge the use of that media themselves is asking someone to give you a falsely positive report. Further, many of the advertising DAMs have been customized to meet the needs of the advertising agency, not the needs of their clients. Worst of all, when you put another organization in charge of your DAM, you're likely just creating another information silo that is separate from the everyday working needs of your organization.

If your agency has offered you access to its DAM, ask about the pricing structure, and then add that to the cost avoidance value of your own. It's always a better deal to retain ownership of your assets than leave them in someone else's hands.

Table 10-4. Sample ROI chart

Costs Associated with DAM	Year 1	Year 2	Year 3
System maintenance	SM	SM + 5%	Year 2 SM + 5%
Staffing	E	E + 5%	Year 2 E + 5%
Upgrades/enhancements	U	U + 5%	Year 2 U + 5%
Total spend	SM + E + U	SM + E + U	SM + E + U
Costs Avoided with DAM			
Asset valuation metrics	$3,345,700	$3,512,985	$3,688,634
Sunset systems cost	$40,000	$40,000	$40,000
Total cost avoidance	$3,385,700	$3,552,985	$3,728,634
ROI	Cost avoidance - spend = ROI	Cost avoidance - spend = ROI	Cost avoidance - spend = ROI

While the above table expresses ROI in a whole dollar amount, those with MBA degrees may be more used to seeing ROI expressed as a percentage with the following formula:

$$ROI = \frac{(\text{Return from Investment} - \text{Cost of Investment})}{\text{Cost of Investment}}$$

You may also hear of DAM ROI expressed as a ratio of return. Ratio of return takes the whole ROI dollar amount and puts it against the cost of investment more simply. For example, if the ROI whole dollar amount was approximately five million, and the cost of investment was approximately two million, then the ratio of return is 5:2.

Conclusion

In the sample ROI chart, each year of DAM deployment has a projected 5 percent growth in asset use and spend. The reality of such figures is often much more complicated. The growth in use of your DAM will largely depend on the quality and quantity of assets uploaded and cataloged in your system. Also, how your DAM team responds to the metrics provided by your user interface and user feedback will determine how well your system is adopted by the organization. The measurements provided by all the metrics discussed in this chapter will feed the numbers used to calculate ROI and provide a positive or negative picture of your DAM for the accountants in the organization.

If you do end up with a negative ROI in the first year or two of your DAM, don't be surprised or alarmed. The initial deployment of your system will result in substantial one-time support costs such as equipment purchase and API construction. Likely you will also be paying hefty fees for vendor visits and educational materials for new DAM team members. Don't despair at these figures; instead, use the sample asset metrics provided here to demonstrate that DAM is a more-than-worthy investment for your organization in the long term.

CHAPTER 11

Building Successful Workflows

Chapter Goal: Strategies for developing efficient workflows to maximize return on investment (ROI) for your digital asset management (DAM) system.

What Makes a DAM Workflow Successful?

Building workflows in your DAM is the best way to use the system as a tool for transparency and accountability. Any process that involves emailing assets or notices about assets from one department to another is likely ripe for a workflow tool that can streamline operations and hopefully speed processes along. After defining some common workflow actions, this chapter will break out three sample workflows common to digital asset management. First though, it's worth examining why DAM workflow implementations succeed or fail.

Successful workflows in DAM systems all share the following characteristics:

1. Visibility

2. Flexible interaction with users and metadata

3. Efficient management of human resources

4. Generation of valued metrics and reporting data

Visibility of Workflow Movement Is Key to Workflow Success

Workflows must be visible and constantly in action in order to be considered successful. In order to be truly used and usable, all workflows are dependent on some sort of notification or publication system that allows users to know when an asset moves from one stage to the next, and that action is required. The traditional way of sending workflow alerts is to link the DAM to an email server, and to have email alerts sent to the relevant users as the workflow moves from step to step. The author strongly recommends that digital asset managers find different ways of sending alerts. If the DAM can be programmed to send alerts via your organization's instant messenger system, or even to text via virtual network, consider sending alerts that way. If your organization uses an internal social network, program your DAM to post alerts to user walls. Having workflow notices live-posted to the intranet landing page or to the DAM's own internal social media feed might be another way of creating workflow visibility. The days of email reliance are waning, and any trick that digital asset managers can invent or program into their workflow notifications to keep the movement of assets visible is fair game.

Successful Workflows Are Fed by People and Metadata

The aim of a DAM workflow should always be to lessen the workload attached to using assets, not to increase it. This again is another area where digital asset managers should be designing DAM actions to match up with tasks, not matching people to a process. As Mark Davey, CEO of IQEquity, puts it:

> *Workflow is a human machine effort. The software needs to adapt and respond to the variables of the user. The user needs to understand the best practice as it relates to workflow, and both need to work within the roles, permissions and rights. After the taxonomy, controlled vocabulary, and metadata has been curated, the workflow build and adoption is a critical component of a successful DAM deployment.*

Mark rightly points out that just as with metadata modeling and controlled vocabulary, the workflow should be adapted to the users, not the other way around. Mark also emphasizes in his own DAM consulting that, when launching a DAM, workflow builds should come ***after*** the metadata modeling, taxonomy, and controlled vocabulary have been set up. For those who wish to build a DAM with a focus on workflows first versus collections first, as mentioned in Chapter 6, focusing on workflows first will not allow you to skip the process of metadata modeling. How the metadata modeling and search experiences of a DAM function will inform, in part, how workflows function.

When building workflows, it's easy to forget that the initial purpose behind implementing a DAM is to make things easier for all concerned, not more difficult. People dislike change and will complain, while machines do exactly as they are told and never gripe. It's easy, given a climate of complaints, to blame the machines or the people using them, but the reason for a nonfunctioning workflow usually lies somewhere between the two. Both people and software must compromise in ideal work situations in order to succeed. The root of many implementation woes can be traced back to insufficient or inflexible metadata; in the case of not enough metadata, people need to give to the machine, and in the case of inflexible metadata, the machine's metadata modeling must be altered in order to make the workflow one that will be adopted by users.

Successful Workflow Implementation Is Backed by Management

Still, some adaptation of work habits by the users is necessary. Managers should decide ahead of the workflow project how much they are willing to back workflow implementation, and what the incentives and penalties for workflow adoption should be. Efficient management of the human resources involved with workflow creation, adoption, and use are critical to success; too often DAMs stumble in a scenario where decisions are made without the buy-in of the workers, and then the workers simply find ways to go around the new workflow process or decide not to use the DAM altogether. The digital asset manager must work with management to make calls on how to adapt the new process to the people, or, if people refuse to work with the DAM at all, how to reallocate jobs around those who refuse to change work habits. It's best to hold large group meetings and create charts of what everyone would like and need in a workflow, so that everyone can see that questions and concerns are being met openly and transparently. The following table is an example.

Person	Would Like in Workflow	Doesn't Want in Workflow
Elle	Timed markings of completed deliverables	Unlimited actions by everyone; concerned about ownership of process
Jack	Notifications when he needs to take actions	His actions limited by dependencies on others
Nikia	Resources to add to projects as they come in	Too many extra steps in her work process
Andrew	Uniform project names	A clock running on his actions

Figure 11-1. *A list of common concerns about building DAM workflows*

In the table, conflicts around DAM workflow implementation become clear for everyone to see. For instance, Elle and Andrew might be at odds, if only indirectly, about what they hope the DAM workflow tool will do for their team. Elle wants the time she turns in her deliverables to the workflow noted, so that everyone can see when she turned in her work. At the same time, Andrew is worried that a workflow in the DAM will create a clock running on his actions, as everyone will be able to see how fast he responds to his stage of work in the DAM. The digital asset manager, the team manager, and the team itself will have to talk out options and expectations around Elle's and Andrew's workflow needs, and once a decision is made, management must stick by it, even if it means reassigning Elle or Andrew to another position. We'll discuss Jack's and Nikia's concerns later in this chapter, as they speak to the actual function of workflows themselves. Still, no matter the solution landed on by the team and management, human resources and the managers involved must fully back decisions once they are made in order for the workflow implementation to be a success.

Successful Workflows Generate Measures

One of the benefits of DAM workflows that sometimes takes organizations by surprise is the ability to generate metrics from workflow actions. For instance, once the workflow is implemented, the business can see the time/money benefits of completing tasks in-house vs. through outside contracted companies. Further, the generation of the everyday metrics (such as the number of projects completed or in process, and the time and resources each takes) is instantly at hand in the DAM. For managers who have spent years compiling reports by typing in dates and projects one by one into spreadsheets, the ability to have measures immediately at hand at any time can be a revelation. Real efficiencies to workflow are often realized in the first year of DAM implementation, leading to the revision of how things are done both inside the DAM and out.

The adjustments that provide efficiencies to work in progress through the DAM are just one more argument in favor of full-time dedicated staffing for a DAM. Without an expert on hand, DAM workflows can't be upgraded to match changes in work patterns and tightened processes. Once workflows are in place and running, the metrics generated in the system will likely influence the way things are done, resulting in more profitable results. If your organization is interested in building true **business intelligence (BI)**, then programming your DAM for meaningful metrics from workflows is a must. None of this work can truly be done by a contractor; only a full-time digital asset manager can gain meaningful measures from workflows.

DAM Workflow Terminology

Before outlining how workflows are built in a DAM, it is helpful to define some of the terms used to describe workflow actions.

Ingest: Digital asset managers often say "ingest" instead of "upload," because the term "upload" just implies the taking in of an asset, whereas "ingest" more commonly means an entire process at the upload time, including metadata generation, autopopulation, and workflow triggers.

Autopopulated metadata: As discussed in earlier chapters on metadata and mass sets, many fields of metadata can be autopopulated on ingest, and when this happens, it is part of a workflow built into the DAM upload tools or application programming interfaces (APIs). Be aware that autopopulated metadata will never be enough to operate a successful workflow; while critical to success, some metadata will always need to be entered and governed.

Actions triggered by creator: Workflows can be designed around the actions taken by specific DAM users, so that when particular people commit assets to ingest, their work begins workflows specific to their jobs.

Actions triggered by source: Just as with **actions triggered by creator**, workflows can be set up by source to kick off certain actions. For instance, a workflow specific to approving marketing assets may begin when assets are pushed through a tunnel from an agency DAM into your organization's DAM. The DAM is programmed so that if a source is X, a task to do is Y.

Content type or **asset type**: This definition in a workflow build will determine the actions the assets ingested follow as they come into the DAM. For instance, video will usually have very different workflow needs than still images.

Autorouting/metadata-based routing: This process refers to actions the DAM takes when specific metadata fields are chosen on ingest. For example, all videos may go into a complex production workflow, while all documents may simply wait for one approval.

Versioning/modifications: Earlier in Chapter 2, the process of versioning was discussed as the DAM's capability to hold an asset as one with the same unique identifier always, even as that asset is changed over time. When a DAM is being used as a collaboration and approval tool, versioning becomes critical. At each step of the workflow a version of the asset will be saved, allowing for the team to step back through the process of creation as needed. If working with video, this results in massive server needs, and the deployment of a redundant array of independent disks (RAID) (see Chapter 4 for a discussion of storage space).

Delivery, output, export: Delivery in a workflow is the pushing of an asset at any stage to another system. This can mean pushing the final, approved version of a video to a distribution system, or it could be pushing a final piece of approved media to a publisher's DAM.

Autorouting, transformation, transcoding, and proxy file generation: These terms all mean essentially the same thing: creating multiple versions of an asset at ingest or at another stage of workflow, all of which are parts of the same asset. As an example, all DAMs create a thumbnail of an asset at upload; this thumbnail image is a part of the asset, not a new asset itself. Likewise, if the DAM is programmed to run a workflow at the ingest of a video that generates both QuickTime and Windows media files to offer to users as download options, these two **proxy files** have been **transcoded** from the original, in a **transform workflow,** although if the DAM does this on its own, as with thumbnails, it may be called **autorouting** instead of workflow.

Syndication: While the death of really simple syndication (RSS) feeds is in contention, those who love content to be autopublished to intranet sites or social networking platforms continue to use RSS tools to increase the visibility of workflow progress. Likewise, when content reaches its final approval stage, syndication may be used to push the new asset or assets in delivery. It may also be called **autopublishing** or may be part of an autopublishing workflow.

Static/dynamic templating: Advanced DAMs may allow for templating to be applied to assets for consistency in advertising, newsletter creation, or sales sheet generation. Static templating applies the template in a fixed way, while dynamic templating allows for the adjustment of elements within the template. These functions are often based on Extensible Markup Language (XML).

Expiration/rights tracking: Many workflows in DAM involve tracking the rights of assets and, when permissions expire or rights must be renewed, publishing results or applying watermarks to the downloadable or viewable parts of assets (for an example of expiration watermarking, see Chapter 6). These workflows often also involve notifications to specific users or user groups when assets expire.

Logging: The term "logging" can apply to two different phases in a DAM. In the first definition, logging is the process whereby metadata is added to sections of content, typically before the editing phase of a project. This identification or cataloging of video content can take place either in the DAM or in separate video-editing suites. Either way, the information generated during logging should be handled in a metadata model that is consistent with the overall metadata governance of all assets in the DAM, and this is sometimes part of a larger workflow. In the second definition, logging can mean the recording of every action taken in the DAM, including ingest, downloads, workflow actions, and so on. Often those seeking to troubleshoot will "check the logs" to see which actions precipitated an undesirable event.

Workflow Implementation Tools End Information Silos

All of these terms defined above speak to the communication of the status of assets in a DAM. Every one of these tools has an impact on how an asset may be used, and this speaks to the true power of a DAM to allow for the movement of collateral and information.

> *Digital Asset Management means a lot of different things to a lot of different people. In entertainment companies like video game developers, we have Digital Asset Management systems involved in the production pipelines for developing the actual games, the assets that go into the games, the source code repository management. There is, of course, the marketing DAMs that manage marketing assets, distribution for sales channels. My involvement is particularly focused on archiving valuable assets, so things like concept art, and also in providing workflow applications for marketing, PR, and web teams. (Source: Rodger Howard, Digital Asset Manager for Blizzard Entertainment, "Another DAM Podcast Transcribed," p. 78)*

Now that the terms have been defined, let's examine how some of them might be used in the most basic of DAM workflows.

Sample Workflow: Photo Ingest, Selection, Retouching, and Approval

Figure 11-2. *A simplified visualization of a photo ingest, review, and release workflow. At each stage, measures should be available: how many products of the shoot were generated, how many were approved, how many needed retouching, how many had legal issues, etc. Ultimately, an ROI for the photo shoot may be generated by the use metrics of images downloaded from the DAM*

Standardization of metadata controls is important for searchability, so all roads will eventually lead to metadata creation/review. Note that the digital asset manager adds keywords after reviewers approve photography, but before releasing the new photographs to a wider audience. The steps in this workflow are as follows:

The photographer puts new products from the photo shoot in a hotfolder.

Action triggered by source: The hotfolder pushes images through the ETL (extract, transform, load) process.

Transformation: The photographs are assigned unique ID codes and assigned to a review access control list (ACL), which dumps to a review folder. Metadata autopopulates from Extensible Metadata Platform (XMP) as much as possible.

Action triggered by source: The photo review ACL users are notified by the DAM of new assets.

Manual process: Users involved in photo review push images into one of the following workflow paths:

Not for release: These images are zipped into a single file; this zip file is assigned metadata indicating that they are originals of the shoot not selected for release.

Retouch: These images are put in the DAM folder or ACL that is used by the in-house or external retouching experts. Once the images have been downloaded and manipulated, they are uploaded again as new versions over the original files, maintaining the ID codes assigned to the assets on ingest. After the new retouched versions are approved, these assets are sent to metadata creation.

Metadata creation: In this workflow, assets have keywords added and metadata proofed before release to DAM users during searches.

Image quarantine: This workflow indicates that images have outstanding legal, metadata, or other issues; this workflow should require manual input from legal or digital asset managers to move the image through steps before release to the metadata creation flow.

Syndication: Users are notified when new assets with specific subject headings or ACLs are added to the system via syndication.

Conclusions

Building successful workflows in a DAM can be some of the most difficult tasks a digital asset manager may face. While handling the sometimes delicate egos and long-held work habits of multiple employees, the digital asset manager must simultaneously ensure that the DAM metadata modeling and content are adapting to search needs and generating the statistics needed to justify the workflow implementation. Visibility of results will only help all these objectives, although visibility can cut both ways; the inevitable breakdown of processes as the kinks (both human and machine) work out will be as public as the successes.

There are a lot of pieces that really have very little to do with the software.

These are issues of what I call "operational design," which is a big catchall that covers everything from organizational alignment, to detailed workflow planning. It really depends on the size and complexity of the organization. I would argue that you're looking at, at a minimum, a few months to be up and running, where you say, "We used to do it this way. Now we do it this other way, with the benefit of this new technology." The technology itself doesn't make that change happen. That's a misconception that a lot of people fall into. Even after doing this for a long time, I still tend to fall into that, too. It's so attractive to think, "We get this thing installed, then we'll be able to do this, this new way and it's going to be great."...

Unfortunately, that change has to be programmatically implemented. There's a lot of upfront work that has to happen before the software actually gets implemented. In some organizations, honestly, it takes years. (Source: Joel Warwick, JAW Consulting, "Another DAM Podcast Transcribed," p. 235)

Be sure before building workflows that management understands just how many parts are in play, and point out that real change takes time. As things go along, it is not unusual to lose a person or process long in place. Things that cannot bend often break. Among some of the common concerns regarding DAM workflows, the conflicts between different workers' needs are obvious; some resentments long boiling under the surface may rear their heads as actions are, for the first time, truly logged in a transparent way. A deft and experienced managerial hand will be needed to ensure that the workflows are truly successful.

True change in established organizations takes time, effort, and the ability to work with both people and new processes. Consider putting forward internal awards of recognition for those most effective at working with DAM workflow changes. Be prepared for penalties that may include reassignment of staff and realignment of team responsibilities. Building and establishing successful workflows is the true measure of a successful digital asset manager, and it is a true test of patience. The investment in time and costs of intensive system and people management in the phased rollout of workflows is, in the end, less expensive than half-measures that may result in a failed effort.

■ ■ ■

CHAPTER 12

Moving Assets into a New System

Chapter Goal: To outline best practices for moving content from older or redundant systems into your new digital asset management (DAM) system.

Digital Preservation and Content Migration Strategies

In the case studies in Chapters 3 and 9, the intake of assets was discussed from the perspective of taking in original materials. But what of managing the upload process of assets and the metadata attached to mass sets that come from another system, or moving *all* the assets from an older DAM into a new one? This chapter will give you an overview of digital preservation practices to ensure data is not lost, and it will discuss how assets and metadata can be prepared for migration into new systems. The practices around ensuring that data and assets can be accessed in the future are referred to as **digital preservation**.

It is important when discussing digital preservation in the context of DAM systems to distinguish between the practices of safeguarding metadata and digital assets from **digitization *for* preservation**, which refers to the measures taken to digitize physical objects for conservation reasons. This chapter will discuss digital preservation in depth before also delving into digitization for preservation, as both forms of preservation are relevant to digital asset managers. DAMs are used to ensure the longevity of both born-digital and older media, so that systems can handle requests for information or searches for visual assets and then reliably return accurate results for decades past—whether that means the past of 10 years ago or the past of 10 decades ago.

Digital Preservation

Digital preservation includes strategies for ensuring data and assets can be accessed no matter what the future may bring. There are three main digital preservation strategies:

1. Technology preservation
2. Digital archaeology, which includes the practices of emulation and refreshing
3. Migration

Technology Preservation

Technology preservation is a relatively rare digital preservation strategy that is practiced mostly in archives and museums. Simply put, technology preservation is the strategy of saving devices so that older media can be read from them, laser disc players being the most famous example of this sort of strategy. At one time, laser discs were thought to be the digital media of the future, and quite a bit of information was layered on to them in complicated hex coding. Within a few years of the laser disc craze, however, machines that could read laser discs were no longer in production.

***Figure 12-1.** Just Some of the machines that are available in the Media Archaeology Lab at the National Digital Stewardship Alliance in Boulder, Colorado. Source: `http://blogs.loc.gov/digitalpreservation/2012/10/ media-archaeology-and-digital-stewardship-an-interview-with-lori-emerson/` (retrieved 10/31/2013)*

Technology preservation is thankfully rare now, as emulation programs have become more commonplace and readily available. While most archives and libraries will keep drives that can read floppy discs, data CDs, and DVDs around just in case, these drives are hooked up to more recent computers. Still, technology preservation will be with us for a long time yet, as some hardware will never be fully able to be rendered onto another platform with emulation programs fully. Consider the original cabinet setups of arcade games from the 1970s and 1980s, where much of the play experience depended on custom button, ball, or joystick setups. Along with the hardware problems associated with these older games is the sad fact that many of even the most popular titles were never fully or faithfully emulated into new platforms. *Donkey Kong*, one of the most popular arcade titles of all time, remains playable in its original form only in machines produced in the early 1980s. When the last *Donkey Kong* cabinet breaks, the ability to play this game in its original form will be lost, and the same can be said for many other games from this era.

Digital Archaeology

Digital archaeology is a complex term; while some, like Lori Emerson at the National Digital Stewardship Alliance (NDSA), assert that the term "digital archaeology" should be thought of in the context of understanding the history of human-computer interaction and development (`http://blogs.loc.gov/digitalpreservation/2012/10/ media-archaeology-and-digital-stewardship-an-interview-with-lori-emerson/`), others, like the members of the Council on Library and Information Resources (CLIR), use the term in a much more narrow sense to mean the practices used to access obsolete information resources. CLIR's 2010 report "Digital Forensics and Born-Digital Content in Cultural Heritage Collections" (`http://www.clir.org/pubs/abstract/reports/pub149`) is, as of the writing of this book, the definitive source for digital preservation practices in the United States, and it is cited often in grant applications and in policies relating to digital preservation. This book will choose to use the term in its technical, CLIR definition, rather than in the humanities-focused, NDSA use, as that is most applicable to DAMs.

The two main tools used in digital archaeology to bring information forward from obsolete media are emulation and refreshing. In **emulation**, a program is re-created in a newer code on a newer computer, so that digital assets can be read, viewed, or simply experienced. To do this, the older media must first be loaded into a new computer, where the emulation program can then take over and render the old code on a new machine. Because these emulation programs are often more a labor of love than profit, the most popular ones are generally available license-free as shareware. Web sites such as Apple Archives, for example (not actually affiliated with Apple Computer), make emulation programs for outdated Apple computers (`http://applearchives.com`).

In **refreshing**, the older digital assets are continually saved again on new discs or within emulation programs in their original code. Refreshing is the act of preserving original code without migration, and it is sometimes desirable when moving the assets or programs to a new platform would substantially change them. An example of refreshing in digital preservation would be the act of saving early digital art in its original code into a new emulation program, so that the art could be experienced in its original context. You can see an example of someone using an emulation program to save and refresh data in a video by Payton Byrd (http://youtu.be/gUs_wvOG8wg).

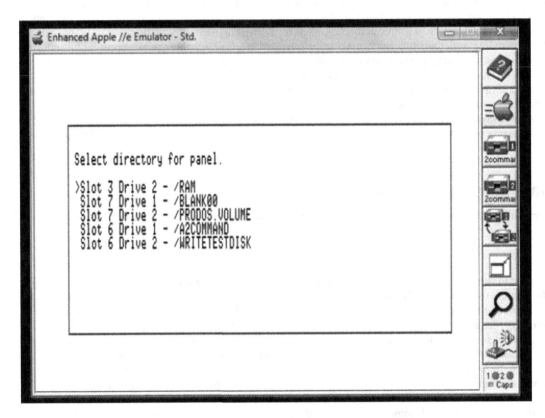

Figure 12-2. Apple emulation, as seen in Payton Byrd's video. Source: http://youtu.be/gUs_wvOG8wg

Migration

Migration is the most common form of digital preservation work done by digital asset managers. This strategy involves moving assets from one platform to another over time, as improvements to search engine function, display, and system performance become available. Commonly, migrations are performed by IT staff as communication and other computer infrastructure upgrades occur. Digital asset managers are performing a form of content migration when transferring assets from one DAM to another as in the Point-to-Point Tunneling Protocol (PPTP) discussed in Chapter 9, but as PPTP is for asset capture, it's usually not referred to as migration. Migration has become so closely associated with digital preservation activities as to be nearly synonymous, even though it is common for IT staff not to bring all content forward in their system upgrades. Because IT staff are primarily concerned with the usability of data rather than its preservation, often files that cannot be used in upgrade migrations are simply shelved in the form of inaccessible hard drives.

How Migration Works

There are as many different strategies for migrating data and assets as there are systems and asset destinations. Any process a digital asset manager can imagine to get assets and data transferred between systems that works is a valid migration strategy. The need for content migration will present itself continuously over a digital asset manager's career, as technology is always progressing and the need to move assets forward will never cease.

The challenge inherent to all migration strategies is the quality control, often called **data scrubbing** in this context, related to cleaning up the assets and data once the migration is done. While the physical migration of assets from one system to another may be as simple as loading assets on a drive and then loading the contents of that drive to the DAM, the metadata work then involved in making the migrated assets searchable can be a considerable effort. Not only may the digital asset manager be dealing with missing or inconsistent metadata, but the data may come in to the new system **dirty**, or showing artifacts of the switch from one platform to another. These artifacts of system upgrade may be as simple as turning each ampersand (&) into a nonsense string (ndSmp) or as complex as rendering entire strings of code into unreadable wingdings.

Strategies are always being presented for the ever-present problems of dirty data in content migration, but over the last decade the process formalized as ETL (extract, transform, and load) has become the most common and the most defined.

ETL (Extract, Transform, and Load) Data

The content migration strategy referred to as ETL breaks the migration of assets down into three main steps.

Extract

The methods used to suck assets and metadata out of the older system are referred to as **data extraction**. In this step, parsing and validation may occur. **Parsing** is the process whereby the ETL program recognizes both programming and natural language processing (NLP) in order to execute commands in the transform part of ETL. For example, having the program recognize that a comma separates keyword terms is to have the program **parse** each term as a comma-separated value. **Validation** occurs during this time as well, as this process checks the incoming data against known rules, validating that the code or assets meet the criteria for parsing. Dirty data usually occur when data or assets fail to be validated, or when the validation piece of the ETL program running during migration fails to flag assets being transferred as not conforming to the programmed routines before the next ETL stage. Macros and programs are commonly available on the Internet to help remove repeating characters in dirty data; search-and-replace routines are also helpful in cleaning errors generated by underscores or em dashes.

Because many systems implemented in organizations before DAMs lack clear metadata standards, dirty data and failure to validate or parse can mean that an ETL isn't able to effectively translate digital assets from an older system into a new one. If an ETL program can't be run in any meaningful way, the digital asset manager will likely have to hire someone to transfer those assets the old-fashioned way (one by one, adding the metadata by hand). While this process seems long and painful, sometimes it really is the only way forward. A silver lining to running into a problem like this in migration is that your DAM team now has an in-house case study for why digital preservation and metadata governance are important to avoiding expensive migrations or data loss in the future.

Transform

If the extraction of assets and metadata was successful, the next step of ETL can progress. In transformation, the metadata and assets can be cleaned, normalized, filtered, enriched, and have business rules applied. **Cleaning** at this step refers to what the ETL program can do to scrub dirty data. Rules can be set up to tell the transform that if X, then Y; so if the program shows blank fields from the original content source as ", ," for instance, you can have the transform programmed to delete all ", ". More common would be to show this as a skipped field, with a rule that would be programmed along the lines of "If ', ,' occurs between instance a and instance c, leave instance b blank (no input)".

The process of cleaning goes hand-in-hand with data integrity checks, and the type of cleaning used as an example above may be referred to by computer scientists as **integrity constraints in a relational data model**. When speaking of data integrity, those building an ETL program for your content migration to the DAM may ask you to break down your data integrity checks into three categories:

1. **Domain integrity:** This piece of ETL programming speaks directly to the metadata crosswalk you will build in order to transform information from the older system into metadata fields in your DAM. If a computer scientist asks you to "build a primary key to ensure domain and entity integrity," what he or she is asking you for is a table where every field in the old system matches up to a destination field in the metadata model of your DAM (see the end of this section for an example). If your ETL programmer asks you for this, you may want to tell him that there will be advanced rules in your parsing of the primary key, as in the referential or entity integrity rules listed below. Domain integrity in specific refers to higher levels of order within your metadata crosswalk, as in "if the data extracted is a jpg, it is ingested as a digital asset; if the data extracted is in HTML code, it is rendered in format XYZ."

2. **Entity integrity:** This is what most digital asset managers are talking about when they discuss **metadata crosswalks**. This is how entities, or the specific data fields, are translated into specific metadata fields. You may also hear of the process of creating a metadata crosswalk referred to as **schema mapping**. In the example of a crosswalk here, note that several fields from a hypothetical SQL document system's metadata model are transferring into the description field of the destination Extensible Markup Language (XML) DAM. This is because much of the data from the previous system will not conform to the rules governing the new metadata model. For instance, in the older system, location could be entered in a variety of ways in a free text field, while our new DAM uses a combo box/controlled list to enable faceted location searching. Because our new location field in the DAM will not accept data that are not part of its controlled list, the free text locations from the old system will have to dump to another free text field–description–in order to retain the data so that someone can go in and properly fix the locations later. Likewise, photos and graphics were given titles in the old system but aren't allowed for in the new, so that information will be kept in the description so that it can still be searched on without muddying the new DAM's metadata waters.

SQL Document System	Crosswalks To	XML DAM
Title	If photo	<description>
	If document	<title>
	If video	<title>
	If graphic	<description>
Author	If any	<creator>
Producer	If any	<agency>
Date	If any	<creation date>
Location	If any	<description> (Note: digital asset managers to scrub these data for controlled location list later)
Referrer	If any	<parent> (Note: digital asset managers to scrub these data for links after ingest)
Tags	If any	<keywords> (Note: digital asset managers to scrub these data for controlled vocabulary after ingest)
Event	If any	<description>
People	If any	<model name>
Use	If any	<rights statement>
File format	Do not transfer; to be read on file ingest	
File name	Do not transfer; to be read on file ingest	
Notes	If any	<description>
Project name	If any	<job code>(Note: digital asset managers to match project names to job codes after ingest)

Figure 12-3. *A sample metadata crosswalk*

3. **Referential integrity:** A referential integrity rule programmed into an ETL will tell the transform if any foreign-key value can exist or not. There may be input in some of the older data sources that doesn't make sense to your new DAM. For instance, perhaps the older system used the up caret (^) to denote specific relationships between documents, or this character existed as a clickable link. The up caret doesn't do anything in particular in your new DAM, but when assets are pushed through to the new system, you'd like the

transform to note the caret character and put any information following it into a specific field. Or maybe you want all the information after the caret ignored. You can even institute complicated rules, where if the caret is followed or preceded by a set of conditions, it is ignored or transformed. Either way, the referential integrity of that foreign character must be defined in the transform to assist with validation.

Other Common Transform Actions

A major advantage to having someone custom-program an ETL for your DAM from an older system is the ability for the program to recognize duplicate files or records. Archivists and librarians call this process of auditing the system for duplicates **duping** or **de-duping**. Computer scientists refer to the process of recognizing duplicates and merging the records in an ETL as **joining**. No matter what this process is called, the ability to have a program scan mass sets for this type of double entry (so common to file storage systems without regular governance) is extremely helpful to digital asset managers. Your ETL can be programmed to join suspected duplicate files or to just put them in a holding access control list (ACL) or collection for review.

For advanced de-duping using bit-by-bit comparison of assets for advanced systems (and advanced digital asset managers), a good write-up of repurposing MD5 and SHA-1 can be found at `http://anotherdamblog.com/2010/02/11/avoid_duplicate_assets/` by Henrik de Gyor. DAM warning: Computers with considerable processing speed and power will be needed to run these algorithms.

Free-form values can be mapped in the transform; commonly this is from radio button or Y/N fields. For instance, if the old system had specific fields such as "Available in Print" as free text, where people could write In Print or Out of Print, but the new DAM just marks this field as Y or N, the transform can include rules that change the metadata to match the new system. This is also known as **normalizing** to IT professionals.

Aggregation can occur through an ETL and is often overlooked in the digital asset manager's usual focus on providing search results for visual assets. Aggregation is the process whereby a transform can conduct mathematical analysis on incoming documentation. For instance, if the DAM takes in sets of survey results from a shared drive, an ETL program can be run that provides aggregated data from these surveys, providing search results across the documents. This coding may also include actions that allow for transposing or pivoting, allowing for data to be examined in many different ways. **Disaggregation**, or the moving of information in a spreadsheet or table into separate return values, is often used in transforms on address or person lookup functions within a DAM. While aggregation sums up results of columns or rows, disaggregation is programming that allows for column-specific or row-specific search returns. The information in disaggregation pulls out specific values, while aggregation adds values together.

Surrogate key values can be programmed into the transform. As an example, say the old system had someone who liked to use underscores instead of spaces between words in titles of documents. In this case, lines of code in the transform that recognized underscores in the title field should be transformed into spaces.

Loading

After the transformation of the assets and data, it's time to load everything into the DAM. Some ETL programs will have no intermediary step between transform and load, with the program running all the way through once extract is started. Other ETLs may extract and transform and then hold the data until the digital asset manager confirms that the DAM is ready for upload. In mass migrations, it's common for the ETL to be set to run when the workday is over and for the digital asset managers to either stay on to watch the thing or to go home and just hope it ran right overnight. If your DAM was purchased with a software as a service (SaaS) agreement, the time to ask about overnight system monitoring is at the time when you're planning to run an ETL. Because a new or foreign program will be running against the DAM, it is not uncommon for hung threads or other system issues to occur during a large ETL. Don't despair or panic when this occurs; just plan ahead and notify system users they may be impacted. Try to stage mass ETL actions for slower times of DAM activity.

Further, do not be discouraged if the ETL fails its first time through or if it produces corrupted data. Simply restore your system from the previous day's backup, and ask the programmer to fix the ETL. Because these are often one-off programs running against older systems that must be migrated for preservation reasons, system issues simply come with the territory. In the following figure, a basic ETL architecture is outlined.

Enterprise Architecture - Information - Patterns

Extraction Transformation Load (ETL) Architecture Pattern

Description

Extraction, Transformation and Load (ETL) is an industry standard term used to represent the data movement and transformation processes.

ETL is an essential component used to load the data into data warehouses (DWH), operational data stores (ODS) and datamarts (DM) from the source systems. ETL processes are also widely used in data integration, data migration and master data management (MDM) initiatives.

Architectural Context

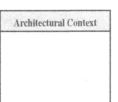

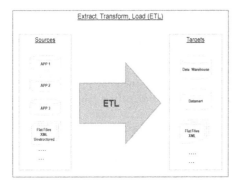

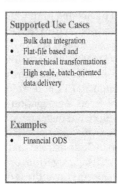

Supported Use Cases

- Bulk data integration
- Flat-file based and hierarchical transformations
- High scale, batch-oriented data delivery

Examples

- Financial ODS

Goals and Benefits	When to use

• The objective of an ETL process is to facilitate the data movement and transformation
• ETL is the technology that performs three distinct functions of data movement:
  o the Extraction of data from one or more sources
  o the Transformations of the data e.g. cleansing, reformatting, standardization, aggregation, or the application of any number of business rules and
  o the Loading of the resulting data set into specified target systems or file formats
• ETL processes are reusable components that can be scheduled to perform data movement jobs on a regular basis
• ETL supports massive parallel processing (MPP) for large data volumes
	• Data movement across or within systems involving high data volumes and complex business rules
	• Load data into data warehouses (DWH), operational data stores (ODS), datamarts (DM)

Strategy	**Limitations**
• ETL processes are in usually grouped and executed as batch jobs • ETL tools (like Informatica PowerCenter) are used to implement the ETL processes • ETL processes are designed to be very efficient, scalable, and maintainable	• Real-time event based transfers • Transactional integrations

Figure 12-4. *The common discussion around ETL. Source:* `http://upload.wikimedia.org/wikipedia/commons/d/d8/ETL_Architecture_Pattern.jpg Licensed CC-NC 1.0 (retrieved 11/2/2013)`

Digitization for Preservation

While the majority of DAM systems are implemented for content that is **born digital**, or created on the computer, a significant portion of return on investment (ROI) for some DAMs comes from the ability to provide access to materials previously unavailable in digital format or to provide the platform for migration from a decaying analog form.

Anyone familiar with media libraries or video storage is likely also familiar with the issues surrounding the storage of film and tapes. Unlike paper documents, which can sit in any climate-controlled facility for decades without readability issues, film and video tape degrade over time, no matter how well they are stored. This is due to issues of **inherent vice**, or the chemical action of agents in the media present at its creation. The Association of Moving Image Archivists (http://www.amianet.org/), or **AMIA**, is an entire professional organization dedicated to the arrangement, description, preservation, and access to film and video, and it has many publications and materials available as resources to digital asset managers who may suddenly find themselves in the unfamiliar and bewildering world of film degradation, vinegar disease, sticky shedding, and bit rot. Their publications and resources can be found at http://www.amianet.org/resources-and-publications/publications, and the online list-serv of AMIA is often cited as one of the best resources available for information about the digitization of magnetic media.

While it is widely recognized that digitization for preservation is a must, not an option, for film and video to prevent content loss as time passes, many fail to think of their photograph collection in the same way. Although the loss over time occurs in different ways than the dramatic failure of film or video to be playable, photographs are all eventually fading resources. Early photographs printed with albumen (egg whites) have a tendency to curl over time as the print constricts on its base paper. The fragility of daguerreotypes, tintypes, and other historic photographic processes is evident to anyone who needs to handle them; more recent photography may be fading due to unstable exposure chemistry. Most families have images in their collection that now appear red, as the cyan and yellow dyes have completely faded out of certain brands of prints produced in the late 1960s through the early 1980s. Further, exposure to sunlight, the particular settings on the developing machine at the local department store, and a variety of other environmental factors mean that photography from the last half of the twentieth century may not last as long as photographic prints from the first half of the century, when developing studios were often more artisanal in nature.

Figure 12-5. *This tintype image of an infant has now degraded past most preservation efforts that might have been used to save the image. Had the tintype been rephotographed and digitized for preservation a decade earlier, it might still be viewed without damage. Source: Private family collection of Douglas Brown. Unknown infant, Brunswick, Georgia, 1889*

Figure 12-6. *An albumen print on paper (left) is losing its edges and should not be handled. By scanning the image in black and white and making it available online (right), the image can be accessed without incurring further damage to the original. Those digitizing for preservation in a DAM might also save the original file as well as the version that has been touched up for Internet viewing. These two files would have the same unique identifier but would be presented as separate versions. Source: Private family collection of Douglas Brown. Lizzie Cook and unknown beau, Brunswick, Georgia, date unknown*

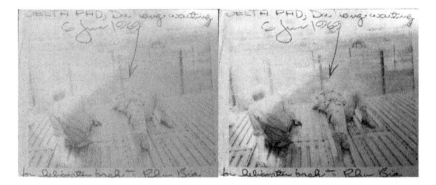

Figure 12-7. *ThisA Kodak print from Vietnam (left) endured less-than-ideal storage conditions, leading to severe fading. Scanning in black and white and enhancing with digital tools (right) allows the soldier's face to once again become visible. Source: Private family collection of Douglas Brown. Dahong, Vietnam, 1969*

Figure 12-8. *Color images processed in the last half of the twentieth century (left) often lose one or more of their pigments as time goes on. In particular, those processed rapidly by machine often become red in hue over time as the cyan and yellow pigments drop out. By digitizing these images, color correction as part of digitization for preservation (right) can occur. Source: Private family collection of Douglas Brown. Laura Bookhultz Brown, Augusta, Georgia, circa 1979*

When digitizing photographs for preservation, take care to use the file format .tiff at the highest resolution and file size that are available to you. The .jpg format, while common, has issues with data compression that will not capture an image at the highest quality.

Just as photographs from the twentieth century won't be visible forever, likewise paper documentation comes with its own preservation issues. While paper in theory can last centuries if stored properly, not all paper is created equal. Carbon copies can become very fragile with age, and documents stored in plastic three-ring binders or plastic boxes of any kind are particularly at risk due to **acid migration**. The PVC plastic found in three-ring binders commonly used in office environments leaches acid over time, causing papers to stick together and degrade.

Further, there are very real health concerns for those working with large collections of paper materials in archives or records management. The best thing I ever did for my long-term health was to move from traditional archives work into the digital realm. While the smell generated from gently acidifying paper is relaxing to those of us who grew up in and around old bookstores and libraries, with that distinctive smell of old books and documents comes other, less desirable things that might be inhaled: mold spores, insect leavings, and the off-gassing from plastics, varnishes, and the mystery chemicals used in the production of a thousand different dyes and adhesives. At this point in time, preservation experts advise that the original papers and prints be retained after digitization for preservation. At some point though, a call must be made. How long should the original be retained after the burden of its care outweighs the benefits of its retention?

Case Study: Three Migrations and a Metadata Model
Problem

You have been hired as the first full-time digital asset manager, and during the first year of the new DAM's implementation, you have been tasked to migrate all assets and metadata from three information silos. Your new employer has just licensed a DAM that he wishes to make the primary search interface for all visual assets in the organization, which up to this point have been stored in a different manner in each department.

The marketing department tried to launch a DAM five years before, but after approximately 5,000 assets were loaded at the time of system launch, the marketing department failed to continue funding or assign full-time staffing to the system, and so it languished.

The video department has logged each of its final products in a "flat-file" system, which provides only metadata entered by producers for each video along with a bar code that identifies where the video lives on backup tapes, drives, or DVDs in a modified closet.

Archives houses all completed visual projects within physical files. A scanning project was run in the late 1990s on a proprietary system no one can access, though the results were saved on gold-backed data CDs. The company spent quite a lot of money on this scanning project at the time and was told that the scans would last forever. As a result, the company then partially defunded the archives, and the photographs and other documents haven't been properly curated since that time.

All of the silo consolidation, of course, will be implemented concurrently with the development of new workflows, definition of ACLs, and constant tweaking needed in new search interfaces and metadata models as theory meets practice in the rollout of a new DAM. Before you lose your mind or quit, remember: you can take each of these tasks on one at a time. The solutions here presuppose that the DAM is already up and running with at least one basic metadata model and that, due to the organization's goal of consolidating information silos, funding for solutions is available, up to and including the hiring of persons to help you get the jobs done.

Solution 1: Content Migration from a Previous DAM

Much like the rush to digitize documents and photographs that led to the legacy scanning project in the archives, the initial rush for marketing or design departments to do something in DAM or content management led to quite a lot of *"shelf babies,"* or DAMs that, once launched, sat on a shelf untouched as those purchasing a system did not understand the ongoing costs and staffing needs associated with digital asset management.

The company from which you are licensing the new DAM system should have programmers on staff experienced with migrating information from older systems into their product via custom ETL processes. Talk with your vendor and see if migration from the older system was factored in as part of the expense of setting up the new product. If not, negotiate a statement of work (SOW) under the terms of your SaaS agreement to have a custom ETL built to walk the older data over. Remember that the cost of the ETL is just part of the effort; depending on the volume and quality of the data, cataloging contractors or programmers may need to be hired to scrub the assets.

Solution 2: Content Migration from the Legacy Scanning Project

The rush to digitize archives collections in the late 1990s resulted in many fly-by-night companies or unscrupulous vendors all too ready to scan documents and photographs, assign metadata, and offer up their final product on gold-backed data discs. Unfortunately, many of these same companies made sure their metadata was only readable through proprietary systems, meaning that while you might be able to get the tiffs (and the scanning may be of dubious quality as well) off those discs, the metadata is another issue altogether.

Do what you can to scrape the tiffs off the gold-backed discs. If you are lucky, the metadata will be there as readable Extensible Markup Platform (XMP) metadata. If not, you have two options: breaking the news that the earlier scanning project must be entirely re-created, meaning a second scanning project, or paying a very large sum to someone who can write an ETL for the older data. The call on whether to re-scan or ETL should be based on the amount of time and effort it will take to salvage the legacy scanning project. **Often, these projects are not salvageable**. Write the legacy program off as a loss, and start over as if it had never happened. Any money the company "saved" as a result of scanning and scaling back archives spending will now be more than spent cleaning up this legacy effort. Be sure to document the cost analysis of your decision thoroughly, in order to hopefully prevent history from repeating itself at a later date.

Solution 3: Content Migration from a Legacy Flat-File System

The video department's flat-file system is one of the many SQL-based products popular with small television stations in the recent past. These systems allowed for the logging of video in a quick and dirty way, and as you scan through the cataloging information in the system you will discover that, indeed, most of the data are dirty: Each producer had its own style of entering notes, and in some cases files are duplicated because one producer couldn't find another's work. To sort out video access for your new employer, you'll have to **implement both digital preservation tactics as well as digitize the videos for preservation and access**.

For the digital preservation/content migration effort, a programmer with a proven track record in custom ETL writing should be hired. After the digital asset manager works with the ETL programmer to ETL the data, the videos can be digitized or loaded to match the metadata records by using the bar codes as a guide. Once the videos themselves are associated with as many records as possible, metadata cleanup can begin. There are many cataloging outsourcing firms available to do this kind of work, as mentioned in Chapter 5, including those that specialize in video, like Apex CoVantage. If the company your organization contracts with to digitize video can't or won't add or edit metadata in your system, and instead tries to talk you into paying to use its proprietary DAM, find another company. Your videos, and their metadata, should reside in one DAM that belongs to your organization. Use the failure of the legacy scanning project as a warning to anyone who tries to talk you into proprietary storage solutions; both digital preservation and digitization for preservation hold long-term access as a primary goal in their efforts.

Solutions Summary

There is more than one solution for each of the migration scenarios listed here, and new techniques and best practices are emerging all the time, as both digital preservation and digitization for preservation mature. In your career as a digital asset manager, you will likely confront migrations just like these, as well as even more challenging projects. One of the main tenets of all preservation work is to make sure that your work doesn't leave a mess for someone else to clean up down the road. This means documenting your processes, following the best practices listed by the Library of Congress, Society of American Archivists, Association of Moving Image Archivists, and American Library Association. Don't reinvent the wheel and thus invent a new preservation or access problem for your successors. Always design your preservation work as if you might win the lottery and retire to your own private island in the morning, to never speak of legacy systems, content migration, or accessibility ever again.

Conclusions

While this chapter approaches digital preservation and digitization for preservation with the understanding that digital asset managers want to migrate and preserve everything, the reality of limited resources (time, money, and people) means that we can't save everything. Prioritize the funds and hours available to getting collections in the DAM based not only on immediate need, but also on the rate at which stored media may be decaying or becoming inaccessible.

There are many workshops, web sites, and publications available on the topics of digital preservation and digitization for preservation. Listed here are just a few resources; remember when approaching digitization for preservation in particular that active professional communities are likely in your area wrestling with many of the issues you may encounter.

- Conservation OnLine (`http://cool.conservation-us.org/topics.html`) contains many reliable links to publications and discussions on both digital preservation and digitization for preservation.

- The Digital Preservation Coalition (`http://dpconline.org`) is one of the most respected organizations in the field, and it offers both publications and training.

- The Library of Congress Digital Preservation web site (`http://www.digitalpreservation.gov/`) regularly publishes on new developments in the field, as well as highlighting the processes being used at the library for projects in progress.

- The National Archives in the United Kingdom (`http://www.nationalarchives.gov.uk/information-management/projects-and-work/digital-preservation.htm`) is often slightly ahead of the Library of Congress in digital preservation measures, but it publishes less frequently.

- The Society of American Archivists (`http://saa.archivists.org/4DCGI/events/ConferenceList.html?Action=GetEvents`) runs regular classes on topics related to digital preservation and digitization for preservation, both in a live online format and day-long classes in person. These classes are taught by professionals active in their fields and are attended by professionals working with active collections.

- The University of North Carolina at Chapel Hill has a web site (`http://digitalpreservation.ncdcr.gov/`) that provides digital preservation education materials within a well-designed web site.

■ ■ ■

CHAPTER 13

Brand and Rights Management

Chapter Goal: To outline how digital asset management systems (DAMs) function in both brand management and rights management initiatives.

Two Sides of the Same Licensed Coin

Earlier in this book, both brand management and rights management came up repeatedly in reference to other subjects. Both were mentioned as the first justifications for why an organization might need a DAM in Chapter 2. In Chapter 7, a brand-request workflow was used as an example of why a separate web portal was desirable for DAM access by outsiders. In the discussion of return on investment (ROI), both brand and rights management figured prominently in Chapter 10. Because the issues of intellectual property (IP), creative governance, and building consensus of ideas are inherent to digital asset management, so brand management and rights management are inherent to DAM systems. More important, brand and rights management are two sides of the same coin: **brand management is IP management by the license holder; rights management is IP management by the licensee.**

"Never impose on others what you would not choose for yourself." (Confucius, Analects XV.24)

Knowing that these two concepts are so closely linked, it behooves digital asset managers in conversation on these topics to point out that we should never expect to impose on others rules and regulations regarding copyright that we would not expect of ourselves. This can be a difficult ethical rule to follow, though, as both concepts of brand and rights management have complex meanings layered with legal jargon and rules that change, and this can lead to frequent misunderstandings and differing interpretations across a single organization, let alone any one industry. This chapter will outline the general rules of rights management and their implications for brand management *as the general rules exist at the writing of this book.* Readers should be aware that as the information age is just now upon us, the way society deals with laws governing image rights, privacy, and copyright are shifting and vary widely from state to state, and even more between countries.

Rentism as an Economic Model

While most readers will be familiar with the three currently dominant political/economic constructs of capitalism, socialism, and communism, many may be surprised that copyright forms the basis of another economic model with nearly as much geopolitical intrigue as the big three: rentism. The concept takes its name from the traditional idea of landlords and renters; the landlord owns the property and dictates how it may be used, while the person who actually lives in the house is a renter, paying a fee for limited kinds of use. The landlord thus extracts wealth from his or her possession not through production of goods or selling of goods but by managing property for others to use. In his article "Four Futures," Peter Frase explains a possible rentism future thusly:

> *Suppose, for example, that all production is by means of Star Trek's replicator. In order to make money from selling replicated items, people must somehow be prevented from just making whatever they want for free, and this is the function of intellectual property. A replicator is only available from a company that licenses you the right to use one, since anyone who tried to give you a replicator or make one with their own replicator would be violating the terms of their license. What's more, every time you make something with the replicator, you must pay a licensing fee to whoever owns the rights to that particular thing. In this world, if Star Trek's Captain Jean-Luc Picard wanted to replicate his beloved "tea, Earl Grey, hot," he would have to pay the company that has copyrighted the replicator pattern for hot Earl Grey tea. (Source: Peter Frase, "Four Futures," Jacobin Magazine, December 2011)*

Rentism solves the problem of how anyone would make money from hot tea ever again once it was available to everyone via a replicator; thus rentism is a reaction against the end of scarcity of consumer goods. Whether you have problems with the ethical and moral arguments underpinning rentism or not, the concept has become deeply entrenched in international law. Treaties and lawsuits over IP are evergreen in the news, and entire subcultures and companies, such as Pirate Bay and Bit Torrent, have become devoted to subverting and avoiding them on the Internet.

The truth is that we already live in the future of the Star Trek replicator, as far as digital assets are concerned. The Internet allows for an infinite number of ways to duplicate any image or text in any format, at any time, for free. However, if you believe that you are bound by ethics and morals to pay photographers, graphic designers, and other creative personnel for the use of their work, then you need to use your DAM to manage both the license your organization takes out to use the work of others as well as the license your organization grants for use of their own IP.

If you do not believe that you are bound by ethics and morals to manage your licenses, both granted and accepted, then you might want to consider that you are most certainly bound by the law. The penalties for IP infringement vary widely but should not be ignored.

> *"Hurt not others in ways that you yourself would find hurtful." (Buddha, Udanavarga 5:18)*

A Quick-and-Dirty Guide to Rights Management

Every DAM should have the ability to associate rights documentation with all assets, period. If your organization stores rights documentation separate from imagery before implementation of a DAM, this practice should cease with DAM implementation. This can occur with the linkage of a legal documentation system to the DAM or by storing scans and/or copies of legal documentation in the DAM as related files to assets. Rights information is critical to the use of assets, so storing assets separate from this information impacts the usefulness of the DAM as an endeavor.

Key to understanding rights management in any country is that at any time, a digital asset manager should be able to pull up the rights associated with an asset. While rights violations sometimes arise out of simple misunderstandings, the unambiguous proof of intent to do the right thing by rightsholders will always save the day. When trying to do right by copyright holders, digital asset managers should keep the following four rules in mind.

Everyone Owns His or Her Own Face

Never publish or distribute an image of a person without his or her permission, ever. While current law allows for **news organizations only** to publish or broadcast images of persons without their consent, for-profit and educational organizations should never do so. While there is "wiggle room" in the law in some jurisdictions for educational or nonprofit organizations to use images of people without their express written consent, it's generally considered a bad idea. A common complaint heard from public relations personnel is that while their organization is for-profit, they are providing material for news organizations and thus shouldn't be bound by the permissions rule. This is false; just because you work in PR doesn't mean that you work for a news organization, and many, many lawsuits have been filed that back this up. If there's one hard-and-fast rule in copyright and licensing, it's that everyone, all over the world, owns his or her own face, and one's face cannot be used without one's express permission.

Digital asset managers often become the unfortunate bearers of bad news when images are turned in to the DAM without documentation of permission to photograph by the people in the pictures. Public relations folk don't like to hear that none of the images of that celebrity visit are usable or that no pictures of all those kids hugging the company mascot can be distributed. Digital asset managers must be polite but firm: no image distribution without legal permissions from the persons pictured. If you are the one put in this uncomfortable spot, make sure that you have company lawyers to back you up. If the company regularly asks you to break this rule, look for another job. An employer that distributes images of persons without permission likely has little to no concern for the rights of others or is operating with a potentially catastrophic misunderstanding of IP laws that could permanently damage your career.

Never Assume a Location Is Copyright-Free

Laws regarding the use of locations in imagery are currently a mess. While this rule applies specifically to the shooting of photography and video, it's also up to digital artists to make sure that images in their "backgrounds" aren't owned by someone else. Once a photographer shot pictures of a couple on an interesting-looking bench in a public park. Later, *it turned out that the bench itself was a copyrighted work of art*, and the artist sued for use of the work in the photograph, which had been used in an advertising campaign. Buildings, park grounds, monuments—an image of anything can belong to someone else. While it is hoped that this legal morass resolves itself in the next few decades, digital asset managers must, in the meantime, make sure that the documentation related to locations and objects is fully documented in their systems.

Different Cultures Have Different Norms

When providing legal documents, waivers, or even signage to those being photographed in order to gain permission for use of their images, don't assume that everyone can read. Don't assume that everyone understands what he or she has consented to. Don't assume that anyone will sign anything at a public and planned event.

Make sure that the content generators in your organization have been provided with consent forms in the local language, are compliant with all local laws and customs, and that someone is on-site who speaks the local language and can answer anyone's questions. In short, treat everyone the way you yourself would like to be treated. If, at an outdoor event, someone shoved a piece of paper written in a foreign language in your face and pushed a pen into your hand, would you sign?

While many digital asset managers would protest that these issues are ones of content creators, marketing, legal, or anyone else but them, the truth of the matter is that while issues of cultural sensitivity may not be strictly the purview of digital asset management, they certainly have an impact on the DAM. Because the DAM is the ultimate media distribution machine, the DAM will be the mechanism that allows for images obtained with or without appropriate consent to be used. Digital asset managers need to know that the actions in which they are complicit are ethical, moral, and legal, just as one does with any aspect of daily work.

Never Assume You Know an Image's Origin

When loading content—especially older content from shared drives—it can be difficult to track down rights information. When older images are loaded without rights information, it's best to make sure they are visible but watermarked against use. Cries of "But we've been using these images forever!" will assail a digital asset manager's ears once a well-worn stock image without documentation is pulled from circulation. Meet these cries with the argument that it's a lawsuit waiting to happen and that it's time they stopped leaning on older images anyway. How to research an image's rights will be discussed later in this chapter. The bottom line should always be that if you don't know where an image comes from, you don't know if you have the rights to redistribute and use that image.

All of these rules are backed up by an international law that was negotiated in Berne, Switzerland, and is commonly referred to as the Berne Convention. First put in place in 1887, this set of rules states that copyright is governed by the country of origin. For example, if a copyright is filed in the United States, that copyright is enforceable in any of the other 166 countries that have also signed the Berne Convention, even if the same copyright law does not exist outside the United States.

When dealing with issues of international copyright law, there exists a shorthand for testing if copyright might apply, commonly referred to as the Berne three-step test:

> *It shall be a matter for legislation in the countries of the eUnion to permit the reproduction of such works [a] in certain special cases, provided that [b] such reproduction does not conflict with a normal exploitation of the work and [c] does not unreasonably prejudice the legitimate interests of the author. (Source:* `https://www.eff.org/sites/default/files/filenode/Three-Step%20Test_FNL.pdf`*, retrieved 11/21/2013)*

Managing Rights Associated with Stock Photography

Stock photography, as commonly purchased from Internet libraries, is often the bane of a digital asset manager's existence, but that doesn't have to be the case. As you look to solve issues related to the use of stock photography, know that these should be addressed at the source: the designers who purchase and license the assets for use. Make the designers feel like heroes; the better they keep up with the provenance of their stock images, the more likely it is that their coworkers can reuse the same image under the same license, thereby saving everyone the time and hassle of tracking down another picture. Draft the designers as allies in your quest for digital asset record completion, and let them know they can take the following actions to document stock licenses.

Make Sure Stock Photography Is Licensed in the Organization's Name

A frequent mistake by those licensing stock imagery is the purchase of use in the name of the designer or contracted company rather than the organization who ultimately owns the web page, publication, or ad where the image is used. The licensee needs to be the entity who publishes or otherwise distributes the image.

Collect a Copy of the License for Every Image

When a stock image is licensed, there should be documentation that comes along with that purchase. If the documentation is not imported with the image, a master license should be available from the stock house, pertaining to either the single image for sale or the overall agreement between the purchasers and the image source. Every stock image housed in a DAM should have a license attached to it, even if that's a single group license to which many images are linked.

Learn Your Legal Team's Opinion on Royalty Language

Some stock image houses make as much from catching "violations" of license terms as much as from honest sales. The rules behind terms such as royalty-free, use seats, and complicated terms of use are not there to help those purchasing images from stock houses; instead they legally tie down the rights to the images as much as possible. Have legal counsel determine which kinds of stock licenses are appropriate for your organization's uses. Due to the increasingly litigious nature of stock houses in the recent past, many organizations have a "zero tolerance" policy toward buying stock images at all.

Stop Sharing Files on Discs and Drives

The source of most image-rights violations is usually a disc or drive that has been passed through the hands of many well-meaning employees, many of whom don't understand limited rights on imagery or assume the images being passed around could never end up accidentally being published outside the organization. By building up a reliable and user-centered DAM, the digital asset manager should eventually make it much easier and more comfortable to search for images than looking on a disc or drive. Until that day of DAM bliss occurs, though, it's best to notify everyone that sharing older image sources could result in copyright issues.

Get a Contact at a Major Stock Studio

If your organization is particularly large, you may have a handler/account representative at one or more of the major stock photography houses. If so, don't be afraid to ask for regular audits or reports of your company's purchases. Further, building a relationship with this contact will help when it's time to update or expand licenses on popular or often-used stock. Account representatives with these types of organizations understand the role of digital asset managers in the management of rights in image libraries, and they will be able to speak with you about concerns you may have with legal language in any documentation or metadata.

Resources for More Information on Copyright

Many classes and resources exist to help digital asset managers in their copyright-management needs, including classes and resources to help determine the rights of an image when ownership is unclear. Below is a short list of some of these resources; many more exist and will likely be published after this book:

American Library Association (ALA) Professional Wiki

Written and updated by professional librarians, this wiki keeps up-to-date links and quick synopsis of current legal issues on its Copyright page.

http://wikis.ala.org/professionaltips/index.php/Copyright

Copyright.gov

This website offers circulars on specific copyright questions as well as specific laws for organizations operating within the United States.

http://copyright.gov

Creative Commons

Devoted to the clear communication of copyright language on the internet, Creative Commons offers many guidelines and publishes blog posts on copyright use and news.

http://us.creativecommons.org/

Kodak Copyright Handout

The Kodak Company has published a page that is often used as a handout by educators to explain copyright. You can access this great document at the following link.

```
http://www.kodak.com/global/en/consumer/doingMore/copyright.shtml
```

Society of American Archivists (SAA)

The Society of American Archivists offers one-day, in-person courses several times a year, generally cotaught by a lawyer and a practicing archivist from a large institution. These classes provide use cases and an overview of current guidelines and laws. Three of the best classes are listed here, but SAA is constantly updating and offering new classes on these topics.

- Copyright: Archivists and the Law

- Copyright Issues for Digital Archives

- Archivists' Guide to Balancing Legal Issues in Photographic Collections

```
http://saa.archivists.org
```

A Quick and Dirty Guide to Brand Management

Brand management is the modern practice of building a company's identity through the controlled use of imagery, color, marketing materials, and other design elements to build a unified public image of a company, person, or idea. The inverse of rights management, the tenets of brand management focus on the distribution of media and rights to others, rather than the management of assets purchased from elsewhere. As the DAM should be the central repository for all documentation of brand principles as well as signature elements associated with an organization's brand, digital asset managers have the role of distributor to play for a brand management team.

Further, DAMs sometimes act as the workflow governance system for requests to use the brand or branded elements from third parties. For instance, a retailer may wish to include brandmarks or branded materials from your organization in a catalog or advertisement. The use of these brandmarks and branded materials—let's say shirts your organization manufactures—will require the retailer to secure legal permission for publication, as your organization will have registered its brandmark and designs as intellectual property.

Brand-request and approval workflows can be deceptively complex, as can be seen in the example used in Chapter 7 on access. Because of this, it is often recommended that a brand-request web site that links to DAM workflow capability and assets is built to stand apart from the DAM but working with it to ensure legal processes and documents are captured. I strongly suggest that if brand requests are made part of the brand-request workflow that a separate site administrator with the responsibility of shepherding brand requests be hired for the brand team, separate from the digital asset managers themselves.

Brand management is its own discipline, with its own strategies and entire MBA courses devoted to the subject. Asking a digital asset manager to not only develop and run a DAM, but also to participate in one of the key actions of brand management is akin to asking someone to tap dance and paint a portrait at the same time. One or the other of these activities will be done quite badly, even if both of them are accomplished.

Brand managers seeking to formalize brand-request processes through use of a DAM should keep in mind that they should only ask others to treat their IP the way they themselves handle the IP of others. Never ask a licensee to keep up with restrictions and paperwork that you yourself cannot track.

"Do to no one what you yourself dislike." (Book of Tobit, 4:15)

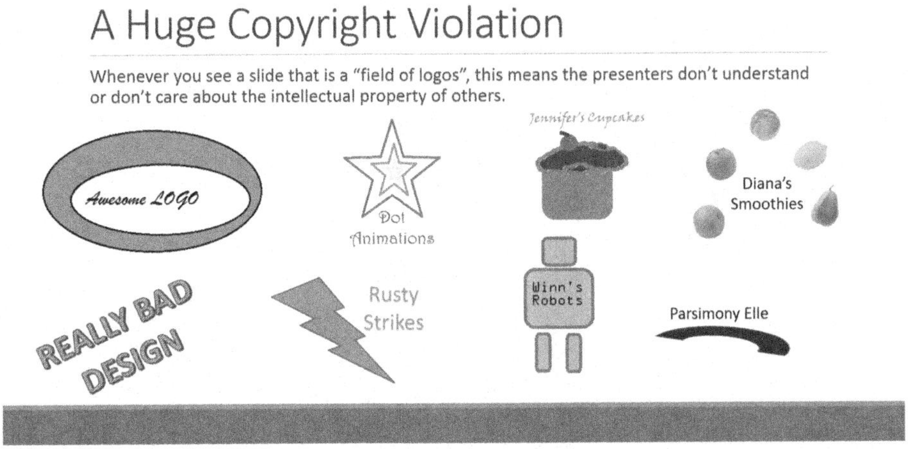

A Huge Copyright Violation

Whenever you see a slide that is a "field of logos", this means the presenters don't understand or don't care about the intellectual property of others.

Figure 13-1. *The dreaded "field of logos" slide often spotted in poorly designed presentations usually manages to violate both design standards as well as multiple copyrights. This type of slide is to be avoided at all costs; even when the appropriate permissions for logo use are secured, it's unoriginal to the point of being tacky. Never let the logos of others speak for you when your own branding and design should speak for itself*

Conclusions

Rights management can quickly become a substantial part of a digital asset manager's job, especially if the brand managers are uninterested or disinclined to examine the legal side of their work. Some organizations are small enough that the digital asset manager can wear a second hat as the brand manager, but this is rare; if a company is large enough to have a brand manager, that role should be one that works with digital asset management without doing the same job. Few brand managers are inclined to obsess over metadata modeling and audits, while few digital asset managers care about trade shows. While rights management in a DAM will be forever linked to brand management as both have intense DAM needs, these two roles are distinct and serve very different needs for an organization.

This chapter has contained quotes from Confucius, Buddha, and the Judeo-Christian text of Tobit. All of these quotes ask for reciprocity in actions; that is, as expressed by the golden rule, we treat others (and their IP) as we ourselves ask to be treated. If your brand-management strategy asks those licensing your organization's branded assets for a heavy burden of permissions, use, and tracking, before implementing workflows, take a good look at how your business handles the assets of others. If we are moving more toward rentism as an economic model in an era where replication makes object scarcity close to obsolete, then the ethical treatment of intellectual property will only become more important.

> *"One should never do that to another which one regards as injurious to one's own self. This, in brief, is the rule of dharma. Other behavior is due to selfish desires." (Brihaspati, Hindu text of Mahabharata [Anusasana Parva, Section CXIII, Verse 8])*

CHAPTER 14

■ ■ ■

DAM Is the Future of Work

Chapter Goal: *To summarize the content covered in the previous chapters, as well as make the case for a digital asset management (DAM) system as a valuable technology for all work environments.*

Figure 14-1. *Office work is a relatively new invention and wasn't always done in beige cubes under horrible lighting in buildings that make people sick. DAM systems offer a way to bring back collaborative work and accountability, using centralized repositories in environments of the workers' choosing. Shown here is the 32B Secretary Treasurer's office, 1937, Clockwise from the left: Elsie Collier, Vera Carr, Moira Smith, Gertrude Lynch, Evelyn Adelman, and Elizabeth Steinman. New York City. Source: SEIU 32BJ Archives,* `http://commons.wikimedia.org/wiki/File:32B_Secretary_Treasurer_Office.jpg`*. Public domain image*

At the beginning of this book, I mentioned that email had been in effect as a commonly available work tool for 25 years. In many ways, email has reached the end of its progression as a method that can stand alone in its capability to facilitate creation and communication. Because tasks passed from person to person in an email system are private to each individual, there is little transparency or metrics to be easily gained within complex, multiparty work conducted via email accounts.

By consolidating digital assets and opening workflows to defined groups, DAMs seek to eliminate the information silos created by individual and inconsistent ways of managing shared drives and tasks. Email has also been doomed from the beginning by the continually increasing file sizes of digital assets that need to be shared; email servers were never designed for asset storage, and so the file-size caps applied by email administration staff rightly prevent their systems from being used as digital archives. However, because workers necessarily need to associate assets with communication information and rights documentation, a new system capable of handling all these items must be put into place, and that system must necessarily be a DAM by definition of the tasks it will be asked to accomplish.

> *Some of the trends . . . I'm seeing, is indeed many . . . organizations are making Digital Asset Management a vital mission in the way they do their business. Which, to the delight of many of the future Demisters, is taking it a step further to do even more, automate work flow, the rights process, the speech recognition, the better search capabilities. The list goes on. (Source: Mary Yurkovik, DAM consultant, "Another DAM Podcast Transcribed," p. 100)*

Systems Will Mature at the Pace That Management Sets

In the DAM Maturity model (`http://dammaturitymodel.org`), every digital asset management system or strategy is judged on a scale from one to five, or ad hoc to optimal. In all the ad hoc measures, whether they relate to people, information, systems, or processes, employees act alone. In all the optimal measures, the centrality of digital governance is present throughout the DAM. This is not to say that DAMs stress uniformity of action across all spheres; indeed, as we have seen in each chapter, there is no one best way to choose a DAM, to model metadata, or even to govern rights. What is best for each organization, type of asset, or way of pushing things through a workflow depends on many factors, even within a single company. Management must thus take the lead in pacing the growth of the DAM from ad hoc to optimal processes.

In many ways, the work habits of the last 100 years have all been the descendants of the industrial age's assembly line. While we have all been directed to work in the same building in order to make effective use of technology, we should each do so in our own cubicles, independent of each other, often seeing only our own narrow piece of production. While an assembly line of workers is fine for turning out guns or sewing machines, it has never quite worked for designers or creatives, and in many ways that's the reason DAM systems have started in those fields. Allowing for collaborative work from a centralized library, regardless of employee location, DAMs put a layer of organization over the chaos that is the often asynchronous and messy group work that produces new and different products, rather than the cookie-cutter stamp of the same product.

For DAMs to be effective, management must stand behind the new technology and workflows in an autocratic fashion, while letting go of the assembly-line processes of the past. The more managers impose accountability via metrics from the DAM, the more they should be willing to let their employees operate in the system freely, from devices and spaces of their own choosing. Good managers will also realize that if they make their workers dependent on the DAM technology, the system needs to be adequately staffed and funded. A DAM without full-time, dedicated staffing will simply make workers miserable, and it is likely doomed to fail without constant care and feeding.

But we cannot get away from the fact that information services are, by their nature, labor intensive and expensive. Before the first customer can find an answer to a question or find an information object, there's content to pay for, staff to pay for, IT infrastructure to put in place, and so on. It's understandable to me when a senior executive asks bluntly, "What am I getting for that six or seven-figure line item called the Corporate Information Center? (Source: Ulla De Stricker, coauthor of The Information and Knowledge Professional's Career Handbook, "Another DAM Podcast Transcribed," p. 184)

Identify Needs and Meet Them

A successful DAM will regularly conduct a needs assessment along the lines of the one outlined in Chapter 2. Regularly polling the desired audience of DAM users about their assets, where assets are stored while being used, and what their ultimate destinations might be will keep a digital asset manager in touch with the audience. While assessing needs, you should welcome any criticism or questioning of methods or of the DAM in place. Even if you disagree with the DAM users in their delivery or objections, understanding what they like or don't about the DAM will help you stay on target in the continual adjustments and redesigns of your user portals and metadata models.

Being professionally active as a digital asset manager or director is key to the success of a DAM as well. Attending events in person is often the best way to see multiple vendor offerings at the same time, and the presentations of your peers will show you how others have deployed new solutions or modified old ones. Because DAM software options are always changing and being upgraded, it's impossible to keep track of new solutions and emerging best practices without peer input from outside your own organization. While online groups like the DAM Foundation or the many LinkedIn groups for digital asset managers keep the conversation going outside of conferences, attendance and literature review are still the best way to stay current in the field. Conferences should be seen as problem-solving opportunities, where seeing new offerings and speaking with peers can help you tackle persistent issues. The proliferation of digital asset manager meetup groups (`http://digital-asset-management.meetup.com/`) shows how eager those entering the new field are for interaction in order to grow their skill sets.

Those of you looking to get into the Digital Asset Management field, I'd say . . . Congratulations. You are definitely future-proofing yourself. Digital Asset Management is exploding right now, not in just television, but in all businesses throughout the world. Knowledge and information is power, so to have that information, to understand as much as you can about specific assets, whether it's secret intelligence, or video files, or audio files, or tax records, it's extremely important. (Source: Clayton Dutton, Vice President of Post Production and Media Operations, Discovery Channel, "Another DAM Podcast Transcribed," p. 77)

Find Your Best Balance in Security and Storage Issues

In Chapter 4, security issues as they pertain to system hosting and storage were examined; a company must find its own balance in the areas of speed versus safety, flexibility versus reliability, flexibility versus consistency, usability versus quality, and accessibility versus security when it comes to choosing where a DAM might live. However, all these same questions might be asked about users as well when discussing the formation of access control lists (ACLs) as described in Chapter 7. While none of the items we pit against each other in our search for the best DAM experience should be exclusive of each other, choices must be made that fit both the needs of the users and the needs of system stability.

To this end, those in charge of DAMs should also always be on the lookout for potential hosting solutions that better meet their user and system needs. Further, in their search for both system stability and access, those in digital asset management should always ask themselves how to meet needs in the future. Just because your organization chooses to contract with a particular commercial solution for its first DAM deployment does not mean that the company is locked into that software licensing agreement forever. Digital asset managers, if for no other reason than the digital preservation reasons discussed in Chapter 12, should continually revisit the ideas behind three types of DAMs (commercial, open source, and home brew) to see if new developments, either in the marketplace or in experienced staffers, have made one of the other choices more desirable.

Finally, a digital asset manager should never lose sight of larger asset management options and choices. When Greene and Meissner published "More Product, Less Process: Revamping Traditional Archives Processing" in 2005, it was revelatory for many government and corporate archivists struggling under the ideals of cataloging each and every piece of paper. Greene and Meissner's philosophy of taking in large amounts of records is the accepted norm for many government archives. While I noted in Chapter 6 that most DAM users reject MPLP as a means of organization, don't forget that the levels of organization–A, B, and C used for preservation at the Kennedy Library– are a middle way, with item-level metadata assigned to digital assets most in need, folder-level description given to collections that have been zipped together by category, and box-level description given to items that are useful to keep but probably never needed in any detailed way.

Further, when overwhelmed with a large number of assets to describe in a small amount of time, those in charge of DAMs must be realistic about the time needed to accomplish the task in a meaningful way. Simply applying level B or C descriptions to all assets in the DAM will lead to an unusable system, but putting out only a few hundred assets a month to users will likely cause some frustration as well. If investment in permanent staffing isn't possible, consider hiring a company that outsources arrangement and description services in order to populate the DAM in a meaningful way.

Economic Concerns, Rights Management, and Lawyers

In Chapter 13, rentism as an economic concept was put on the same level as capitalism. While many reading this book may think that presumptuous, the down-in-the-trenches everyday work of digital asset managers is ruled by legal concerns, waiting on calls with lawyers, and explaining to designers why they can't use certain images in which another company's logo happens to appear.

CAREFULLY READ THE FOLLOWING TERMS AND CONDITIONS BEFORE USING THIS PRODUCT.

LIMITED LICENSE AND RESTRICTIONS: In consideration of the purchase price paid by the buyer ("Buyer") of this Photo Image Compact Disc ("CD") to Disney Photo Imaging LLC ("Seller"), Seller hereby grants Buyer a worldwide, perpetual, royalty free license to reproduce, prepare derivative works of, distribute, and display the digital photo files contained on the CD ("Photo Files") solely for personal, non-commercial use. Buyer agrees that he/she will not (and will not permit another person or entity to) sell, transfer, or use in any commercial manner (i.e. for the purpose of receiving or facilitating the receipt of financial remuneration or any other consideration), the CD, the Photo Files, and/or photographic prints created therefrom ("Photographs"). Buyer acknowledges and agrees that he/she receives no rights or ownership interest of any type in or with respect to any intellectual property owned by Seller and its affiliates, or any third party, displayed in or as part of any Photo File or Photograph and that all such rights remain the property of their respective owners.

LIMITED WARRANTY: Seller warrants to Buyer that the CD will be free from defects in workmanship and materials under normal use, for ninety days from the original purchase date. This warranty is not transferable from the original Buyer to any other person. This warranty excludes damages caused by mishandling, misuse, neglect or any other cause beyond the range of the intended use (i.e., placement in a computer cd drive), and damage caused by accident, fire, or acts of God.

EXCLUSIVE REMEDY: Should a covered defect occur during the warranty period and Buyer notifies Seller, Buyer's sole and exclusive remedy shall be to receive a refund of the purchase price of the CD.

WARRANTIES EXCLUSIVE: THE FORGOING WARRANTY AND REMEDY IS EXCLUSIVE AND IN LIEU OF ALL OTHER WARRANTIES, EXPRESS OR IMPLIED, INCLUDING WARRANTIES FOR MERCHANTABILITY, FITNESS FOR A PARTICULAR PURPOSE, CORRESPONDENCE WITH DESCRIPTION, AND NON-INFRINGEMENT, ALL OF WHICH ARE EXPRESSLY DISCLAIMED.

LIMITATION OF LIABILITY: SELLER SHALL NOT BE LIABLE FOR INCIDENTAL, CONSEQUENTIAL, INDIRECT, SPECIAL, OR PUNATIVE DAMAGES OF ANY KIND, LOSS OF INFORMATION OR DATA, OR OTHER FINANCIAL LOSS ARISING OUT OF OR IN CONNECTION WITH THE SALE OR USE OF THIS CD, WHETHER BASED IN CONTRACT, TORT (INCLUDING NEGLIGENCE) OR ANY OTHER THEORY, EVEN IF SELLER HAS BEEN ADVISED OF THE POSSIBILITY OF SUCH DAMAGES. SELLER'S ENTIRE LIABILITY SHALL BE LIMITED TO THE REFUND OF THE PURCHASE PRICE PAID.

GOVERNING LAW: This License shall be governed by the laws of the State of Florida.

© DISNEY

Figure 14-2. This printed agreement comes with all the images purchased on a CD through Disney's PhotoPass service. When I bought images of my Disney World vacation though this service, I entered into this contract, giving me the right to publish the contract here–but not the images themselves, as that might constitute resale. This contract originally contained a Disney PhotoPass logo in the upper left-hand corner, which was cropped out of this publication in order to avoid logo use without permission. The legal language and laws cited here prevent the resale or publication of images, but not the republication of this document.

Rentism, of course, plays a major role in any DAM deployment that isn't home brew all the way, which is to say nearly all of them. Even if your organization chooses to build an open source or home-brew DAM instead of licensing the software for a commercial solution, it is highly likely that the video playback features or other add-ons will mean recurring fees for your DAM team. A DAM's return on investment (ROI) models are very difficult to chart because they are a center of cost avoidance, not profit generation.

If rentism continues to expand in our society as a viable way for creators to profit from their works, then look for lawyers to become permanent parts of DAM teams and creative teams. As things stand today, it really isn't a bad idea to have a lawyer on staff for creative departments, if not solely for the DAM itself. In previous decades, many would scoff at the idea of an embedded, full-time lawyer, as the cost of this type of staffing would overwhelm any benefit of cost avoidance with the DAM. Luckily for us (and unluckily for lawyers), wages for those with law degrees have decreased dramatically in the past decade, as the supply of new lawyers has outstripped the demand for their work. Many large firms now have the unofficial practice of letting go more experienced lawyers at a certain wage price point and then hiring fresh recruits right out of school at lower wages. This puts experienced legal counsel on the market at often quite reasonable prices, and more creative and DAM teams should realize that having a lawyer on their side is an affordable and helpful addition.

The Future of DAMs

As DAMs grow more common and trendy in the marketplace, there has been a deluge of systems that claim to be DAMs that aren't. Earlier in this book both Microsoft's SharePoint and Adobe's WCM (previously CQ5) were called out as systems that market themselves as DAMs but that lack full DAM capabilities. As I sat down to review this conclusion, I received an email announcing the publication of a white paper on connecting SharePoint to Adobe's WCM. Via a white paper, SDL was touting an application programming interface (API) that allows the two half-DAMs to connect, thereby making more of a whole (`http://www.sdl.com/campaign/wcm/SharePoint-Connector/Product-Brief-Download.html`). This API mashup is a sad comment on the DAM industry's lack of ability to promote itself; while many dozens of DAMs that could do just about any job better than the two mentioned above are available, large name brands are able to sell inferior wares based on their already established contracts with organizations.

Further, the fact that this API offered connecting a workflow and storage tool to a web content management tool in order to provide a more DAM-like experience highlights two paths that are emerging for the future of DAMs. These futures may be seen as the micro and macro futures of DAM development.

The Micro Future of DAM

DAMs today are made up of what Theresa Regli of The Real Story calls "a cocktail of ingredients." The base DAM technology must be augmented by separate email servers, video playback services, transcode engines, and custom APIs in order to give DAM users the experience they want. Because each organization has different needs, each DAM cocktail is a highly customized piece of work, with all the different pieces altered to work together in highly specific ways. The API that connects SharePoint and the Adobe WCM shows us a vision of the micro future of a DAM, where each department in an organization buys and maintains its corner of the overall digital asset management strategy of an organization, with or without an overarching ECM (enterprise content management) system in place.

Vendors often encourage the DAM micro approach, as it allows for each vendor to build small systems that can be sold to many different people with a reliance on the buyer to buy other products to reach their goals of optimized digital asset management. By keeping systems broadly generalized, vendors can charge for customizations and coders can busily work on sellable APIs. In this DAM future, those manufacturing the systems are clearly in control of the marketplace.

The Macro Future of DAM

Many digital asset managers wish for one system that "does it all." If we continue with Theresa Regli's analogy of the current state of affairs being custom mixed DAM cocktails, what many digital asset managers wish for would be the equivalent of a wine cooler. Prepackaged to have a profile with mass appeal and available already chilled, a system that comes with an email server, the ability to transcode and play back video, and a tool to resolve RGB color conflicts would have to take the gamble that whatever programming path it takes to accomplish these tasks would be just fine with its buyers. In fact, just as with the custom API mentioned earlier, some DAM vendors do offer some of these services already bundled.

Many are quick to point out that by offering bundles, the onus of negotiating and holding the individual licenses for each piece of software reverts to the DAM vendor and not to those using the licenses (the actual digital asset managers). These issues are, of course, tied up with the concepts of rentism, and the best way out of the mess is for a large corporation to buy up the rights for all pieces of the chain. So far, this seems unlikely, though not impossible, as the economy seems to be moving toward a model of access rather than ownership. At the time of this writing, Microsoft's attempt at integrating SharePoint continues to struggle, and the closest off-the-shelf product on the market like a fully integrated DAM platform exists within Google's cloud-based products. Though lacking in the ability to synchronize the products offered in Drive, YouTube, and Google Apps, when taken together as a whole, Google offers many small businesses all the tools for a DAM without a connective tissue named a DAM. Google's attempts at workflow tools, such as the under-used and now retired Wave, seem to make its systems the mirror of Microsoft's efforts. While SharePoint offers top-of-the-line workflow capabilities, it falls down on many accessibility options, exactly the area where Google excels. Neither mega-corporation has the answer to a fully integrated DAM platform yet.

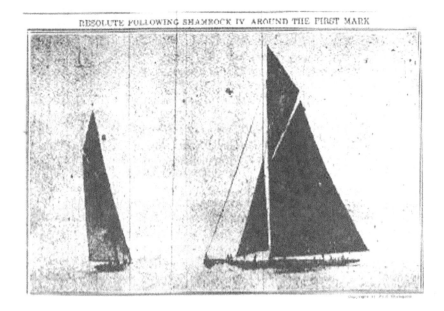

RESOLUTE FOLLOWING SHAMROCK IV AROUND THE FIRST MARK

YACHT RACE PICTURE CABLED TO LONDON

Two Photographs of Tuesday's Contest Transmitted by Telegraphy to Daily Mirror.

TEST OF NEW INVENTION

Shamrock and Resolute Shown to English Readers by Aid of "Coding" Machine—Process Not Yet Perfect.

LONDON, July 23.—Two pictures of Tuesday's race between the Shamrock IV. and Resolute, described as having been transmitted by photo-telegraphy, are printed by The Daily Mirror. The newspaper admits they are imperfect and not wholly accurate, but asserts that when the experimental stage of transmitting photographs by telegraph is passed and the apparatus is developed it will be possible to transmit pictures by this process to any part of the world.

The printing of photographs of the International yacht race, sent from New York, in The London Daily Mirror the day after the race, is the first long distance test of photograph transmitter, a new invention that is controlled and owned by The London Daily Mirror. The pictures, reproduced in London, were such as to assure the success of the new device, it was said, although it remains to perfect the new machine.

H. G. Bartholomew, a Director of the Mirror, who came to New York to set up the machine and to conduct this end of the test, said yesterday that he had received word that the photographs transmitted had been satisfactorily reproduced in London.

The machine for "coding" the photograph so that it can be sent by cable is about half the size of an ordinary desk and as high. Mr. Bartholomew would only discuss the transmitting and reproducing machines in the most general way. He said he did not at this time care to go into the details of construction or the principle involved except to say that the principle was based upon selenium resistance.

The photographic plate containing the view of the yacht race was developed and placed in the machine which has been set up here. What comes out is not a photograph, but a typewritten message, meaningless lines of letters which look like a code cable. The advantage of this is that it can be turned in at any telegraph office for transmission by cable without explanation just as though it were a commercial message. When this is received in the Mirror office it is placed in a machine much like an ordinary typewriter. This, instead of reproducing the letters, punches a series of holes in a tape.

This hole punched paper and an undeveloped plate are placed together in the reproducing machine. After the final operation the operator takes from the machine an apparently undeveloped plate. When this is placed in the producing bath there appears a negative of the scene that was photographed 3,000 miles away.

Every shade of the New York negative is reproduced and through selenium resistance the densities of the negative are duplicated upon the undeveloped plate down to the smallest particle of an inch. Mr. Bartholomew said.

"The tests have been in every way successful," he said. "The photographs reproduced well, but, of course, something was lost in the sending. What remains now is to perfect the machine."

The New York Times
Published: July 24, 1920
Copyright © The New York Times

Figure 14-3. *The first images transmitted by digital means were done so in 1920 using the Bartlane cable picture transmission system. There is some disagreement regarding the nature of the first picture successfully sent, as this labor involved quite a bit of trial and error. Images were shades of gray, and success was sometimes difficult to define. Source: July 24, 1920, issue of the New York Times*

Conclusion

Digital asset management is a rapidly developing technology with not just the possibility of changing the way we work, but with the express goal of doing so. A natural outcome of our need to organize the items with which we work and the processes we execute to get our jobs done, DAMs are set to be the future of work for many creative fields, as well as many other spheres of content and object creation.

At the speed of developing technology, it is entirely possible that by the time this book has been out for a few months that another major name brand may have entered the DAM market with the best integrated DAM platform yet. Or, if we follow the micro theory of DAM development, perhaps a killer API with the ability to cross-link many different digital creation and distribution platforms may have been released.

Although I followed the path of library science into digital asset management, I believe the expansion of the DAM field to be the most exciting of all the information science developments in the past decade. For those of us truly fascinated by the arrangement, description, preservation, and access of information–for those of us who prepare information to become usable history in its own time–nothing could be more exciting than the intensive management of assets to meet user needs. There's just no telling where the future of DAM will lead us, but I can't wait to see what comes next.

CHAPTER 15

■ ■ ■

Glossary of Terms

What follows is a brief glossary of some terms found in this text. Online, Ralph Windsor generated the building of a more global glossary of DAM terms and definitions; you can read this collaborative work at http://damglossary.org/. Likewise, *A Glossary of Archival and Records Terminology* by Richard Pearce-Moses provides more depth to much of the terminology behind preservation and archives vocabulary; it can be found at http://www2.archivists.org/glossary.

Accession—to accession a group or collection of digital assets is to take these assets in for the purposes of inventory, arrangement, description, and access. When working with a DAM, it can be helpful to use the term "accession" instead of "upload," because accession makes clear there is much work to be done before these assets are ready for searches and use. Example: *Sarah added the papers of retiring managers to the list of assets accessioned for the year. Later, Sarah and Jamal would prioritize accessions for the year according to the available budget for DAM ingest workflow.*

ACL—access control list. Rules and permissions built around both users and assets that allow for assets to appear or be hidden from search results. A detailed description of ACLs, along with visualizations, can be read in Chapter 7.

Actions triggered by creator—workflows can be designed around the actions taken by a specific DAM username or usernames, so that when particular people commit assets to ingest, their work kicks off workflows specific to their jobs.

Actions triggered by source—just as with actions triggered by the creator, workflows can be set up by the source to kick off certain actions. For instance, a workflow specific to approving marketing assets may begin when assets are pushed through a tunnel from an agency DAM into the tour organization's DAM.

Administrative metadata—these metadata give the who, what, when, where, and how of asset creation. Examples would include the camera type, date stamp, GIS coordinates, and shutter speed automatically embedded in each cell phone picture.

API—application programming interface. Custom APIs allow for DAMs to interact with other software and/or programming languages (such as HTML5) for specific purposes. An example of an API would be a portlet on a web site that allows for image uploads to the DAM along with a legal agreement.

Appraisal—the first step in determining if a collection of assets should be taken in to the DAM. A collection appraisal should happen before collection acquisition.

Archive, archival, archiving, archivist—these commonly misused words pertain to the profession, materials, and processes around the arrangement, description, preservation, and access of original source information.

ASP—application service provider. This acronym is commonly used in service and licensing agreements by IT or DAM vendors.

Autopopulate metadata—part of a workflow built into the DAM upload tools, metadata may autopopulate from embedded data in the asset itself. Many DAMs autopopulate the date of creation, asset type, and file name into their metadata models from information contained in XMP or other information embedded in the background of a digital file.

Autorouting—this process refers to actions the DAM takes when specific metadata fields are chosen on ingest. For example, all videos may go into a complex production workflow, while all documents may simply wait for one approval.

Backups, backing up—a routine action taken to copy all assets and metadata in a DAM to a secondary source for storage in case of emergency.

BAM—brand asset management systems are DAMs that focus on aspects of brand management, including brand workflows and the maintenance of brandmarked, copyrighted, or intellectual property. These systems may include HTML interfaces meant to guide external users through the brand-request process for licensing purposes.

Berne Convention—the international agreement that serves as the basis for contemporary copyright law.

Born digital—any asset that was created in a digital format before having a physical format. Used to differentiate items that have been scanned from items that were created with computers or digital cameras.

Brand management—a business discipline centered around the unification and control of an entity's image and copyrighted materials. While rights management in a DAM focuses on the management of licenses bought from others, brand management in a DAM often focuses on granting licenses and the care of associated documents and workflows.

Click-wrap agreement—sometimes used as a synonym to TOS (terms of service), a click-wrap agreement can be any legal verbiage that a user agrees to with a click.

Cloud—a term often used in place of "Internet access through server storage," because the word cloud has positive connotations, and the idea of storing and accessing things on the Internet is scary to some people. Also, using the word "cloud" allows for salespeople to draw a puffy little cloud on their diagrams of storage, again bringing in the good associations instead of thoughts of the bad scary hacker people or the National Security Agency merrily hashing through one's cloud-stored data.

CMS—a content management system, as the term is commonly used at the time of the writing of this book, is generally a system that allows for shortcuts in the publication of web pages through entry forms. Because a sophisticated CMS might contain a small image library, and because these systems are commonly used for web publications, there is often confusion about the differences between a CMS and a DAM. A DAM stores assets and may offer up a URL of an image or content for a web page to hotlink to, but it is not a web-page creation machine by itself. A CMS is a web-publication tool for those who wish to create web pages in a quick and relatively easy way. A CMS is not designed for use in the long-term storage of digital assets, nor is it typically able to handle workflows or complex searching and sharing functions.

Content type or asset type—this definition in a workflow build will determine the path of actions the assets ingested follow as they come into the DAM.

Controlled vocabulary—an approved list of words and terms to be used in the metadata records of assets in order to produce uniformity in search results.

Copyright—a total mess in the age of freely available replication technologies.

CSV—comma-separated value. Spreadsheets in CSV form allow digital asset managers to work with metadata in a flattened way for speed. By utilizing the ability to sort, copy, and replace terms in mass actions in spreadsheet form, CSVs are the strongest tool many digital asset managers use at this time to work with mass sets of assets.

DAM—digital asset management system. Software that provides unique identification numbers to assets so that complex metadata records may be attached, parts such as thumbnails may be generated, and statistics, sets, and workflows may be generated.

DAS—direct attached storage. Storage directly attached to your server, typically used for backups, and is often just a hard drive that lives on the same computer as your server.

Delimited value field—this term is sometimes used when speaking about drop-down lists/combo boxes or yes/no fields. Delimited here simply means "controlled or defined," so a delimited value field is one with a specific set of terms specified. It is the opposite of free form value.

Delimiter—a delimiter is a value, such as a comma, that tells the program where a term or command ends. Commas, pipes, or vertical bars are delimiters in CSV sheets to separate terms.

Delivery—delivery in a workflow is the pushing of an asset at any stage to another system. This can mean pushing the final, approved version of a video to a distribution system, or it could be pushing a final piece of approved media to a publisher's DAM.

Digital archaeology—a broad term used in digital preservation to mean bringing older, sometimes inaccessible, data or programs forward into current software environments for preservation and access.

Digital asset management strategy—a broad term used to explain policies and practices governing all DAM systems, DAM-like systems, asset storage, and digital preservation and access efforts for an organization, including disaster planning and future planning.

Digital asset manager—a member of the information science community working primarily with digital assets, and usually with a DAM system. The primary responsibilities of a digital asset manager are the building, curation, and adaptation of metadata and metadata models to facilitate the manipulation and use of digital assets under their purview. Arrangement, description, preservation, and access of digital assets and DAMs form the main part of their work, with education and reference services also considered to be large parts of this job title. See Chapter 5 for more information and job models.

Digital preservation—any action taken to ensure that digital assets remain accessible for the future.

Digitization for preservation—the act of scanning a physical object in order to create a digital copy for use after the physical version has ceased to be usable. As photographs from previous centuries fade, digitization for preservation becomes necessary.

Direct search—a search box that allows for free form user input.

DM, or document management—this type of system focuses solely on the management of legal or human resources documentation. Most are not capable of image management or do not allow for the types of mass actions seen in DAMs.

Dublin Core—the fifteen core elements of most DAM metadata models; the official standard as codified by IETF RFC 5013 (http://tools.ietf.org/html/rfc5013), ISO Standard 15836-2009 (http://www.iso.org/iso/iso_catalogue/catalogue_ics/catalogue_detail_ics.htm?csnumber=52142), and NISO Standard Z39.85 (http://www.niso.org/kst/reports/standards?step=2&gid=None&project_key=9b7bffcd2daeca6198b4ee5a848f9beec2f600e5).

ECM—an enterprise content management system. This type of DAM governs and pulls metrics from many different smaller DAMs and systems as part of an overall digital asset management strategy.

Emulation—the act of building a program or environment that allows for an older program to run as it originally was presented.

Escapement—the act of escaping, or a means of escape. This refers to the part of a timepiece connecting the wheelwork with the pendulum or balance, allowing a tooth to escape at each vibration.

ETL—extract, transform, load. ETL programs are commonly used in migrations or as part of tunnels that walk assets and metadata from one DAM to another.

Expiration/rights tracking—many workflows in a DAM involve tracking the rights of assets, and when permissions expire or rights must be renewed, publishing results or applying watermarks to the downloadable or viewable parts of an asset (for an example of expiration watermarking, see Chapter 6).

Expiration workflow—a workflow or utility that notifies users and digital asset managers of rights or use expiration.

Faceted search—a faceted search is implemented most often through the HTML user interface of a DAM, rather than through any subtlety of the search engine itself. Still, an index must allow effective customization in order for DAM search interfaces to allow for faceted filtering, continuous facets, hierarchical facets, and faceted recommendations. See Chapter 9 for more on faceted search types.

File type—the construction of a file denoted by the extension after the file name (for example, .jpg, .tif, .PDF).

Flat file system—any system that stores just metadata in order to catalog or otherwise describe physical or digital objects stored elsewhere. A card catalog is an example of a physical flat file; an online library catalog that identifies physical books without connecting to electronic copies is a digital flat file.

FPO—for placement only. Often seen in watermarking workflows.

Free form value, free text field—this term is sometimes used when speaking about metadata or search fields where any input is allowed. Free form here simply means "***not*** controlled or defined," so a free form value field is one with no terms specified or free text specified. It is the opposite of delimited value.

Full text search—a search that encompasses all metadata.

GUI—graphical user interface. A way of interacting with computers via pointing with finger, stylus, or mouse. DAMs often have both a programming layer and a GUI; the GUI is usually written for the Web.

Hosting—to store code, software, or other data on a server accessible to the Internet. To host a web site is to store its code on your servers. For example: The original city web site was hosted by Geocities, and so it is no longer accessible; the city council now has the web site hosted by the state.

HTML—the common coding language of web sites. The current standard is HTML5, which makes the embedding of video much easier and more common.

Information silo—any storage of information that prevents easy access (e.g., a shared drive with no obvious organization to outsiders).

Ingest—digital asset managers often use "ingest" instead of "upload," as the term "upload" just implies the taking in of an asset, whereas "ingest" more commonly means an entire process at the time of upload, including metadata generation, autopopulation, and workflow triggers.

Internet—an invention that changed the world much in the same way that the printing press did.

IPTC—International Press Telecommunications Council. The London-based organization that maintains technical standards for new organizations. In digital asset management, IPTC is used to refer to a specific set of XMP standards for the embedding of metadata in images.

Item type—a broad category used to organize assets for faceted searches and to distinguish between differing metadata models. Common item types are documents, images, and videos.

Kennedy levels—published by Henry J. Gwiazda in the journal *Restaurator* in 1987, the method of accessioning collections at the Kennedy Library in Boston in such a way as to prioritize the time spent arranging and describing collections. The Kennedy levels are as follows:

Level A: processing each item individually

Level B: processing each folder of items

Level C: processing each box of items

Latency—the time between action and reaction in systems (e.g., the time it takes a web page to load).

Lightbox—a common term that photographers use for collections within a DAM, inherited from the practice of lining up slides or negatives on traditional lightboxes before the advent of digital photography.

Logging—the term "logging" is applied to the process whereby metadata are added to sections of content, typically before the editing phase of a project. This identification or cataloging of video content can take place either in the DAM or in separate video editing suites. Either way, the information generated during logging should be handled in a metadata model consistent with the overall metadata governance of all assets in the DAM, and this is sometimes part of a larger workflow.

MAM—media asset management system; typically this is a DAM devoted to storing videos.

Metadata—information about a thing, apart from the thing itself.

Migration—moving digital content, assets, metadata, or files, from one platform to another, typically for digital preservation reasons.

MPLP—More Product, Less Process. Introduced in an article, "More Product, Less Process: Revamping Traditional Archives Processing," by Greene and Meissner in *American Archivist* in 2005, this idea embraced box-level processing and downplayed the importance of very detailed finding aids. It is now the standard in most government archives.

MVS—multiple virtual storage. This IBM protocol for data storage replaced the VSAM (virtual storage access method). You may hear this term mentioned in discussions of data migration or digital preservation.

NAS —this can mean either network-attached storage as in a network-based computer data storage system, or network access server, also known as a terminal server.

Navigational search—a GUI search strategy that can include linked keywords or other fields, cross-referencing of assets, and web-site design strategies linked to asset discovery.

Needs assessment—a document or graph generated at the beginning of the acquisitions phase of collections processing, noting the generation, delivery, and storage points of assets.

NLP—natural language processing. This category of search strategies and tools pertains to how a search engine handles language input and output. NLP as a category contains the following executables:

- Supported languages

- Entity extraction

- Document clustering

- Sentiment analysis

- Auto-categorization (by language)

- Stemming

OAIS—open archival information system.

OCR—optical character recognition. OCR technologies allow machines to "read" text for character recognition, as opposed to seeing documents as images without letters and words.

Offline—any system or information not stored in such a way as to be accessible to the Internet or any other network of systems. Offline storage is often used for backups.

Open source—any program or work freely available and redistributed without cost.

PaaS—platform as a service; another kind of software vendor licensing agreement.

PPTP—Point-to-Point Tunneling Protocol; sometimes used to build ETL functions between information systems.

Process metadata—metadata used in workflows.

Provenance—the custody chain of an asset; where an asset came from, and who had ownership or care of it in the past.

Proxy file generation—by creating multiple versions of assets at ingest or at another stage of workflow, all of which are parts of the same assets. As an example, all DAMs create thumbnails of assets at upload; the thumbnail image is a part of the asset, not a new asset itself. Likewise, if the DAM is programmed to run a workflow at the ingest of a video that generates QuickTime and Windows media files to offer users as download options, these two proxy files have been transcoded from the original, in a transform workflow—although if the DAM does this on its own, as with thumbnails, it may be called autorouting instead of workflow.

RAID—redundant array of information (or inexpensive) disks. A method for storage of very large amounts of assets or data.

Reference service—the critical digital asset management service provided by individuals for DAM users.

Refreshing—in a DAM, the act of saving assets and information over again as-is on newer media to prevent loss through the physical degradation of storage.

Relevancy strategies—the weighting of search results for a more robust search experience necessitates relevancy strategies. Common relevancy strategies include the following:

- Statistical relevancy

- Natural biasing

- Field weighting

- Popularity biasing

- Multiple relevancy profiles

Rights management—the professional practices around maintaining and providing access to legal documents governing the storage, distribution, and use of creative materials.

ROI—return on investment. Numbers used to justify the costs of systems and labor related to business.

SaaS, SaS—software as a service, or service and support. Contracts typically used with software vendors who also offer help desk, systems monitoring, and speedy issue resolution on a fee-based structure.

SAN—storage area network. Storage servers connected to the DAM or other systems.

Scalability, scalable—the ability to grow or shrink traffic, functionality, or storage as needed.

SEO—search engine optimization. While often used in the commercial Internet world to mean the boosting of a web site in search engine rankings, SEO is used in DAMs to refer to the practices around optimizing metadata and user interfaces for the best user experiences in searches.

SERP—search engine results page.

Server—a network or computer that runs programs that serve up content to the Internet or a closed network.

Shelf baby—the nickname given to any DAM system that has been deployed and then neglected due to lack of staffing or attention.

Static /dynamic templating—advanced DAMs may allow for templating to be applied to assets for consistency in advertising, newsletter creation, or sales sheet generation. Static templating applies the template in a fixed way, while dynamic templating allows for the adjustment of elements within the template.

Stemming—resolving a word to its root form in order to conjugate all derivate terms for search function.

Structural metadata—the metadata that allow a computer to render an object as intended.

Syndication—Likewise, when content reaches its final approval stage, syndication may be used to push the new asset or assets in delivery. May also be called autopublishing or be part of an autopublishing workflow. While the death of RSS feeds is in contention, those who love content autopublished to intranet sites or social networking platforms continue to use really simple syndication (RSS) tools to increase the visibility of workflow progress.

Tab-delimited value, tab-separated value—an older spreadsheet upload format preceding CSV (or comma-separated value).

Time—a dimension used to measure the progress in space and the duration of events.

TOS—Terms of Service. Commonly offered in a click-wrap form, these legal agreements ask users to give over certain rights and claims in return for use of a site or service.

Transcoding—the translation of an audio or video file into new file formats. A transcode engine is the program that accomplishes this task.

Transformation—the modification of assets using a DAM; while this can refer to flipping, cropping, or other editing tasks, it commonly refers to actions that take place in migrations or in the ordinary passing of assets from one system to another.

User access web page—a web page customized to meet the search needs of the audience that pulls information and assets from the DAM.

Versioning—in Chapter 6, the process of versioning was discussed as the DAM's capability to hold an asset as one with the same unique identifier always, even as that asset is changed over time. When a DAM is being used as a collaboration and approval tool, versioning becomes critical. At each step of the workflow a version of the asset will be saved, allowing for the team to step back through the process of creation as needed. If working with video, this results in massive server needs, and the deployment of a RAID (see Chapter 4 for a discussion of storage space).

VSAM—virtual storage access method. This is an IBM protocol for data storage, which was later replaced by MVS (multiple virtual storage). You may hear this term mentioned in discussions of data migration or digital preservation.

Watermarks, watermarking—the process of rendering an image visible but not usable by overlaying an image or embedding a code. This process may be automated by building a watermarking workflow.

WCM—web content management system. A system for storing content that can be linked and used on web pages, typically not containing discrete search or sharing functions.

Weighted search results—search results that have been programmed to show up for users in such a way as to favor the weight of one metadata or metric field over another. For example, causing more recently created content to show at the top of a search results page is to have search results weighted by creation date.

WYSIWYG—what you see is what you get, pronounced "wizzywig"; sometimes used in conversations about programming user interfaces, APIs, or GUIs.

XML—this programming language is the current digital preservation standard endorsed by the Library of Congress. For best digital preservation results, all metadata should be downloadable as XML in order for best migration results. XML coding allows for uploading and downloading of metadata in CSV format.

CHAPTER 16

Bibliography

Chapter Goal: A list of resources and links related to the text. Sources are in alphabetical order, with the chapter and page numbers for this text listed as well.

Abbot, Leala. The DAM List. http://goo/gl/vltq9H; Chapter 3, p. 18.

AI Topics. http://aitopics.org/; Chapter 9, p. 95.

American Library Association (ALA). ALA Professional Wiki. http://wikis.ala.org/professionaltips/index.php/Copyright; Chapter 13, p. 141.

Apple Archives (not affiliated with Apple Computer, Inc.). http://applearchives.com; Chapter 12, p. 124.

ArchivesSpace. GitHub page regarding APIs. http://archivesspace.github.io/archivesspace/doc/fileAPI.html; Chapter 2, p. 19.

Atlanta Georgian and News. "Sun Time Right Time, Legislature Decides." July 12, 1911; Chapter 2, p. 8.

Bachana, Joe. "Another DAM Podcast Transcribed." http://anotherdampodcast.com/2012/06/28/joe-bachana/; Chapter 3, p. 20.

Barnes, Bowden, Keathley, and Griffith. "The Sorting of Competing Metadata Models in Digital Asset Management." *Journal of Digital Media Management*, vol. 1, issue 1, 2012; Chapter 7, p. 82.

Bartel, Tim. Photo of kitten in computer. http://commons.wikimedia.org/wiki/File:Computer-kitten.jpg; Chapter 4, p. 27.

Bitunjac, William. "Another DAM Podcast Transcribed." p. 162. Chapter 1, p. 2.

Brown, Stephanie Willen. "The Reference Interview: Theories and Practice." Originally published in *Library Philosophy and Practice*, 2008. http://www.webpages.uidaho.edu/~mbolin/willenbrown.htm; Chapter 7, p. 73.

Byrd, Payton. "A2 Command Demo." 2011. http://youtu.be/gUs_wvOG8wg; Chapter 12, p. 125.

Conservation Online. http://cool.conservation-us.org/topics.html; Chapter 12, p. 136.

Council on Library and Information Resources. "Digital Forensics and Born-Digital Content in Cultural Heritage Collections." 2010. http://www.clir.org/pubs/abstract/reports/pub149; Chapter 12, p. 124.

Creative Commons. http://us.creativecommons.org/; Chapter 13, p. 141.

Daf-de (wikimedia user: DAf-de). Graphic of nested sets. http://commons.wikimedia.org/wiki/File:Nestedsets.svg; Chapter 8, p. 76.

DAM Maturity Model. http://dammaturitymodel.org/; Chapter 1, p. 5; Chapter 14, p. 146.

Davey, Mark. Interview with author on workflow. 11/1/2013; Chapter 11, p. 116.

DB-Engines Ranking of Search Engines. http://db-engines.com/en/ranking/search+engine; Chapter 7, p. 75.

de Gyor, Henrik. "Another DAM Podcast Transcribed." http://anotherdampodcast.com; Chapter 1, p. 6; Chapter 3, p. 20; Chapter 12, p. 129.

De Stricker, Ulla. "Another DAM Podcast Transcribed." p. 184. Chapter 14, p. 147.

Diamond, David. DAM Survival Guide Blog Post. http://damsurvivalguide.com/2013/09/20/why-no-one-trusts-your- content/; Chapter 3, p. 18.

Digital Asset Management News. http://digitalassetmanagementnews.org/; Chapter 3, p. 19.

Digital Preservation Coalition. http://dpconline.org; Chapter 12, p. 136.

Disney's PhotoPass Agreement. Walt Disney World Theme Parks, 2008. Chapter 13, p. 149.

Dublin Core Metadata Initiative. http://dublincore.org/; Chapter 8, p. 82.

Dutton, Clayton. "Another DAM Podcast Transcribed." p. 77; Chapter 14, p. 147.

Electronic Frontier Foundation. "The Three Step Test." https://www.eff.org/sites/default/files/filenode/Three-Step%20Test_FNL.pdf; Chapter 13, p. 140.

Emerson, Lori. "Media Archeology and Digital Stewardship: An Interview with Lori Emerson." http://blogs.loc.gov/digitalpreservation/2012/10/media-archaeology-and-digital-stewardship-an-interview-with-lori-emerson/; Chapter 12, p. 124.

ETL (Wikipedia user ETL). Graphic of ETL Architecture Pattern. http://upload.wikimedia.org/wikipedia/commons/d/d8/ETL_Architecture_Pattern.jpg, Licensed CC-NC 1.0; Chapter 12, p. 130.

Frase, Peter. "Four Futures." Jacobin, December 2011. https://www.jacobinmag.com/2011/12/four-futures/; Chapter 13, p. 138.

Fuda, David. "Another DAM Podcast Transcribed." Chapter 1, p. 4.

Ghaphery, Jimmy. "Mock Reference Interviews." http://www.people.vcu.edu/~jghapher/interview/index.html; Chapter 7, p. 73.

Gray, Charlie. "Marketing, DAM, and the Digital Supply Chain." Presentation at Createasphere NYC 2011. http://vimeo.com/31506629; Chapter 10, p. 97.

Greene and Meissner. "More Product, Less Process: Revamping Traditional Archival Processing." *American Archivist* 68: 208–263. 2005; Chapter 7, p. 66; Chapter 9, p. 92; Chapter 14, p. 148.

Gwiazda II, Henry J. "Preservation Decision-making and Archival Photocopying: Twentieth-century Collections at the Kennedy Library." *Restaurator* , vol. 8, no. 1, pp. 52–62, 1987; Chapter 6, p. 55; Chapter 9, p. 91; Chapter 14, p. 148.

Hirzinger, Florian. Photo of CERN servers. http://commons.wikimedia.org/wiki/File:CERN_Server_02.jpg; Chapter 4, p. 29.

Howard, Rodger. "Another DAM Podcast Transcribed." p. 78; Chapter 11, p. 119.

Keathley, Elizabeth. "Results of the DAM Foundation Salary Survey: Who We Are, What We Do, Where We Work and How We Are Paid." *Journal of Digital Media Management*, vol. 2, issue 1, 2013; Chapter 5, p. 35.

Klee, David. "Another DAM Podcast Transcribed." p. 243; Chapter 4 , p. 34.

Krogh, Peter. *The DAM Book: Digital Asset Management for Photographers*. 2009; Chapter 4, p. 25.

LaForet, Vincent. "To Delete or Not to Delete: 'THAT' Is the Question." http://blog.vincentlaforet.com/2008/08/28/to-delete-or-not-to- delete-that-is-the-the-question/; Chapter 4, p. 34.

Library of Congress Digital Preservation Website. http://www.digitalpreservation.gov/; Chapter 12, p. 136.

Lovins, J. B. "Development of a Stemming Algorithm." *Mechanical Translation and Computational Linguistics* 11, 1968: 22–31; Chapter 9, p. 95.

Magoulas, Roger, and Ben Lorica. "Introduction to Big Data." *Release 2.0* (Sebastopol, CA: O'Reilly Media, 2009); Chapter 10, p. 109.

McKeever, Stacey. "The Myth of Done." Presentation at Henry Stewart, Los Angeles, 2012. Verified by phone with author, 10/15/2013; Chapter 6, p. 55.

Mennis (Wikimedia user Mennis). Graphic of SAN vs. NAS. http://en.wikipedia.org/wiki/File:SANvsNAS.svg; Chapter 4, p. 33.

Munroe, Randall. XCKD. http://xckd.com; Chapter 2, p. 15; Chapter 4, p. 31.

Murphy, Austin (Wikimedia user Austinmurphy). Photo of Super DL Tape. http://en.wikipedia.org/wiki/File:Super_DLTtape_I.jpg; Chapter 4, p. 32.

Mynarz, Jindřich. "Towards Usability Metrics for Vocabularies." http://blog.mynarz.net/2013/07/towards-usability-metrics-for.html; Chapter 10, p. 110.

National Archives and Records Administration. "NARA Reproduction Fee Schedule." http://www.archives.gov/research/order/fees.html; Chapter 10, p. 98.

National Archives UK. http://www.nationalarchives.gov.uk/information-management/projects-and-work/digital-preservation.htm; Chapter 12, p. 126.

New York Times. "Yacht Race Picture Cabled to London." July 24, 1920; Chapter 14, p. 152.

Ohio Reference Excellence. http://www.olc.org/ore/2intro.htm; Chapter 7, p. 73.

Open Source Digital Asset Management. http://opensourcedigitalassetmanagement.org/; Chapter 3, p. 19.

OSHA. Rules applicable to server room construction. https://www.osha.gov/pls/oshaweb/owadisp.show_document?p_table=STANDARDS&p_id=10704; Chapter 4, p. 28.

Owens, Trevor. "Media Archeology and Digital Stewardship: An Interview with Lori Emerson." http://blogs.loc.gov/digitalpreservation/2012/10/media-archaeology-and-digital-stewardship-an-interview-with-lori-emerson/; Chapter 12, p. 124.

Photo Marketing Association International. "Copyright Guidelines" (aka "The Kodak Copyright Handout"). http://www.kodak.com/global/en/consumer/doingMore/copyright.shtml; Chapter 13, p. 142.

Public Broadcasting Metadata Dictionary Project. http://www.pbcore.org/elements; Chapter 8, p. 86.

Reference and User Service Association (RUSA). http://www.ala.org/rusa/development/referenceinterview; Chapter 7, p. 72.

Releford, Dallas. "Setting Up a Sever Room." http://www.techrepublic.com/article/setting-up-a-server-room-part-1-the-basics/; Chapter 4, p. 28.

Riley, Jenn. "Seeing Standards: A Visualization of the Metadata Universe." http://www.dlib.indiana.edu/~jenlrile/metadatamap/; Chapter 7, p. 82.

Service Employees International Union 32BJ Archives. Photograph of the Secretary Treasurer Office. New York City, NY, 1937; Chapter 14, p. 145.

Society of American Archivists. http://saa.archivists.org/; Chapter 13, p. 142.

Special Interest Group on Information Retrieval Workshop on Faceted Search Call for Participation. https://sites.google.com/site/facetedsearch/; Chapter 8, p. 83.

State Library of Iowa. "The Steps of a Reference Interview." http://www.statelibraryofiowa.org/ld/i-j/infolit/toolkit/geninfo/refinterview; Chapter 7, p. 73.

United States Bureau of Labor Statistics. Labor Force Statistics from Current Population Survey. http://www.bls.gov/cps/cpsaat11.pdf; Chapter 5, p. 40.

United States Copyright Office. http://copyright.gov; Chapter 13, p. 141.

University of California, Davis. "Server Room Best Practices." http://vpiet.ucdavis.edu/bestpractices.cfm; Chapter 4, p. 28.

University of North Carolina at Chapel Hill. "Digital Preservation Best Practices and Guidelines." http://digitalpreservation.ncdcr.gov/; Chapter 12, p. 136.

Van Rijsbergen, C. J. *Information Retrieval* (Butterworths, 1979). Chapter 9, p. 94.

Vatant, Bernard. "If It's Used, It's Usable." https://plus.google.com/+BernardVatant/posts/Qx3UKffNETt; Chapter 10, p. 110.

Warwick, Joel. "Another DAM Podcast Transcribed." p. 235; Chapter 11, p. 121.

Web Exhibits.org. http://www.webexhibits.org/daylightsaving/d.html; Chapter 2, p. 8.

Yurkovik, Mary. "Another DAM Podcast Transcribed." p. 100; Chapter 14, p. 146.

Zaveri, Amrapali, Rula Anisa, Maurino Andrea, Pietrobon Ricardo, Lehmann Jens, and Auer Sören. "Quality Assessment Methodologies for Linked Open Data." http://www.semantic-web-journal.net/content/quality-assessment-methodologies-linked-open-data; Chapter 10, p. 110.

Index

■ E, F, G, H, I, J, K, L

■ M

■ N

■ O

■ P, Q

Get the eBook for only $10!

Now you can take the weightless companion with you anywhere, anytime. Your purchase of this book entitles you to 3 electronic versions for only $10.

This Apress title will prove so indispensible that you'll want to carry it with you everywhere, which is why we are offering the eBook in 3 formats for only $10 if you have already purchased the print book.

Convenient and fully searchable, the PDF version enables you to easily find and copy code—or perform examples by quickly toggling between instructions and applications. The MOBI format is ideal for your Kindle, while the ePUB can be utilized on a variety of mobile devices.

Go to www.apress.com/promo/tendollars to purchase your companion eBook.